Those Who Walked Before

How Ice Age Footprints in New Mexico Retell the Stories of the First Americans

MATTHEW R. BENNETT
DAVID F. BUSTOS
DANIEL ODESS

University of New Mexico Press

THOSE WHO WALKED BEFORE

Albuquerque

Printed in the United States of America

ISBN 978-0-8263-6941-3 (paper)
ISBN 978-0-8263-6942-0 (ePub)

Library of Congress Control Number: 2025944774

Founded in 1889, the University of New Mexico sits on the traditional homelands of the Pueblo of Sandia. The original peoples of New Mexico—Pueblo, Navajo, and Apache—since time immemorial have deep connections to the land and have made significant contributions to the broader community statewide. We honor the land itself and those who remain stewards of this land throughout the generations and also acknowledge our committed relationship to Indigenous peoples. We gratefully recognize our history.

Cover artwork by Davide Bonadona; © Matthew R. Bennett
Designed by Isaac Morris
Composed in Change and Semplicita

Contents

Foreword | vii

Acknowledgments | ix

Chapter One. First Sight of White Sands | 1

Chapter Two. How to Study Tracks? | 25

Chapter Three. Cinematic Snapshots | 58

Chapter Four. How Old Is a Footprint? | 91

Chapter Five. Stepping from the Past into the Future | 125

Chapter Six. A Journey of Footprints | 150

Postscript. Definitions, Methods, and Additional Details | 157

Notes | 178

Index | 193

Foreword

The discovery of ancient human footprints at White Sands National Park has caught the imagination of the public, especially when they were dated recently to the height of the last ice age. This pushed the antiquity of human presence in the Americas back far beyond previous estimates. It is a discovery that is not without controversy, and as with any new scientific idea, there are always naysayers. This book is about those footprints and the scientific journey behind their discovery. It is not a contribution to the scientific debate around this discovery or its dating. Instead, it is aimed at the general reader who wants to find out more and share in the discovery of these amazing footprints. Join us via these pages as we tell the story of this discovery and explore the implications of these footprints for the peopling of the Americas.

Just a quick word about the way the book is set up. Each chapter focuses on a different part of our story, but in places it is hard to find the right approach. Some folks will want more depth and detail on the methods we use, while others won't. To solve this problem, we have created a postscript with information that some readers may find interesting but others won't! We suggest that you delve into this postscript as and when you wish, or need it.

Matthew R. Bennett
David F. Bustos
Daniel Odess
April 2025

Acknowledgments

This work reflects the authors' opinions and does not necessarily reflect the views of the National Park Service. The paleo-art within this book was created by Karen Carr, unless otherwise stated. Karen has a long-standing association with White Sands, and you will see her work in the visitor's center, but the paleo-art within this book was commissioned and paid for by Bournemouth University. Sharon Gloshay, a member of the White Mountain Apache Tribe, contributed her thoughts within the book, and we are grateful for her insight and support. She is an amazing friend and archaeologist. We are also grateful for the support of Kim Charlie (Acoma Pueblo).

The authors are part of a large research team, and many different people have contributed in different ways to this work over the years. We thank you all for the pleasure of your company on this journey. To name but a few and in no particular order: Edward Jolie, Kathleen Springer, Jeff Pigati, Tommy Urban, Sally Reynolds, Dave Love, Bruce Allen, Joe Watkins, Carol Ellick, Vance Holliday, Vincent Santucci, Alison Smith, Dave Horne, Jonathan Holmes, Bruce Huckell, Leloni Begay, Daniel Bird, Christopher Franco, Andrew Gentry, Patrick Martinez, Claire Connelly, Cecilia Calvert, Austin Coffman, Jackson Jakeway, Marie Sauter, Amber Kalsuh, Molly Murphy, Allison Harvey, Richard Green, Hannah Strehlau, Abigail Hunt, Michael Everett, Sarah Maryon, David Dennis, Dick Mol, Scott Hays-Storm, Greg McDonald, Neffra Matthews, P. Willey, Tom Nobel, and Cyrus Green and the representatives of the tribes and pueblos that have joined us in the field and shared their knowledge over the years. We would like to thank Randy Best for his interest in (and support of) our work. Part of this research was funded by the UK Arts and Humanities Research Council. The book benefited from insightful and constructive reviews by Edward Jolie and Vance Holliday, for which the authors are grateful. We would also like to thank our commissioning editor, Sonia Dickey at the University of New Mexico Press. We would like to thank Vance Holliday for providing images and copyright approval for Figures 2.13 and 5.2. Chester Zoo in the United Kingdom provided permission to use Figure 3.6A. Figure 4.10 is in the public domain (Creative Commons license), courtesy of Dartmouth Electron Microscope Facility, as is Figure 1.5, by Robert Bruce Horsfall (from William Berryman Scott, *A History of Land*

Mammals in the Western Hemisphere [MacMillan, 1913]). The authors hold the copyright for all other images and artwork.

Matthew would like to thank his wife and research collaborator Sally Reynolds, along with his children, Zoë, Alex, Samuel, and Edward. During the writing of this book, both his mother, Gillian Bennett (1939–2023), and his father, Andrew Bennett (1939–2024), passed away, and he wishes to pay homage to their support. As a severely dyslexic individual Matthew struggled in his early years, but his parents introduced him to the pleasure of books, which transformed his life to such an extent that he now views dyslexia as a privilege, not a handicap. It allows him to see the world differently from most. David, another dyslexic, would like to thank Andrea and his children, Cisco (David Jr.), Diego, and Mylo, for their support and encouragement. He would like to acknowledge all the help from Patrick Martinez, who contributed to multiple parts of this story: "Everyone needs a Patrick." Floyd and Maryann Mac Ernie provided encouragement and are thanked for their general interest in science. Financially, David acknowledges support from the Western National Parks Association. Daniel would like to acknowledge his sister Joan as a source of inspiration and joy in good times and bad.

CHAPTER ONE

First Sight of White Sands

Ellis Wright, a government trapper, was out hunting in the fall of 1932. The sun was hot, and the dust was rising on the salt flats of White Sands in New Mexico. He was an expert in reading animal tracks—after all, his livelihood depended on it. Stopping to mop his brow, he saw a line of tracks in a shallow gully a few yards ahead. With interest, he stepped forward but then stopped short, before shaking his head slowly. The outline of a human foot was cemented into the gypsum rock.[1] In all, there were 13 such tracks forming a short trackway. The exact location has been lost, but the prints may have looked like those in Figure 1.1. Wright was sure they had been made by a human, but something nagged at him. They were simply too large—perhaps 22 inches long. Feeling uneasy, he scanned the horizon. What could have made such large tracks? Bigfoot, perhaps? Wright returned a few days later with a small group of folks. They confirmed his finding, but were at a loss to say who made the tracks other than a giant human. So the story of the White Sands footprints starts with Bigfoot.

And there the matter rested for some 75 years, until the hero of our story, a quietly spoken and keenly observant guy from New Mexico called David Bustos, started to see tracks in the sands. David arrived at White Sands National Park as a biologist in 2005 and in time became the resources manager.[2] His first encounter with the footprints left him puzzled. He recalls:

> It was a warm winter day in 2005. I was working in the interior of the park repairing a fence, far beyond the dunes and out on the salt flats. Something caught my eye, a slight change in soil color. I saw my first print. At first, I thought they were recent prints made by cowboy boots, wide at the front and narrow at the heel, but they seemed too deeply impressed in the soil, and it was strange that they

were so far out on the salt flats. I thought nothing more about it at the time, but the discovery nagged at me for years. Fifteen years later, these tracks would become part of the longest fossil footprint trail in the world, but that is to come in our story. In 2006 we found the first fossil prints of extinct Ice Age animals in the park—prints of mammoths and camels.[3] They were infilled with cornflake-size gypsum (selenite) crystals and were eroded out of the shore by waves when Lake Lucero flooded after a rare storm. As the waves washed away the sediment to expose the prints, they glistened and sparkled like diamonds in the sunlight. But as soon as the prints were exposed, they were washed away.

In 2007 came the first academic paper to describe the mammoth tracks.[4] Large oval-shaped depressions and easy to spot, mammoth tracks are each about the size of a large pizza in diameter and are part of a rich fauna that became extinct at the end of the Ice Age.[5]

The Tularosa Basin

We are racing ahead in our story, and should perhaps take a moment to give context to this unique place called White Sands. One word describes the sands of the Tularosa Basin, where White Sands is located: *white*. So white, in fact, that the gypsum sand dunes shimmer in the heat as they constantly move in the wind, marching forward with the breeze. The dunes are paired with a vast plain of sand called Alkali Flat (Figure 1.2A; geologists call salt flats playas). Alkali Flat is the former bed of a giant lake that once filled the Tularosa Basin during the Ice Age and is referred to as Paleolake Otero.[6] Lake Lucero is a modern remnant of this ancient lake and is found at the southern end of Alkali Flat after rainfall.

If you live in a modern house, chances are its internal walls are clad in drywall boards made from compressed gypsum. Gypsum is composed of calcium sulphate and is formed by the evaporation of salt-rich water, a bit like the limescale that builds up in a kettle over time. When it rains, Alkali Flat fills with water, and it has nowhere to drain. Consequently, it evaporates slowly to leave a crust of gypsum. This bloom of salt is eroded

Figure 1.1. The moment Ellis Wright found the first footprint at White Sands in 1932, reenvisioned by artist Karen Carr. The depiction of Ellis Wright is based on photographs provided to David Bustos by his family.

by the wind and deposited on the adjacent dunes, which are constantly being supplied with tiny sand-size gypsum crystals. In places, groundwater rich in salt emerges onto the flat and evaporates to form beautiful crystals of selenite (Figure 1.2B)—crystals that apparently promote calm, mental clarity, and well-being. The name derives from a Greek word meaning "moon stone," and the pale translucent crystals scatter the surface of the flats in places.

Alkali Flat lies in what geologically we call a rift valley. A rift valley forms when the earth's crust is pulled apart and is defined on each side by a series of large fractures known as faults. The Tularosa Basin is a rift valley in the sense of being a topographic feature and being defined by a series of faults on either side. It is one of a series of such basins that form the Rio Grande Rift system, which runs from the San Luis Valley in Colorado south into Texas and onward into Chihuahua in Mexico.[7] The Tularosa Basin is on the eastern side of this rift system, east of the Rio Grande. To the west, the basin is defined, south to north, by the Organ, San Andres, and Oscura Mountains, and on the east by the Hueco Mountains, Otero Mesa, the Sacramento Mountains, and Sierra Blanca. The southern end of the basin is defined by the Rio Grande, and it becomes narrower to the north (Figure 1.3). The rift cuts ancient Precambrian rocks at depth, as well as marine sediments of Permian and Tertiary age. The former contain thick evaporite strata, formed when Permian seas dried up to leave thick salt layers. This contributes to the gypsum-rich groundwater within the basin.[8] A rift valley typically fills from the sides as its flanks are eroded, feeding large river fans that build out toward the center of the basin. In this case, the floor of the basin contains a range of lake and river deposits, including at-depth deposits of an ancestral Rio Grande that once routed through the basin.

Toward the end of the Ice Age, Paleolake Otero filled part of the Tularosa Basin. Its age and history are not well-known, but it may have been present as early as 42,000 years ago and persisted in some form until around 16,000 years ago.[9] When the gypsum dunes fit into this ancient landscape is not well-dated, but dune formation probably commenced at least 8,800 years ago.[10]

White Sands National Monument, as the site was known until 2019, was signed into law by President Herbert Hoover in 1933 and opened its doors to the public in April 1934. In its first year, it received more than 34,000 visitors.[11] The original declaration under the 1906 Antiquities Act set aside 142,987 acres to conserve part of what was believed to be

Figure 1.2. A: Alkali Flat, which was an ancient lakebed, is now a dusty salt flat or playa. B: Selenite crystals are beautiful slivers that look like a sliced loaf of bread.

the largest gypsum dune field in the world. But the military soon became its neighbors, and at first the military had unrestricted access over the whole area. In 1942, just months after the attack on Pearl Harbor, more than 1.2 million acres of the Tularosa Basin were designated as the Alamogordo Bombing and Gunnery Range. In 1945 the range was used to test the first nuclear bomb (the Trinity test), detonated approximately 77 miles north of Alamogordo. Part of the range closed at the end of the Second World War but reopened as Holloman Air Force Base in 1958. Testing continued at the White Sands Missile Range, which became home to the earliest US rocket tests. Therefore, White Sands can claim to be the birthplace of America's space program. Congress upgraded the monument to a national park in December 2019 and extended its remit to cover both geological and cultural resources as well as the dune field.

The part of the park that visitors see is largely restricted to the gypsum dunes. Most people enjoy their beauty, go sledding on the dunes, or simply hang out there. The other part of the park is Alkali Flat, and this area is still in co-use with the military. It contains unexploded ordnance from decades of military use and is regularly closed for missile tests. The flats can be accessed only with permission and by using one of the National Park Service's utility terrain vehicles (UTVs). It is here that the footprints are found. Within David's resource management team, they are described as "ghost tracks" because they appear and disappear. If conditions are just right, you can see the outline of a track as a slightly darker, or sometimes lighter, shade of gray gypsum sand. It is the contrast in moisture, and salt, between the track infill and the surrounding area that identifies the tracks. Mammoth tracks often stand out clearly (Figure 1.4), but smaller human tracks are also visible under the right conditions. It takes practice to see them and an element of faith, because when it becomes too dry or too wet, they disappear.

Searching for Tracks: David's Quest

Let us return to our story and reconnect with David, who as the years passed was gaining confidence in identifying the large circular tracks of mammoths and the kidney-shaped tracks of giant ground sloths. He also

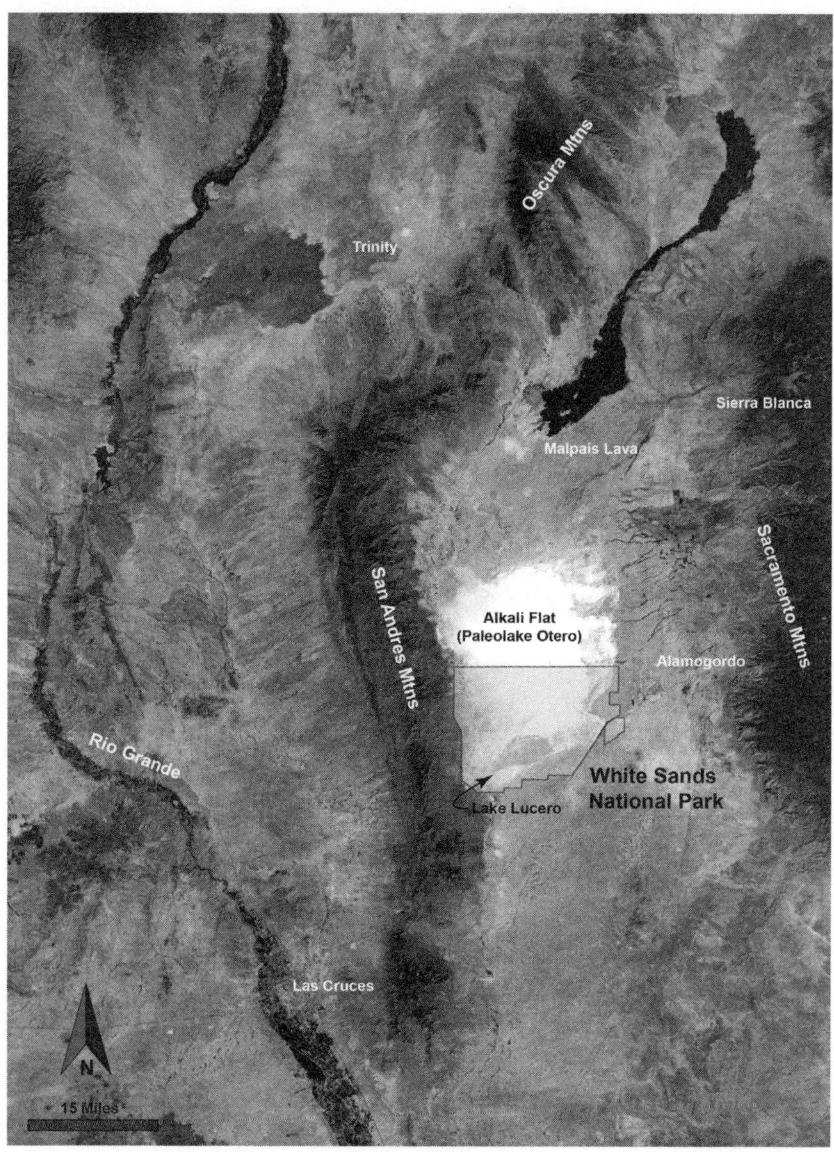

Figure 1.3. A map showing the location of White Sands National Park within the Tularosa Basin, New Mexico. Base image courtesy of Google Earth.

Figure 1.4. A set of mammoth "ghost prints" on Alkali Flat. Note that the skyline has been adjusted to obscure the precise location.

found beautiful tracks of a big cats, dire wolfs, and lots of camels. With the help of the Washington office of the National Park Service, David set up a paleontological program and had the US Geological Survey provide an unmanned aerial vehicle, a fancy drone. With the help of a great deal of interns and seasonal staff, this work led to the discovery of many mammoth and camel tracks. Perhaps the largest discovery was an area some 8 miles long and 2 miles wide of closely spaced mammoth tracks, forming a giant trample-ground. David recalls,

> So we knew that we had a handful of prints, maybe 10 to 15 trackways. And I had talked to a lot of geologists and other folks about the tracks on Alkali Flat. They said there couldn't be any out in the center of the flats because the lakebed had all been scoured away. All right, well, I guess there's no track out in the middle of the salt flats. But one day we went out there following the prints of a lost boy who had roamed miles out into the middle of the salt flats. And while looking for this

boy, we came across this large area of mammoth tracks that formed a huge trampled area. Oh, and we did find the boy too!

But nagging away at David was the idea that there were human tracks as well, something different and bipedal. After many false dawns and disappointments, David eventually got folks in the Washington office of the National Park Service interested in the idea that there might be human tracks alongside those of the Ice Age animals. Reaching out to Dan Odess, who was then an assistant director at the Park Service, he arranged for a team from HABS-HAER[12] to come out and do some basic mapping. It was the first systematic study and the first use of LiDAR (light detection and ranging, which involves using a plane or drone and lasers to map topography) at the site. While it did not lead to any clear conclusions about the tracks, it was an initial step on a journey. In the summer of 2016, the centenary of the Park Service, David reached out to human footprint expert Matthew Bennett. A British geology professor working at Bournemouth University on the south coast of England, he has established himself, by happenstance more than design, as an expert in human footprints. For example, he had worked on the 1.5-million-year-old footprints found at Ileret in northern Kenya, as well as at other sites around the world.[13] But it was his research handbook on fossilized locomotion[14] that was the stimulus for a tentative email. It was the start of a friendship and a new chapter in the story of the White Sands footprints. Matthew joined David at White Sands in January 2017 along with lots of other folks to evaluate two questions: Were there human tracks at White Sands? If so, how could we establish their age?

David recalls,

I had become familiar with the tracks out on the salt flats. They would appear and fade with changes in the weather, ghostlike. There was something walking upright on two legs (bipedal), and in places I was sure that a mammoth track overprinted the tracks. If this was the case, then they had to be old and formed prior to the extinction of the mammoths. At this point I remembered the cowboy boots. If they had toes, then they must be old. Who else would be walking out on the salt flats without shoes? So as soon as I could, I rushed out to the location with Patrick Martinez, a biological technician at the time, and started to brush one of the tracks out. After about

35 minutes, a human foot began to emerge, with toes and a clear arch. Patrick would have none of it: "David! You are making the print up. You're brushing out the shape you want to see!" I handed him the brush and suggested he set to work on what would be the matching track, a left to the right I had uncovered. He brushed this way and that and slowly a track emerged, despite everything he did to prevent it. It was a left track with toes and a heel. The tracks were infilled with sand made of coarse-grained gypsum crystals, and this brushed out easily. The sediment in which the track was made was much finer and more compact. We laughed and joked—we had a human track, but who would believe us?

I started to research human footprints, devouring everything I could find, and during this time I came across Matthew's book. The book provided an overview of the topic of human footprints. I knew it was a long shot, but I reached out to Matthew in the hope of getting his help. To my surprise he responded, and after a few online meetings he agreed to travel out in January 2017 to look at the prints.

The weeks leading up to the visit were exciting. We would have other experts—paleontologists and folks who specialized in dating sediments—visiting as well. It was a busy time organizing folks' travel, booking rooms, and hiring cars. A few days before, the weather forecast began to hint at rain. At first it was just an outside chance of rain, but as the event came nearer, so did the probability of rain. The weekend before the event, it began to rain, a real downpour flooding part of Alkali Flat. We thought about canceling the trip, but with so many people traveling, this was not a real option. The vans got stuck on the way out to the site. The tracks we had prepared were lost to the rain. The ghost tracks began to disappear. It was not a great start!

Matthew adds,

I arrived a day late, and David kindly met me at the airport in El Paso. He is that sort of guy, always there to help. I have to say I was uncertain of what I would find and was really put out that there was a large posse of people at the meeting. I am an introvert at heart and crowds are not my thing. Jet-lagged and tired, I listened to David, park superintendent Marie Sauter, and Vincent Santucci, head of the Park

Service's national geology program, outline what evidence they had and what help they needed. Some dates on ditch grass seed layers (*Ruppia* spp.) were way out there (20,000-plus years old) and much older than any accepted age for humans in the Americas. The dates stirred up a tornado of speculation, but in truth, as I pointed out in my rather blunt way, they could prove nothing! The prints they had found so far possessed no stratigraphic relationship to the dates. After a couple of days of chatting, we were taken into the field, my first experience of a ride across the dune on a UTV, which I have to say is a totally amazing experience and one I cherish on every visit to the park. But I was not impressed by the footprints. Yes, I could see tracks of mammoths, but little else. David took us to this amazing box made of aluminum, about the size of a large door lying flat on the sand flats and maybe 3 inches high. He hoped it would have preserved some of potential human tracks he had excavated a few months before with Patrick. It was like one of those trapdoors you see in sci-fi films, the entrance to a giant subterranean bunker. In fact, it had some poorly excavated tracks, which had gotten damp and did not sell themselves to me. I was not impressed and was undoubtedly rude given my direct manner. Poor David.

David continues,

I remember telling my wife that Matthew didn't think much of the footprints but loved the metal bunker! We had put the metal cover in to try and protect the tracks that Patrick and I had excavated a few months earlier. But with all the rain, water had got in and turned the tracks into a wet mess. It is no wonder no one believed them. I felt as if it was the day that my dog had died. My new friends and colleagues let me know that the tracks were not likely human or, more to the point, the tracks that they had seen would not convince a skeptical crowd.

Dan adds,

I arrived a day early for the meeting to take advantage of David's kind offer to show me around the park. I had been working with David by phone for a few years to try and help him figure out how

> to document and preserve the tracks he was finding, but this was my first chance to meet him in person. I was immediately struck by his quiet, soft-spoken manner, deep curiosity about the natural world, and genuine humility. I was also struck by his incredibly keen eye for subtle detail and something that is just a little out of place. It is his keen powers of observation and his ability to notice when something looks just a little different than it did when he last passed through an area that has been critical in discovering the tracks.

Matthew recalls,

> I felt bad. David was such a nice guy, and there I was shattering his dreams. He took me and Marie Sauter on a UTV tour the day after everyone left. It was there that he showed me some amazing giant ground sloth tracks on the west side of Alkali Flat. Ghost tracks for sure, but they were clearly made by a huge animal. I was impressed and gave David and Marie a commitment to be back to study them and to put White Sands on the map as a track site. My message was clear: Forget the humans. Forget trying to date stuff. Focus on what you do have, which is some amazing giant ground sloth and mammoth tracks. I would be back in April.

This is how the next installment of the footprint saga started. And yes, Matthew was back in April 2017, and with David and an intern named Jackson, they started to work on the west side of Alkali Flat on the sloth tracks. Matthew remembers,

> Boy, was it cold! The early morning drive across Alkali Flat in the open-top UTV was bitterly cold, so much so that I could feel the tears in my eyes begin to freeze. It is the coldest I have ever been at White Sands, and it can get cold. We started to work on a set of ghost tracks that were clearly made by a giant ground sloth. That was our mission, to study ground sloths. We had only been working there for a couple of days when David called me over to look at the small impression he was brushing out. If you break the surface crust over a ghost track, you can then brush out the infill with a little care and the occasional prod from the end of a paintbrush. The secret is to let the brush define the track rather than poke and prod too much.

> Anyway, David called me over. He had a deep track, maybe 7 inches long, with a nice, rounded heel, and the forefoot went deep, and at the bottom there was the faint outline of a set of toes. It was a human track and typical of someone walking on soft mud. The forefoot tends to sink deeper as you push forward in the last phase of stance. It was perfect, in fact. People expect fossil tracks to have clear anatomical form, just like the wet tracks you make getting out of the shower on the bathroom floor, but real tracks are not like that. The ground is soft and deforms under pressure from the foot. A messy track like the one that David had found is far more convincing and real than one with a perfect set of toe pads. I remember swearing as I walked back to the sloth track I was working on. They did have human tracks after all, and more to the point, they were clearly associated with extinct Ice Age animals. I have made over 20 visits to White Sands since April 2017, and nothing quite compares to that moment of excitement. I was so pleased for David and for the park.

White Sands also has more conventional types of archaeology, most of which postdates the end of the Ice Age. There are some amazing hearth mounds, which give important insight into how this landscape was used in the past. Light a fire on gypsum, and if it burns for sufficient time, it drives water from the crystal structure of the gypsum beneath and forms something akin to plaster of Paris. Now add a bit of rain and it will set hard. Campfires made on the gentle windward slopes of gypsum dunes therefore create hard areas of cemented sand, and as the rest of the dune, made of loose sand, continues to migrate in front of the wind, the cemented area is left in the rear as an upstanding mound. Artifacts, food, and charcoal are sometimes cemented into these hearth mounds, and they can be found throughout the dunes at White Sands. They record human occupation in what is known as the Archaic period in American archaeology.[15] Hearth mounds can be dated by charcoal via a technique known as radiocarbon dating (discussed in detail in a later chapter), but the exciting part of this is that the hearth dates form a distinctive pattern. This pattern mirrors the forward movement of the dune field as it migrated. Folks appear to have lived just inside the leading edge of the dune field and moved forward as the dunes migrated. Consequently, the hearth mounds get younger in the direction in which the dunes moved. In effect, people lived at the boundary between two habitats: the dunes, which would have afforded protection from the wind and elevation to scan the horizon, and the flat plain in front of the dune field, which would have been ideal for hunting. Humans across the world have often chosen mosaic habitats, and living on the edge of ecological boundaries affords the best of both worlds. This is potentially instructive with respect to the older footprints at White Sands. The Tularosa Basin has three major habitats: the former lake floor with its distinctive resources, the alluvial fans built up by seasonal streams that flow from the jagged mountains that define the basin edge, and the mountains themselves. Each of these three habitats would have offered different types of material resources for the people of the basin, and each habitat might have had advantages in different seasons. Living on the boundary of all three might have had real advantages.

Track Sites Around the World

We return to the story of the White Sand footprints in the next chapter, but from that fateful day in April 2017, the study of the human tracks gathered pace and has not stopped. Footprints are not always on the radar of conventional archaeologists, who are usually more concerned with material culture—the stuff often left behind as rubbish. Footprints tend to be the preserve of geologists and especially those who study sediments (sedimentologists), deducing how those sediments were deposited and in what sort of environments. For example, clays tend to mean quiet water, while gravel indicates a river and the larger flows of water necessary to move large stones. Human footprints were once considered to be "freak acts" of geological preservation, but this view has changed. The discovery of the Laetoli footprints in northern Tanzania by Mary Leakey in the late 1970s rocked the archaeological world.[16] There, ancient footprints preserved in volcanic ash record the footfall of one of our ancestors (*Australopithecus afarensis*). Footprints were suddenly all the rage, especially when another set assumed to be those of *Homo erectus* was found about the same time at Koobi Fora in northern Kenya.[17] But despite discoveries of tracks in European[18] and North American caves,[19] interest waned. Over the last 20 years, this has slowly changed with the realization that human tracks are quite common in the geological record[20] and with the advent of tools to capture and preserve them in three dimensions. The pace of discovery has increased, since discovery breeds awareness, and where once footprint surfaces were undoubtedly destroyed in the quest for stone tools, folks are now taking more care. The study of human tracks is a branch of ichnology, derived from the Greek *ikhnos*, meaning "trace" or "track." Some archaeologists see this evidence as inferior, preferring artifacts such as stone tools, but this is slowly changing.

At this point, it is perhaps worth stopping for a moment to describe the different types of footprint evidence found at White Sands and to explain how this site differs from other track sites around the world. Why is White Sands special as a track site? The simple answer is the size of the site. Most track sites around the world are quite small. For example, the original humanlike tracks at Laetoli in Tanzania cover an area of just 30 by 7 feet,[21] although other animal tracks extend over much larger areas.[22] The longest trackways at Ileret in Kenya are only a few feet long.[23] The tracks on the edge of Lake Natron, again in Tanzania, are more extensive, but we are still talking a few hundred square yards at most.[24] The tracks at cave sites both in Europe[25] and North America[26] are again limited to a few feet in area. At White Sands, tracks extend over tens of hundreds of yards. In fact, the scale differs over several orders of magnitude. White Sands probably contains hundreds of thousands of individual tracks based on a conservative estimate and may well harbor many more. It is this difference in scale that is important. Hunters on the savanna of Africa can track animals over many miles and can see the interaction of one animal with another from the trackways they leave. At White Sands, you can follow trackways for similar distances and literally indulge in paleo-tracking. That is what makes White Sands unique, and currently, it is the only track site like it in the world. But such dried lakebeds are common in Africa and across the American Southwest, and many of these sites have yet to be studied in the same way as those at White Sands. In time, we might find other track sites like White Sands, but for now it is unique. One word of caution is important here: The number of footprints does not equate simply to the number of animals. A small group of animals visiting the same site repeatedly and milling about can leave a lot of tracks.

During the Ice Age, North America had a diverse and rich fauna, including several large animals often referred to as megafauna. The definition of megafauna varies. For some scientists, it means an animal that weighs more than 100 pounds. For other scientists, the animal must weigh more than 2,205 pounds. The reason for this variation is because *mega* is a relative term. An ostrich, for example, is mega compared to a chicken, but not when compared to an elephant. Irrespective of definition, the fauna at this time was different and is richly recorded in the La Brea Tar Pits in California, which is found in Hancock Park, a suburb of Los Angeles (Figure 1.5). Here, natural tar rose to the surface and trapped Ice Age animals as they ventured close to the edge of the tar pool. In North America at this time, there were several different types of elephant-like animals, variants of the woolly mammoths that roamed in Europe, including Columbian mammoths, mastodons, and gomphotheres. There was a giant armadillo (glyptodont) and various species of giant ground sloths. In fact, giant ground sloths were diverse across the Americas at the time, with more than 40 different species in four families.[27] Giant ground sloths were nothing like Sid and Sylvia of the *Ice Age* film franchise; they were much larger animals, weighing more than 800 pounds and often exceeding 2,000. From the fossil record, two genera are known from New Mexico: *Paramylodon* and *Nothrotheriops*, either or both of which may have been visitors to White Sands.[28] The most distinctive thing about sloths is their mode of locomotion. With long wolverine-like claws designed to rip into trees, they have adopted a way of walking on the outside edge of their paws. As they walk, their front feet are overstepped by their hind feet such that one composite track is normally produced, and therefore their trackways often appear bipedal. Various camels, horses, and bison were also part of this rich fauna. The significance of this megafauna is that at the end of the Ice Age, more than 38 species went extinct, and we don't entirely know why.[29] Some people point to climate change,[30] while others implicate human hunting.[31] It is a point we will return to in a later chapter, but for now it is simply important to recognize that these Ice Age animals are part of the footprint record at White Sands.

At White Sands there are tracks of giant ground sloths; Columbian mammoths; probably mastodons, camels, bison, dire wolves, and dogs of all sorts; and occasional big cats. This, however, is not an accurate record of the White Sands fauna. Tracks of smaller animals are almost totally absent. For example, where are the birds? After many years of study, only a couple of bird tracks have been found. Were birds simply absent from the margins of this lake or wetland? The answer is no, since footprints selectively sample the fauna present. This is sometimes referred to as the Goldilocks principle of footprint formation.[32] For a footprint to form,

Figure 1.5. A saber-tooth cat (*Smilodon californicus*) and a dire wolf (*Canis dirus*) fight over a mammoth (*Mammuthus columbi*) carcass at the edge of a tar pit at La Brea Tar Pits. Illustration by Robert Bruce Horsfall (from William Berryman Scott, *A History of Land Mammals in the Western Hemisphere* [MacMillan, 1913]).

the mud must be firm enough to hold the weight of the animal so that it won't flounder or sink, but soft enough for the sediment to deform under the weight of the animal to leave a track. Conditions have to be just right. If the mud is firm, it will sample only heavy animals able to deform the surface; things that are light, like birds, will go unrecorded. Moreover, a tiny print of a wading bird is more likely to be disturbed and buried in the sand by rising waters than is a track that is much bigger and deeper. The mud at White Sands must have been quite firm to allow the tracks of large mammoths to be left. In fact, there is evidence to suggest that the best tracks were formed during drier periods, when the water levels fell to reveal mud, which baked hard to preserve the tracks. As the water rose again, depositing sand over the tracked surface, the slightly indurated (cemented and hard) tracks were not easily washed away.

The range of different types of track preservation at White Sands also makes it different from other track sites. The first type of tracks present can be described as pedestal tracks. These tracks have epirelief; that is, they stick up above the surrounding area. This type of track forms a flat-topped pedestal where once there was a track depression. The depression became infilled to the brim and cemented to form a hard surface. The surrounding softer sediment was then eroded to leave the pedestal upstanding. The cementing agent is normally calcium carbonate, although at White Sands it is actually dolomite. Dolomite is magnesium carbonate and is precipitated from a mixing of fresh and salt pore waters (pores are gaps between sand grains), coupled with repeated wetting and drying. Algal growth may also help, creating dolomite a bit like magic. Key in this process is the growth of algae in the damp recesses of a footprint, which can help trap sediment, especially where the algae have "sticky" filaments.[33] This hard infill forms the pedestal as the ground around the track is lowered by erosion (Figure 1.6). We don't really know what Ellis Wright found back in 1932, but our suspicion is that he saw one of these tracks—but made by a giant ground sloth, not Bigfoot. It is worth noting that pedestal tracks are almost impossible to excavate, although in some cases they can be inverted to reveal some anatomical detail. Their main value is that they provide a marker for foot placement.

Others tracks at White Sands are cemented tracks that have a combination of both positive and negative relief. The scientific term for negative relief (depressed footprints) is *hyporelief*, but it is not often used. These tracks are cemented, often by dolomite, and usually have a shallow pedestal form but also contain some negative relief. The original outline and shape of the track is visible in negative relief, but aspects are also picked out by positive relief. Look at the track in Figure 1.7. The forefoot, instep, and hindfoot of the track is defined in negative relief, but the toe pads stick upward. These tracks represent an intermediate form between pedestals, where the track morphology has been completely infilled, and more traditional tracks in negative relief. There are examples, particularly of mammoth tracks, where carbonated cements are less apparent and the sediment layers appear to have been simply consolidated by compression. Again, excavating these tracks is not possible because they are basically rock, but they do provide a bit more information than pedestal tracks do.

The final type of track at White Sands is that which still preserves the negative relief of the foot, just like the tracks you might leave if you walk on a beach today. The tracks are usually infilled with sediment, but this sediment is not cemented and with care can be removed via a brush or small dental probe. These are true tracks formed by the indentation of a foot into soft sediment, and both the fill and the surrounding material

Figure 1.6. Upstanding "pedestal" prints made by a giant ground sloth from White Sands Missile Range, just north of White Sands National Park.

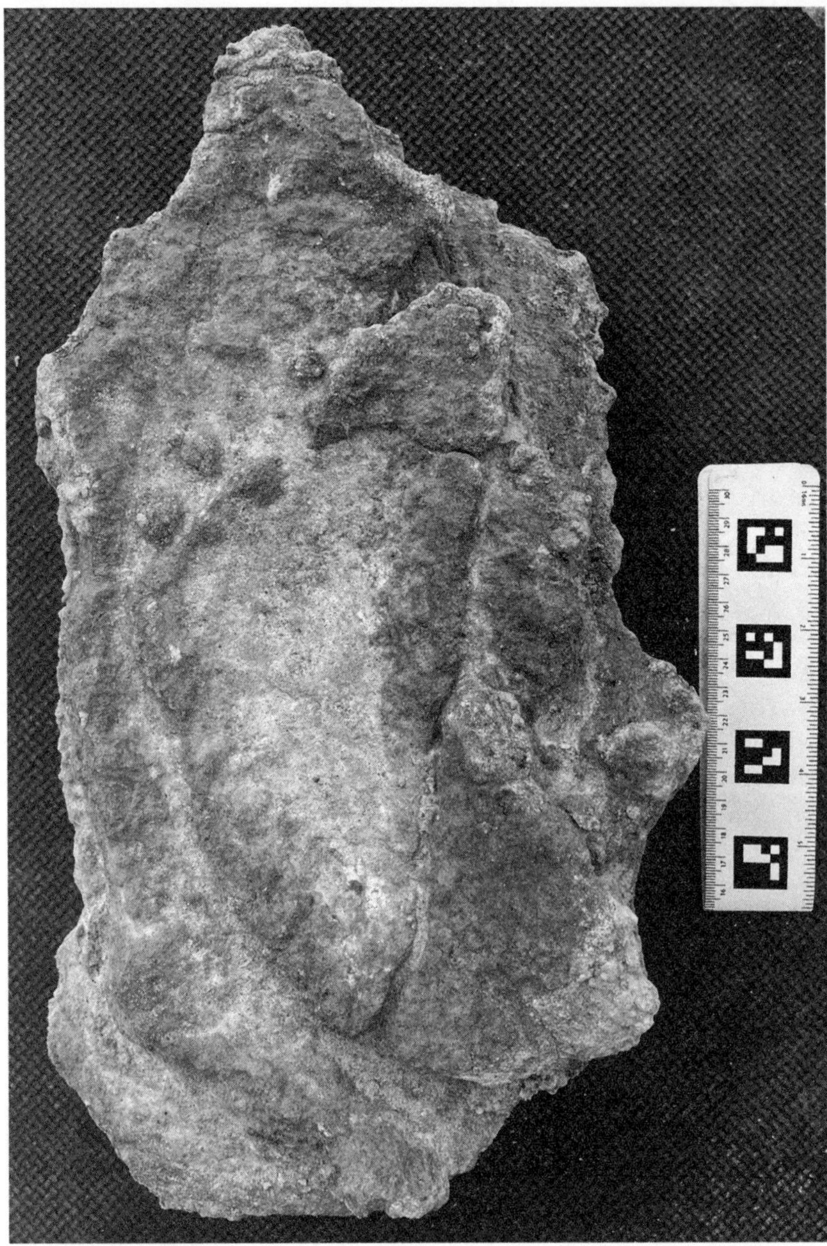

Figure 1.7. A human footprint at White Sands National Park composed of both negative and positive elements. Note the overall dish-shaped form of the main track. In contrast, the toe pads are upstanding.

may remain unlithified, although not in all cases. At depth, these types of tracks commonly occur on indurated gypsum-rich silt layers and are infilled by softer clays and/or fine sands. The track in Figure 1.8A, for example, shows a human footprint imprinted into a more compact gray silty clay, which has then been infilled by reddish fine silty sand. In this case, the track is simply revealed by removal of the infill, thereby uncovering the original surface prior to burial of the track (Figure 1.8B). The track is not visible prior to removal, and it is crucial that the excavator reveals the surface topography rather than slicing down through the surface. In other situations, footprints can be recognized on the playa surface by faint changes in color and might appear or disappear with moisture changes, as described above.

Why Were Humans at White Sands?

The footprint story at White Sands is one of water—abundant, predictable water in a region where it was sometimes hard to find. Humans have always been drawn to water. We drink it; cook with it; swim, bathe, play, and boat in it. We use the plants that grow in water and the animals that come to drink at the water's edge. In an arid landscape, water means life. For the small bands of humans who made their way into the arid West, places like Lake Otero provided stability and resource security. They offered reliable and predictable food and water within a new, uncertain, often changing landscape. Such stability helped ensure survival. Over time, it also fostered regional social cohesion. "We'll meet again at the big lake when the days grow short and the cranes arrive," people might have said to one another.

The predictability afforded by such places allowed groups to come together and linger, trade and socialize, play games, form and renew friendships, resolve disputes, and arrange marriages. These activities cemented ties among bands of people whose territories were scattered over thousands of square miles. Ultimately, they fostered a sense of shared identity reaching beyond the extended family groups that people spend most of their time in. As the centuries passed and language and customs inevitably changed, the differences that evolved between distant groups ultimately led to the emergence of distinct tribal nations. Even today,

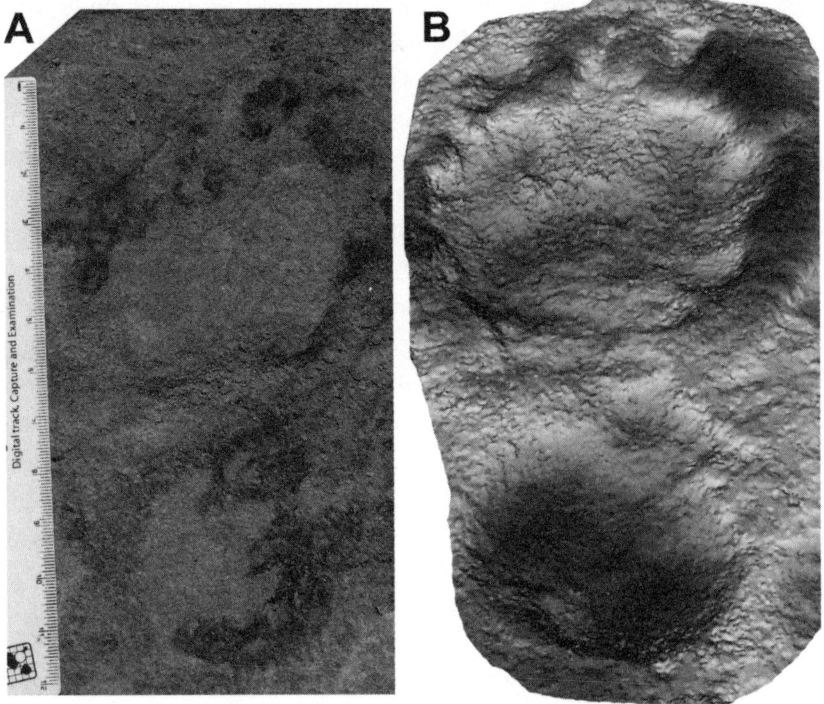

Figure 1.8. A: A large adult left footprint infilled by sediment at White Sands. B: A three-dimensional model of the same track from a more oblique angle. The scan is color-rendered by depth: the blue (darker) colors show low areas and the brown and yellow (lighter) colors show high areas. This is a large foot, with a length of around 260 mm, which in the United States is approximately a male size 8. Notice how the actual excavated track (A) is smaller than the surface area of the colored sediment.

long after Lake Otero dwindled to become a seasonal playa called Lake Lucero, 32 Native American tribes and pueblos still have ancestral ties to White Sands.

We know little about those early Native American ancestors, the first people to walk the shores of Lake Otero. We do not know for sure when they first arrived, where they came from, or the route they took. Nor do we have any real idea what language they might have spoken. And we do not know what they looked like or what their genetic makeup might have been. The oldest genetic samples reported in the Americas postdate the footprints at White Sands by more than 10,000 years. The nearest sample of comparable age comes from southeastern Siberia, near Lake Baikal.

We also do not know what sorts of stone tools they might have used because we have yet to find any that are clearly in situ. For many archaeologists, finding stone tools is important because of what they can tell us about how people made and used them. Tools are designed for specific tasks and food sources. Their shared characteristics tell us about technological and information sharing, and the use of different raw materials can tell us about trade, as well as patterns of movement. There is a lot of information to be deduced from the simplest of tools. So why haven't we found any stone tools? The answer is a bit of leap, but bear with us. You can usually find a stray coin in the fold of a sofa. Why? Because that is where you sit and rest. Yes, you might sometimes find a coin while walking, but it is less of a sure thing. Even the longest trackway at White Sands represents only a few minutes of time, maybe 30 minutes at most. The odds of a forager dropping (and not picking up) a valuable stone tool, transported from rock outcrops many miles away, are low. Find an overnight camp with a hearth and the odds will increase. So the absence of tools reflects the residence time of someone in the landscape. While members of the track team would love to have additional data that might come from finding ancient stone tools, we can still learn a great deal from the tracks themselves. In fact, there are things we can learn from tracks that we probably couldn't learn any other way.

Visiting White Sands

White Sands makes for a great day out, with beautiful dunes set in front of a jagged mountain skyline. Whether you are there to look at the sands, take pictures, sled on the dunes, or simply chill with friends and family, you will have a good experience. Sadly, you will only see a small portion of the park, since much of it has restricted access and is still in co-use with the military. While you can trek to the edge of Alkali Flat to look out onto the former lakebed, you can't go farther due to the unexploded ordnance that scatters the flats. This is where the tracks are located, in a strange way protected by the presence of the military and its missile debris. But over the last few years, the National Park Service has been working to bring the tracks to the visitor's center, improving its exhibits and displays of the tracks. Recently, the Park Service also upgraded its Ice Age Trail, which visits a small playa a few hundred meters wide in front of the dunes. Her,e you can get a sense of what Alkali Flat is like, and while the surface is broken, there are fossil tracks on it. The display boards tell the track story and give a sense of the megafauna that once roamed the park.

CHAPTER TWO

How to Study Tracks?

Do you count your steps? If you do, you likely know that the average person takes between 8,000 and 10,000 steps a day. Let us multiply that over a lifetime, and most of us will leave more than 200 million potential footprints. Yes, many steps will be taken in shoes, and most of the footprints won't survive, but theoretically some could be preserved. If a smartphone is the equivalent of an ancient stone tool and you update to the latest phone model each year of your life, there is a chance of you losing up to 70 phones. We should therefore find more footprints than smartphones in the geological record of the future.

The footprints you leave on the bathroom floor getting out of the shower are clear when first made, but are gone in a few seconds as the water evaporates. A set of footprints left on a holiday beach will be washed away by the sea or trampled by other beachgoers. But a footprint made on a mudflat and left to bake in the sun before being covered by a rising tide stands a chance of being preserved. It turns out that ancient people liked wet mud on the banks of lakes, seashores, along rivers, and on the floor of caves—all places that, given an element of luck, might preserve and fossilize a track.

The process is aided by algae, which favor damp places. A freshly formed deep footprint is damp and may even pool water, all of which is ideal for the growth of algae and bacteria. Mats made up of sticky algal filaments trap sediment and help stabilize the walls of a footprint, facilitating their infill and preservation.[1] Repeated wetting and drying may also aid this process by precipitating salts that cement the sediment grains. In this way, footprints get preserved on bedding surfaces between layers of sediment, and over time these layers are compressed, hardened, and in some cases turned into stone. Footprints were once thought to be rare acts of geological preservation but in truth are far more common than initially believed, and this is testified to by a dramatic increase, over the last 20 years, in the discovery of fossil footprint sites around the world.[2] We have the tools, as we see later in this chapter, to study tracks, and discovery breeds awareness in archaeologists and geologists of their presence, which in turn leads to more careful observation and discovery. In this chapter, we explore some of the methods and considerations in the study of footprints and at the end give some suggestions as to how you can get involved.

Looking from Above and Looking Below

The challenge at White Sands is finding the tracks. They can be elusive—visible one day and not another. The area is also vast. Our secret weapon is David Bustos and his team, who are out on Alkali Flat regularly. They see the ancient lakebed in lots of different states, sometimes covered with water and other times baked dry. A few weeks after rain, when the salt crusts have bloomed and been eroded by the wind, is a good time to see the faint outline of tracks. But having a curious mind and eagle eyes helps. David once spotted a gold wedding ring dropped by a visitor on the dunes from a speeding UTV!

Satellite images also help. Mammoth and sloth tracks are big enough to show up in a library of satellite images taken at different times of the year. It is just a matter of working through the historical image library to find a year when the tracks pop out. Our experience suggests that where there are mammoth tracks, there will be human tracks too. While the use of drones is restricted within the national park, in the missile range, high-resolution drones are being used to locate tracks. But searching for tracks visually can be frustrating, as thin layers of blown sand move across the lakebed, hiding the surface, and one is often left wondering what lies at greater depth.

Geophysics offers us an innovative solution. Geophysics is exactly what the word says: using the physical and electrical properties of the ground (*geo*) to see below the surface. For example, geologists search for oil by sending sound waves into the ground and monitoring their reflections from different geological layers. Sound waves travel at different speeds in different rock types and are reflected to the surface by bedding surfaces

Figure 2.1. A ground-penetrating radar survey looking for footprints. The ghost prints of a human are visible in the background. The lines in this survey are just 3 inches apart. The survey lines made by the wheels of the instrument will be gone in a few days. Tommy Urban, the team's geophysics expert, is at the helm.

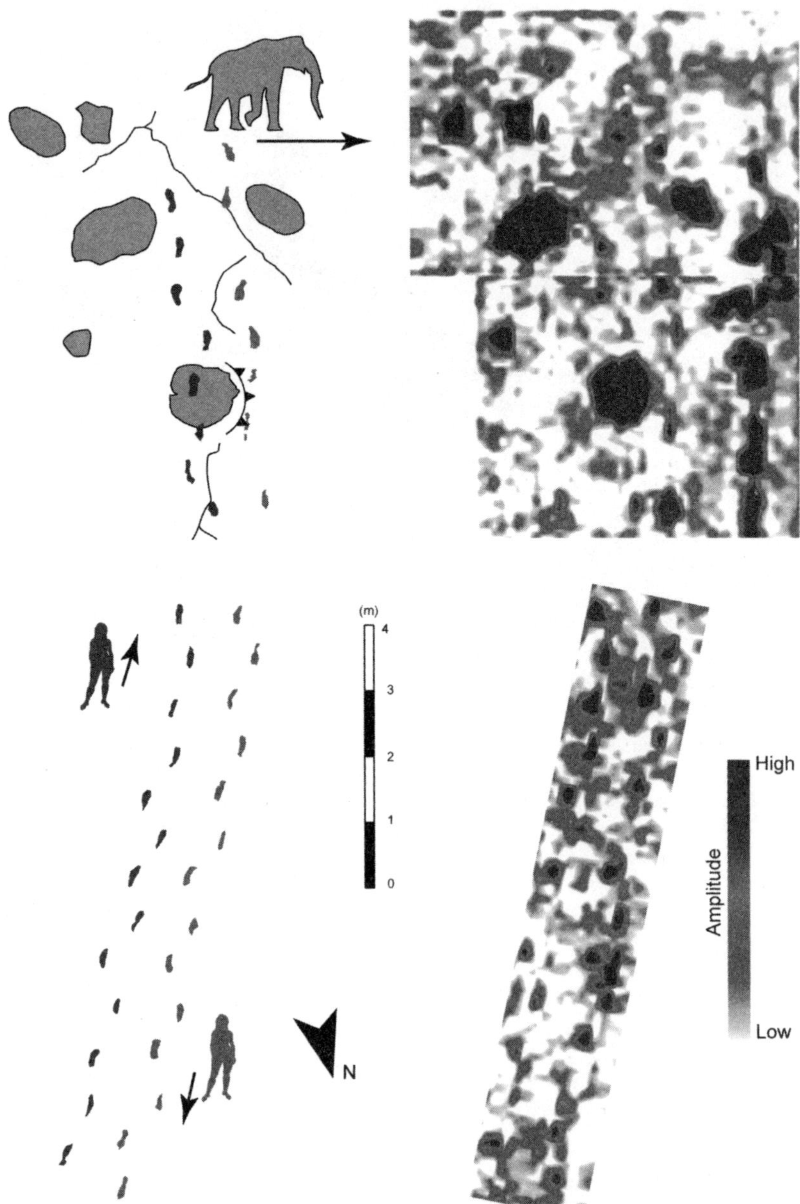

Figure 2.2: The type of output produced by a ground-penetrating radar survey. On the left is the known pattern of footprints in this area. On the right is the processed radar signal. The red (darker) colors show areas of higher signal amplitude and the location of tracks. The large red areas are mammoth tracks. The smaller ones are a double trackway (Urban et al., "3-D Imaging").

between layers. The reflected layers are called reflectors and indicate a change in the properties of the wave and by inference in the geology. Archaeologists use electrical properties in much the same way to image buildings buried below the ground. Here, a combination of different ground properties, as well as the pore water salts, are the key variables. Sediment has gaps between the grains called pores, and these usually contain water with dissolved salts. These salts vary the electrical properties of the ground; more salt leads to greater ground conductivity. One such technique is ground-penetrating radar, which sends a signal like a souped-up mobile phone into the ground. As with the sound waves of more conventional geophysics, the speed at which this signal travels is determined by the sediment properties, in this case electrical properties, and the signal is reflected to the surface when those properties change. Different signal frequencies penetrate to different depths, but in general you can view the subsurface to a depth of a few yards and in three dimensions, if you use a grid of intersecting survey lines and interpolate between those lines. Finding a buried wall is relatively easy using ground-penetrating radar because it is big and piles of rock contrast nicely with adjacent soil in terms of their electrical properties. Your survey lines only need to be spaced a few yards apart to capture the structure. But a mammoth track is much smaller, perhaps 24 inches in diameter, and a human foot is typically less than 12 inches long. If you are going to capture something that small, the spacing between your lines needs to be as little as 3 inches or less.[3]

Ground-penetrating radars come in different shapes and sizes. Some are mounted on small sleds about the size of a dinner tray. Others are larger and are carried on wheels, on a setup looking like an old-fashioned pram (Figure 2.1). When we first started to experiment with this type of work, pioneered by brilliant geophysics expert Tommy Urban from Cornell University, we got a pile of gym mats and marked out long lines 3 inches apart. The mats, designed to cushion the floor of a garage or basement, had jigsaw lugs on the sides that allowed the mats to be linked together. We would lay down a square of mats on the desert floor, say 20 × 20 feet, and use the grid of lines drawn on the mats to drag the radar across the surface. The technique is time-consuming but accurate, although the wind is a trial, and if chasing windblown mats were an Olympic sport, the research team would win gold. With changes of equipment, we progressed in time to a pram-mounted radar in which the lines are a wheel width apart. Whatever equipment is used, it is slow work and, given the scale of Alkali Flat, dispiriting, but it does provide a means of imaging footprints without the need to disturb the ground (Figure 2.2).

Ethics of Disturbance

So we find footprints. What happens next? Well, to be honest, nothing happens without a clear scientific reason to disturb the surface and not before discussions with the Indigenous peoples affiliated, via their tribes and pueblos, with White Sands National Park. Disturbing the ground is seen as an invasion of ancestral ground, and as a research team we respect this view. Some Indigenous people welcome excavation as a way of telling the story of their ancestors and reaffirming their long-standing association with the Americas, but others don't. There are different ways of knowing—one based on Indigenous oral traditions and another based on science. Neither is more important than the other, but sadly public interest and therefore conservation funding tend to favor science. Modern competitive society values dramatic science—the oldest, the biggest, the best. Such claims make careers, gain media attention, and attract the funding to make even bigger claims. But competition is not always healthy, and being first can encourage folks to lose respect for the people whose story they are telling. It is sometimes hard to remember that other worldviews are valid and that ancestral claims to the land need to be cherished.

Consequently, as a research team we try to work on the minimum number of tracks, or the smallest area, needing to be excavated to make

Figure 2.3 (*opposite page, above*). A 3D model of a series of modern dog tracks made on a beach. Note how one animal can make a range of tracks depending on its motion, in this case as it watches for a thrown ball. The model was made using the smartphone app Scaniverse (v3.0.3) with the USDZ output visualized and rendered in the free software Blender v4.1.

Figure 2.4 (*opposite page, below*). A series of 3D models of tracks made by the same individual walking at a similar pace on different substrates. Note how variation in the substrate causes variation in the morphology of the track created. The models were made using the smartphone app Scaniverse (v3.0.3) with the USDZ output visualized and rendered in the free software Blender v4.1.

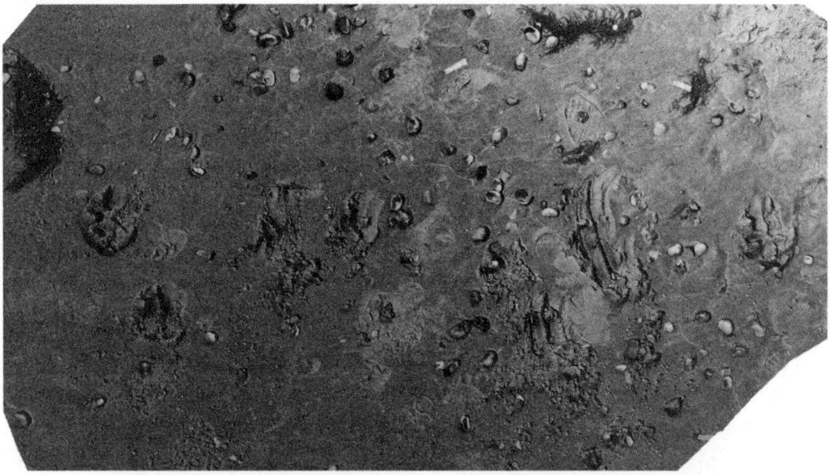

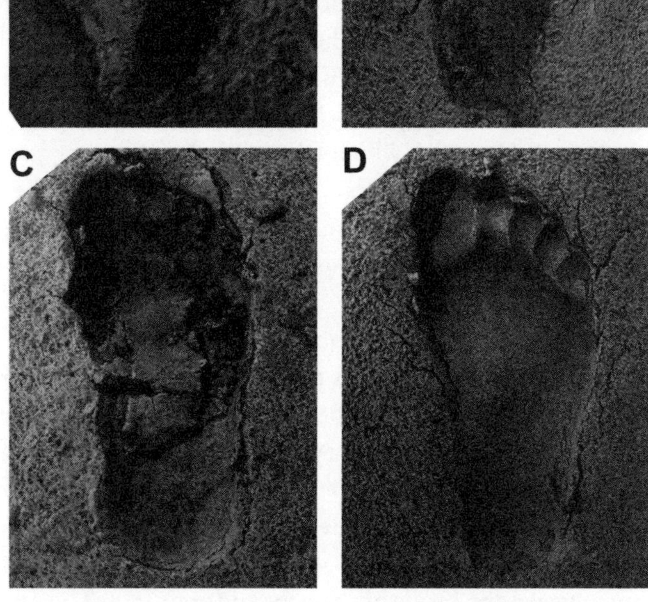
A
B
C
D

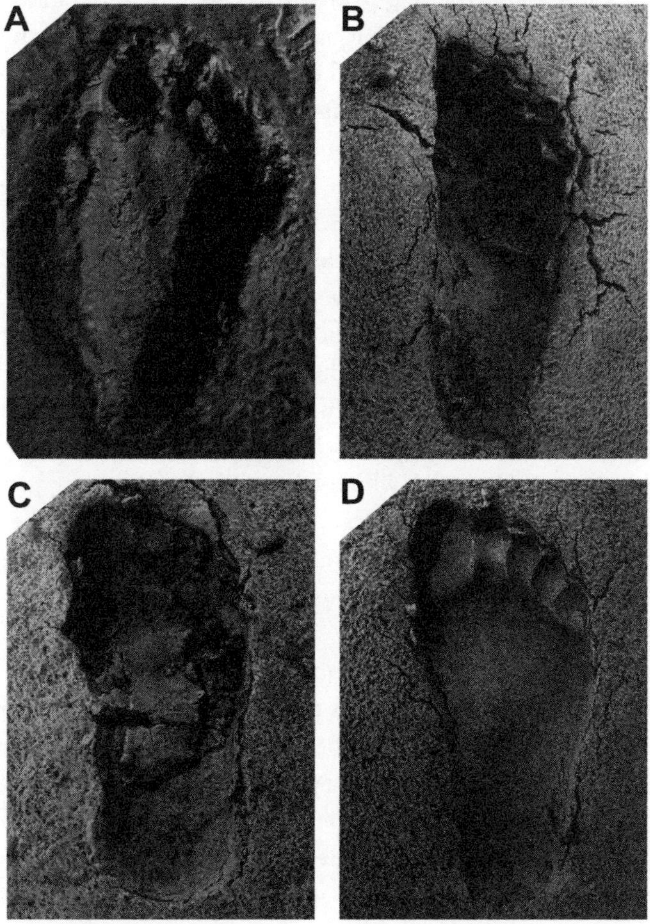

a particular scientific point. Determining that number is often difficult, however. Will one track do? Probably not; a few tracks in a clear trackway are needed to demonstrate that a set of tracks was made by a human, for example. If you want to say something about the individual that made those tracks, you need more. But how many more? In theory, the morphology of a track should reflect the foot that made it, but two interacting forces complicate this: the movement of the foot and the deformation of the sediment into which it presses. If you walk in a perfect line on a treadmill that measures the pressure your foot puts on the belt, the pressure patterns should be similar if you move your body in the same way with each step. But turn your head to one side to chat to a friend or scratch your nose, and that pressure pattern will change. Let us move this experiment to the beach and look at the dog prints in Figure 2.3. They show one dog bounding playfully on the beach; it has left a range of tracks with different morphologies. The sand is level and uniform, but it need not be, and this adds another variable to the mix. Consider the tracks in Figure 2.4, made by the same individual walking at a constant rate but on different substrates; the tracks are quite different. In the first track, the mud is wet but there is a firmer layer below. Consequently, the wet sediment is displaced to the sides, forming ridges around the track. The next track to the right is deep and the sediment is clearly soft, so compression is the key type of deformation taking place to create the footprint void. Effectively, the sand grains have been pushed together tighter to make space for the foot. These two tracks lie on a continuum between the two main ways you can create a footprint—either by displacing sediment out of the track and to the side, or by compression, which compacts the sediment beneath the track. So two variables—the substrate and the combination of the anatomy and motion of the track-maker—can both impact the morphology of the track that is created (Figure 2.5). But there is one more variable we need to consider: taphonomy.

Taphonomy is the branch of paleontology that deals with the process of fossilization. In our context, it is the natural processes that impact on a track after its formation, and it begins as you begin to withdraw your foot. The simple act of withdrawing your foot from a track may cause the side walls of your footprint to widen, on average by about 5 percent. In deeper tracks made in soft mud, the reverse is true. Have you ever tried to pull your foot out of a tall boot and lost your sock? This is caused by the suction between the inside of the boot and your foot. The same is true

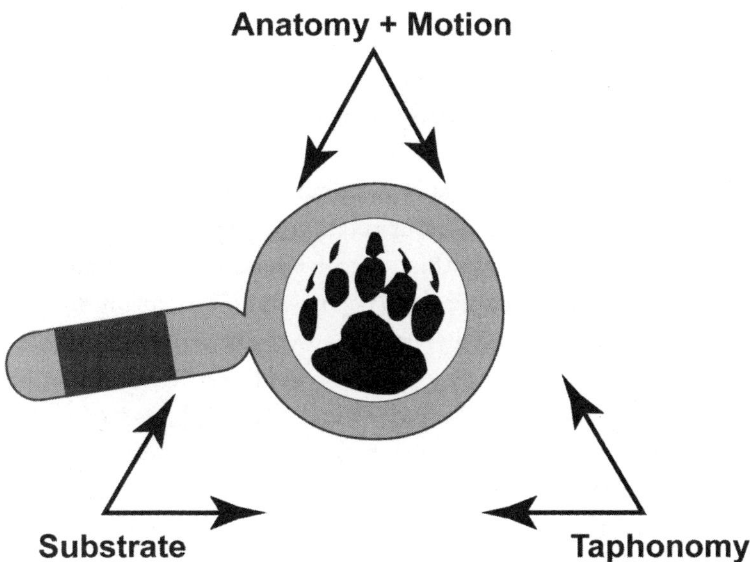

Figure 2.5. The morphology of a footprint is a function of the interaction of three variables: the shape or anatomy of the foot and its motion; the sediment or substrate properties of the ground; and the taphonomy, or processes, that happened to a track after it formed. The latter variables may involve changes made as the foot was removed or the fossilization process itself.

in a deep footprint, since as you draw your foot out, suction between the sole of your foot and the base of the track draws the side walls together, making the print narrower. The side wall of a deep track may also slump, a process helped if water pools in the track base and undermines the walls. If the track survives the first few moments, it may be trampled by someone walking behind the original track-maker—perhaps a child dawdling behind—or later, a herd of animals may trample it away. The point here is that these three variables—substrate, motion and taphonomy—cause lots of intra-trackway variability. Consequently, one individual can create lots of tracks, each with a different morphology. Say you find a fossil track. How do you know that track represents the foot of the individual who made it? Some folks argue that you need literally hundreds of footprints to accurately characterize the individual who made them. We have done some experiments around this via a research paper with the colorful title "When Is Enough, Enough?" It includes data from White Sands.[4] The answer is that it is a question of diminishing returns; you get a reasonably consistent idea of a track's morphology with between 10 and 20 examples per individual. In many cases that is not possible, and you must work with what you have.

The other aspect that must be factored into any discussion of sample size is the importance of crosscut relationships, where one track overprints another. Seeking out this type of relationship is important and can influence the area that needs to be excavated. To explain this, we had better take a walk on a lonely beach. As we walk, enjoying the solitude, we notice that someone walked by a few hours earlier, leaving a line of footprints. The tracks are still fresh in the sand. In places a small dog has left a track on top of a human print, and in other places a human track partially obscures the print of a larger dog. Logic dictates that the larger dog came first, then the human, and then the small dog last. That is the order in which the tracks are superimposed on one another. We have an order of events based simply on the crosscutting pattern of one track with respect to another. We don't know what the precise time interval between these events was, however, or whether the human was walking two dogs, one that raced ahead and one that lagged. But we do know that the three animals passed around the same time, since the prints look fresh and have not been washed away by the tide.

At White Sands, if we find a human track overstepped and therefore crosscut by a mammoth, we know the mammoth came second. Equally, a human track on top of a mammoth track tells us the mammoth passed by first. We know that mammoths became extinct in North America at the end of the Ice Age, so logic dictates that a human print crosscut by a mammoth track must be at least that old. That is the power of simple

Figure 2.6 (*opposite page, above*). Two surface scrapes at White Sands. A: A bunch of tracks and marks made in organic-rich sediment and infilled by silts and sands of different colors. B: Track of a cow-like animal, and beyond it, the outline of a human track. These tracks are within half an inch of the playa surface.

Figure 2.7 (*opposite page, below*). An excavated track surface at White Sands with golfing tees and labels attached to each print. This system allows the excavators to record individual prints. The numbers simply come from the order in which labels were picked out of the bag!

A
B

T082
T083
NCPTT
T006
T081

crosscutting relationships, and without recourse to complex dating methods, we have a relative order of events. We know that the human tracks at White Sands at least date from a time before mammoths, or giant ground sloths for that matter, became extinct. When we put all these considerations together, we can work out what is ethical in terms of disturbance. In part it depends on the scientific question being asked, but ultimately it is through consultation with our Indigenous partners that this decision is made.

Beginning to Brush, Dig, and Preserve

Most of the work we do is either on naturally occurring benches that stick out of small cliffs (bluffs) or on the floor of the playa. Yes, we have dug some deeper trenches, but this is unusual at White Sands. The strategy recognizes the importance of having a plan. The first step is to pause to create a plan. Then you work to assess and preserve what is present while recovering or recording the tracks before finally reviewing your work. This is not a how-to guide for budding ichnologists, but it is worth emphasizing a few of the key things we focus on in the field to give an idea of how we do our job. We include a bit more discussion of excavation strategies in the postscript should you be interested.

An archaeologist is taught to grid a surface, and in each square, you take the surface down one trowel-scrape at a time. Cultural artifacts or bones are identified in situ where possible and mapped. Additionally, the material from each layer is then passed through one or more screens (giant sieves) to pick out smaller cultural items, such as tool flakes, along with big bits of bone, wood, or seeds. If you find something of interest, in theory you know which grid square and at what level within that square the item came from. The aim is often, although not always, to keep the surface horizontal, lowering it in salami slices. The aim of ichnology is rather different. The ichnologist aims to uncover the ancient surface on which the track-maker walked and specifically to unearth the three-dimensional topography of that surface and the tracks on it. Rather than going down in salami slices, the work is about following subtle changes in sediment color, texture, or induration to pick out the original relief. Finding that surface can be difficult. At White Sands, the simplest tracks to uncover are near-surface tracks infilled by a different color of coarser sediment packed into the track. We start by scraping back the ground to remove the surface crust of salt- and water-splashed silt to reveal the undisturbed layers beneath. Amazingly, and it never ceases to surprise us still, this is often just a few inches below the surface. In some locations at White Sands, this process reveals dark, organic-rich sediments marked with tracks that are infilled with differently colored silts (Figure 2.6). When you find something like this, it is amazing, because laid out in front of you is a two-dimensional map of the tracks. Matthew recalls,

> Your mind wanders on the playa. I often chuckle to myself because the tracks laid out in two dimensions in this way remind me of a set of dirty footprints on a kitchen floor. I imagine the scene: A mammoth or camel steps in from a garden and walks across the clean floor, leaving a trail of footprints, just like a dog might today. In my daydream, the irate owner of that floor glowers at the mess the animal has made! On the playa, the surface mud dries quickly and the color fades, as it does on the kitchen floor. Sometimes it can feel like a memory game; you see the pattern of tracks laid out in color for a few moments. When you come to excavate them, you must remember their location when the color is gone. We can bring back the color with a water spray bottle, which can help redefine the prints, but it is never as good as when it is first revealed.

We use wooden golfing tees to mark out tracks and give them a unique code (Figure 2.7). Over the years, the system has evolved from tees used to hold down small wooden squares to tees with neat circles stuck on the top where a golf ball would normally sit. We avoid anything made of metal—firstly because it is not biodegradable, but mainly so we don't leave any metal that might interfere with a later geophysical survey. Our sites quickly resemble mini-golf courses. Keeping good records is essential, but not always as easy as it should be. Writing can be a challenge with your hands smeared in sunscreen, to which dirt naturally adheres, and once you add a few grazed fingers into the mix, the page of your notebook becomes a tapestry of indiscernible scribbles and unpleasant stains. But the main problem is that things change and evolve as you uncover each track; you find one footprint and then go looking for the next step, and slowly you work from the most obvious tracks to those that are shy. There are three important things to record. First is the stratigraphic level. Where does the tracked surface you have uncovered sit within the stratigraphy? This is about tracing the surface to an adjacent trench or placing it within a graphic log or scale drawing of the sediment layers. (We discuss this process for those interested in more information in the postscript.) We do this normally by literally tracing the top surface of a layer into the nearby bluff or cliff, but over a longer distance, we also use something known as lithostratigraphy, which involves matching unit characteristics, such as color and grain size, and bedding.

The second element to record is the placement of the tracks across the surface, and for this we need a scale map. You can make a map in a variety of different ways. There are laser theodolites, for example, which are very accurate. A prism, usually on a pole, is placed on the point you want to record (say, the location of a track), and the lens in the theodolite is focused on the prism. A laser then records the travel time from there back to the prism, which gives distance, while the angle of the theodolite to north is also recorded. The two numbers give you a placement (x, y coordinate) for the point below the prism. These days, geographical positioning systems (GPS) can do the same job. You probably have a GPS in your smartphone, but such systems tend to be less precise, and if the distance between tracks is only a few inches, then GPS is not a great solution. Systems called dGPS (*d* stands for "differential") can measure to a fraction of an inch, but there can still be a level of error. All these solutions involve expensive, bulky, and power-hungry equipment, and in truth, you can get the same level of accuracy using old school methods. For example, you can lay out a grid of string and chalk lines or use a quadrant (a wooden square with a grid of strings). Simply measure the offset of a track from each line in the grid; this allows

Figure 2.8 (*opposite page*). The morphology of a track is a combination of elements, including size, form (triangles, circles, etc.), and topology, which is the variation in depth across the track. Depth variation tells you about the pressure applied by the foot in different places. It is important to also note that one animal (in this case, a dog) can leave lots of different track morphologies, and you must look at this variation to distinguish one animal from another. Among the tools we use to analyze a track are shape statistics that remove the complication of size. A Generalized Procrustes Analysis is a common solution. It transforms prints mathematically, so they are superimposed on top of each other with size removed.

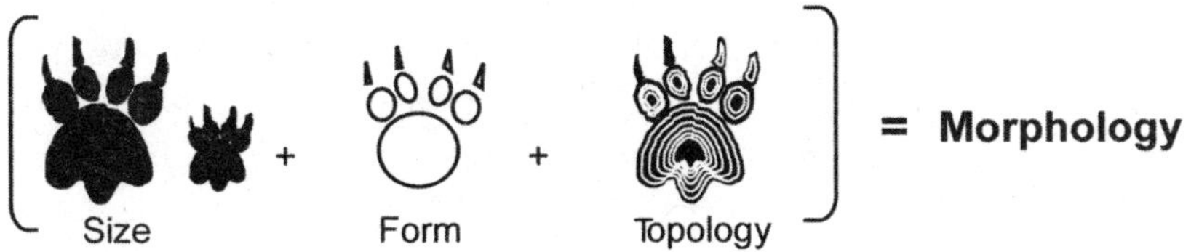

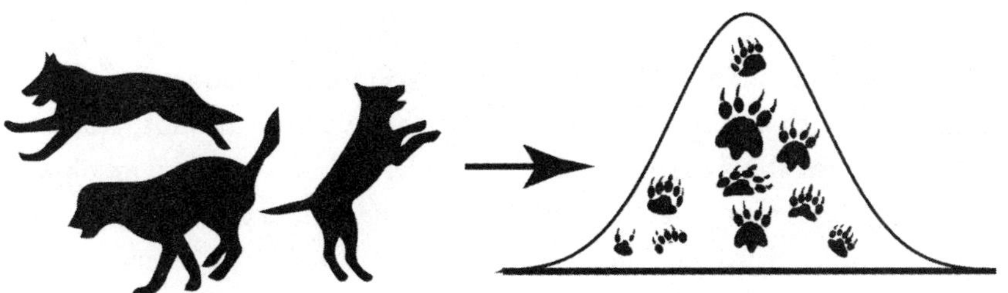

One playful dog

Lots of different print shapes

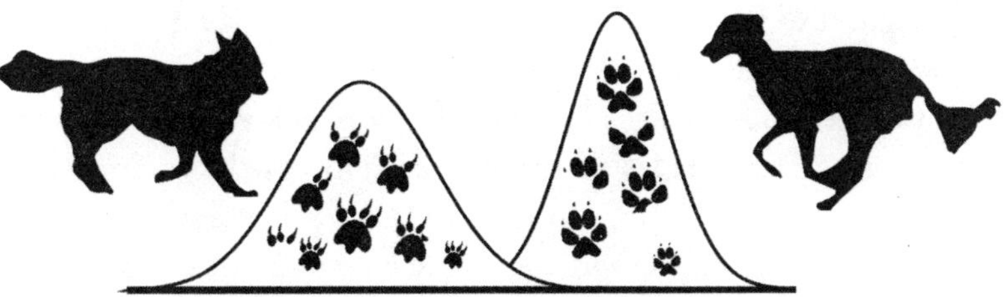

Two species of dog separated by print shapes

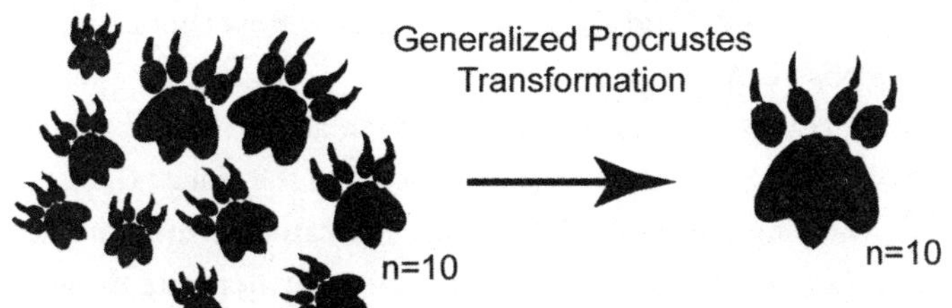

Ten paw prints: different sizes, different orientations

Ten paw prints: superimposed, with size removed

you to place it accurately. Other old school methods simply involve tape, pencil, and a sheet of graph paper on a clipboard.[5] Young geologists are not as well-versed in such techniques as those who were taught a while ago and have had a long history of equipment failure and batteries dying in the middle of nowhere. The other solution is to get high up above your subject. A small drone can take a vertical photograph, and if there are sufficient square scales within it, you can manipulate the image so that it is orthogonal (at a right angle) to the ground. Step ladders, kites, and high poles with GoPros are other options. You want your photographs to be taken from above rather than at an angle, and you can turn an oblique image into one that is vertical given a few squares laid out on the ground.

At White Sands, we use photogrammetry to create what is called an orthomosaic. We take a lot of pictures from different angles over the subject using a high pole with a GoPro set to Time Lapse mode, so that it takes pictures every couple of seconds as you move the pole. We infill this with more pictures from lower angles. For an area that is just a few yards square, we literally take hundreds of pictures. We then use photogrammetry software to stitch these images into a mosaic, which is rectified such that the mosaic is at right angles to the surface. This works well for small areas, and with correct scaling using scale bars you lay down across the site, you can get accurate measurements. Such measurements include the distance between tracks (step length) and the distance between two right or left tracks (stride length). These variables are important to estimate walking or running speeds, and if you want to know how this is done, we refer you to the postscript.

We now have tracks in stratigraphic position and a map of the track distribution from above, so next we need to focus on the tracks themselves and specifically their morphology. To do this, you can take measurements in the field, such as track length and width, with a ruler, but these days the best solution is to create a three-dimensional model of each track and to take the measurements digitally from that. Technology developed over the last 20 years allows you to record a surface, or an object for that matter, in three dimensions. Initially, at the turn of the century, this was done mainly by optical laser scanners. These bits of kit emit a laser that is reflected by the surface. The laser travel time gives you distance, a three-dimensional point in space. Those points have x, y, and z coordinates, where z is the distance from the plane of the scanner. In this way, you can create a cloud of points across a surface and interpolate between these points to create a perfect replica of that surface. Initially, the equipment was expensive, bulky, and needed to be shielded from light, more suited to the laboratory than the field. One of the authors remembers taking such a scanner into the field in Africa only to see it explode in a fireball when hooked up to a broken generator. But over time, this method has been replaced by digital photogrammetry. The development of enhanced computer performance was the key here, along with digital photography. If you take multiple oblique photographs from different angles around a surface with a footprint on it, modern software can now recognize shapes and combinations of pixels on each image, which via some fancy trigonometry allows you to place both the combination of pixels and the camera in three-dimensional space relative to one another. Do this for enough computer-recognized shapes on all the images and you end up with a cloud of points that accurately depict the surface and the footprint. The advances in this field are such that you can now produce a passable three-dimensional model with just a smartphone.

Dinosaur footprints tend to be preserved in rock—for example, in mud that was once soft but has over time been cemented by natural salts precipitated between the grains of sand and clay. Even then, it can be a challenge to preserve such sites from the wind and rain. The famous 3.66-million-year-old Laetoli footprints made by an ancient human ancestor in Tanzania are preserved in volcanic ash, which due to a freak of chemistry cemented rapidly after deposition. But the White Sands footprints are preserved for the most part in sediment, which—while sometimes cemented by dolomite and often compressed hard—is still quite soft and will yield easily to the wind and rain. In fact, the White Sands footprints are eroding fast, in part due to climate change, and geologists are in a race against time to preserve this amazing resource before it is gone. How can you preserve the impossible?

The harsh reality is that you can't. You can only rescue and record what is there. This is why creating accurate three-dimensional models is so important; you preserve the impossible by creating a perfect replica that can be used for scientific study, 3D printed for display and education, and archived for posterity. In an interesting circular development, three-dimensional laser scanners have gotten smaller and much more robust in recent years, such that our research team is now using a combination of photogrammetry and laser scanning.

What Can Footprints Tell Us?

Before we go much further, we had better clarify what a footprint can and crucially cannot tell you.[6] The morphology of a track is the sum of different components, namely size, form, and topology (Figure 2.8). Size is easily understood—is one track bigger or smaller than another? And if scientists are using the same measuring system, tracks can be compared. The slight issue there, however, is that scientists are free thinkers and tend not to follow the same measurement rules.

Take the length of your foot, for example. The heel is easily defined at the apex, but which toe do you measure to? Some folks favor the first toe, or hallux, as it is called. Others favor the second toe because it is more in line with the apex of the heel.[7] And some folks measure to all five toes. This is before we come to any other potential measurement, such as heel width, ball width, or the size of your big toe! Most measurements these days are made digitally, either on vertical photographs or, better still, on three-dimensional track models. The next component of morphology is form, which basically breaks down a track's shape into component shapes. For example, a cat print consists of a big oval and four smaller circles. This can help when we're comparing tracks, especially where two species make similar impressions. The final component is the topology of a track, which is its three-dimensional shape, often portrayed via contour lines or depth shading. Implicit in track studies is the substitution of depth for pressure; those areas that are deepest in a track should equate to those areas where the foot has pressed down most. It helps sometimes to think of a track's topology as a micro-landscape; just as the contours on a map portray the location of valleys, basins, and peaks, so do the contours on a three-dimensional model of a track. Together, size, form, and topology give you the morphology of a track (Figure 2.8).

Numbers can help describe morphology. Over the last 20 years or so, the study of anatomy has been revolutionized using spatial statistics to describe elements of anatomical shape.[8] The math has been around for some time, but the computing power needed to run it had to catch up. The technology is called geometric morphometrics and is beyond the scope of this book, but it is worth a paragraph because it lies at the heart of modern ichnology. Every time you take a measurement, you place mental landmarks, points, on the item to be measured—the start and end point

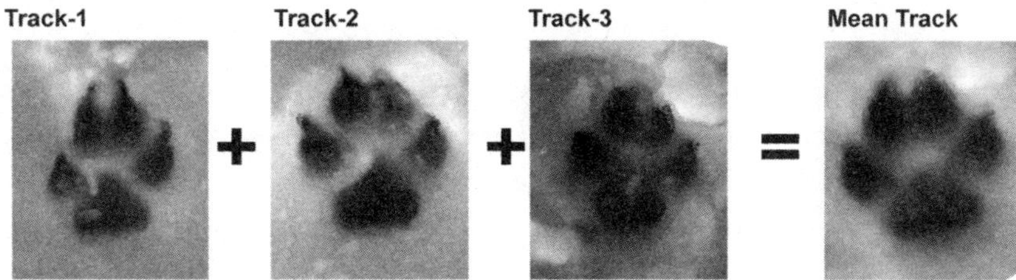

Figure 2.9. Creating a mean track. We begin with a series of 3D models, color-rendered by depth (Tracks 1 to 3). By superimposing these images one above the other so that the same anatomical points correspond in all three, we can compute a mean track (instead of picking the track that best suits your argument). This is a powerful way of reducing variability in analyses (Bennett et al. "Laetoli's Lost Tracks").

of a line, if you like. If you are measuring lots of footprints, you measure from the same point every time and effectively place a landmark. If you place lots of landmarks across a footprint, you have a network of points defined by the distances between the landmarks. We can also define each of these points via x and y coordinates. Let us imagine a picture of the footprint. The left-hand bottom corner of the picture is equivalent to the origin on a graph. At this point, the distance, or number of pixels, along the horizontal (x) axis is 0, and the distance on the vertical (y) axis is also 0. We can define any point on the photograph by measuring the number of pixels along the horizontal and vertical axes, and that gives that point x and y coordinates expressed as the number of pixels. Every picture has a different origin point and scaling, so the coordinates between pictures may not be comparable. Also, some footprints are bigger than others, and if you want to compare anatomical form, we need to remove size. Why is this important? Well, if you are studying the shape of hands, for example, and have a sample of 60 handprints to compare—each with a different size—these size differences may obscure any common shape traits that exist. To solve this, we need help from a Greek innkeeper named Procrustes. He was famous for allegedly stretching his clientele to fit the beds in his inn or, if they were too tall, shortening their limbs. His name is now given to a mathematical transformation that removes size from a set of shapes (making them all the same size) and brings all examples in the set into a common alignment with a common origin (Figures 2.8 and 2.9). Once this transformation has been done, you explore the differences between examples in terms of variation in their anatomical forms. You do this type of analysis by placing landmarks on a shape and using those landmarks to transform it. We can use a similar transformation to align multiple three-dimensional tracks to produce a mean track.[9] Matthew remembers,

> I started to explore the application of shape statistics, something called geometric morphometrics, back in 2008, when I was trying to compare the tracks of two of our ancestors. I was working on the 1.5-million-year-old tracks at Ileret in northern Kenya at the time.[10] We believed these were made by *Homo erectus*. I was comparing them to the tracks at Laetoli in Tanzania, which dated from 3.66 million years and were made by an earlier ancestor (*Australopithecus afarensis*). I had all these textbooks and learned papers about this technique and how it had transformed biological description of anatomy, but I just couldn't find, or get to work, a software package that would do the analysis. I was really frustrated, feeling stupid and limited by my own mathematical knowledge, when I came across a brilliant piece of freeware called PAST,[11] developed by Professor Øyvind Hammer of the Natural History Museum at the University of Oslo. It was a transformational moment and opened a door for me. I can't thank him enough!

We have already noted how tracks vary within a trackway, something called intra-trackway variance, and this is a bit of nuisance when you are trying to compare one trackway with another. But you can overcome this and create a mean track by using landmarks. A three-dimensional track that is color-rendered by depth—say, light gray for high areas and dark gray for low—is essentially a grid of pixels. The color represents depth. If you now place landmarks on multiple tracks and use them to transform each colored scan, you end up with a stack of scans one on top of the other in similar orientations. Take each pixel in the stack and create an average value for that pixel. You now have a set of pixels that represent a mean print (Figure 2.9).[12] In short, there are lots of sophisticated analytical tools you can employ to describe individual footprints and whole trackways, and crucially to compare one trackway or track statistically with another. This is at the cutting edge of modern ichnology and is often referred to as computational ichnology.

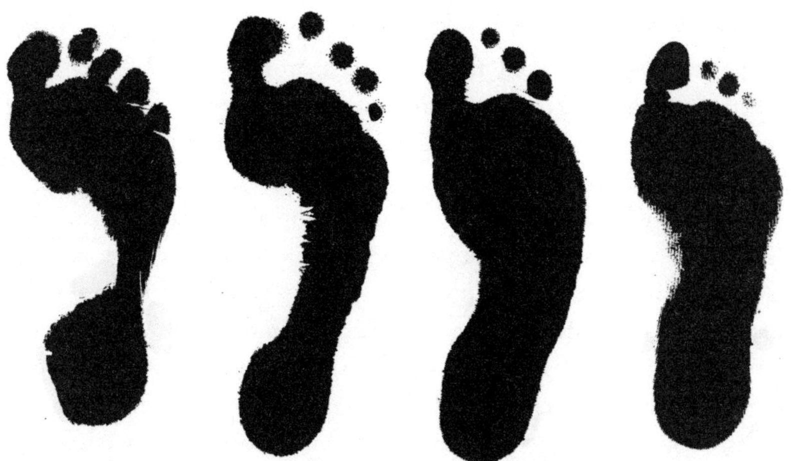

Figure 2.10. A series of modern human footprint silhouettes. Note the diversity of anatomical morphology. It is quite common for the smallest toe not to register (see the rightmost example) and for the longitudinal lateral arch to vary in morphology (that is, some people are flat-footed).

As with most sciences, there is an unspoken rule to try and separate factual observation from interpretation. We see a dog make a footprint, and we refer to it as a dog print, but in the past, did dogs have the same print morphology? The answer is probably yes, but that may not hold for all tracks. What we have here is an interpretative leap: "This looks like a dog print, so it must have been made by a dog." A more objective approach is to say we have a central pad around which are four smaller pads with claws. Our interpretation is that we have a dog track. The need for caution comes from the fact that, as we have seen earlier, a dog bounding about on a beach as its owner throws a ball will create many different track morphologies depending on the dog's motion and the properties of the sand. This poses a bit of a problem for the classification of tracks; one track-maker can leave many different track morphologies.

Animals and plants are classified according to the Linnaean system devised by Carl Linnaeus (1707–1778). It is a hierarchal system in which a species is defined by a dual identifier: the genus followed by the species. So, as *Homo sapiens*, we belong to the same family as our ancestor *Homo erectus*. Our even older ancestor *Australopithecus afarensis* (better known as Lucy) was part of a different family, but both *Homo* and *Australopithecus* belong to a large group known as hominins. We only have one thing to place in the species category, despite the wealth of anatomical variability there. But with tracks, *Homo sapiens* can make lots of different marks, whether by standing on tiptoes, walking on heels, dancing, or jumping. In trying to classify tracks, ichnologists refer to an ichnotaxa that is morphologically objective and without an immediate inference of a track-maker. This system was developed largely for invertebrate traces—those made by arthropods crawling about on the ocean floor. Now folks have tried to apply this to human footprints, defining an ichnotaxa for modern human footprints and also one for older tracks. They have even gone as far as to define type-specimens. The ichnotaxa and associated type-specimen for modern human tracks are based on the Acahualinca footprints in Nicaragua,[13] while those for older *Australopithecus afarensis* tracks reference the famous footprint site at Laetoli in Tanzania.[14] The idea is that folks compare their specific example (the track they have found) to the type-specimen and thereby show it is the same ichnotaxa. Whether this is helpful or not is questionable, due to the morphological diversity present in human tracks, but it is common practice when looking at dinosaur tracks and invertebrate traces. The key message here is that if you don't know what the track-maker is, you should be cautious in making the final interpretative leap. A good example involves the mammoth tracks we find at White Sands. Technically, they are the tracks of proboscideans, members of the order to which modern elephants, mammoths, and mastodons belong. Mastodons were smaller versions of the Columbian mammoths that roamed across the Americas during the Ice Age, but the footprints made by these animals

Figure 2.11 (*opposite page, above*). A three-dimensional model of a modern barefoot track viewed obliquely and made on a damp gypsum playa, just like that at White Sands. Note how elongated the toes are due to slippage and the movement of sediment to the rear of the footprint behind the rotating and slipping ball of the foot. Sediment has been pushed up on the lateral edge, or outside, of the track, and a small block has fallen into the track to cover part of the toes. There are also cracks at right angles to the print margins. This is a real footprint in every sense of the word, but differs from what folks often think they look like (cf. Figure 2.10). Prints by the same maker are seen in Figure 2.4.

Figure 2.12 (*opposite page, below*). The tortuosity of giant ground sloth trackways in the presence or absence of a human track. Each dot is a sloth print. The human foot symbols mark places where a human trackway comes close to or crosses a sloth trackway.

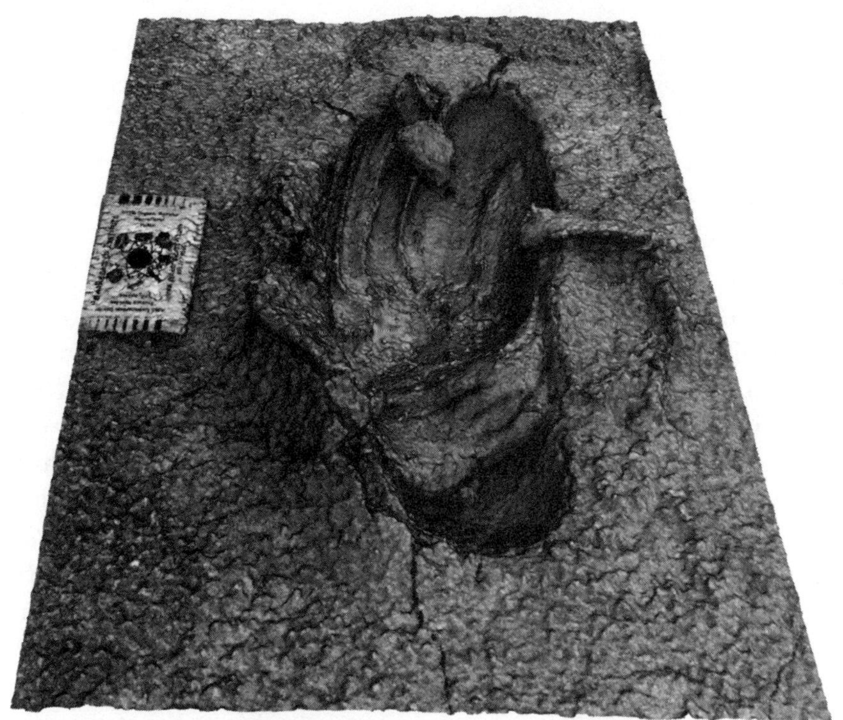

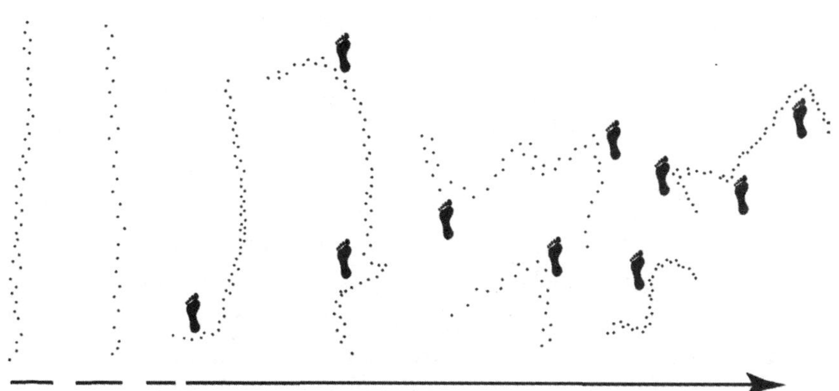
More human tracks

are virtually the same. And bits of fossil mastodons have been recovered from the White Sands Missile Range in the past,[15] so we know they were present on the landscape. Mammoths were more common and therefore are the likely track-maker we see at White Sands in such numbers, but we can't be sure. This is one example where rushing to name a track-maker can lead folks astray.

Linked to this question is a fundamental one for the work at White Sands: How do we know the tracks are made by humans? To be scientific about this, we need criteria on which to base this interpretation. Recognition of human footprints should be based on multiple criteria. First, a track should have good anatomical form, such as toes, a heel, and an instep. Figure 2.10 shows a range of modern human footprint shapes in which the main anatomical features are present. These tracks are probably like the ones you make when you step out of the shower with wet feet, and a fossil track should in theory show some of these features. In practice, however, the sediment properties on which the subject walks have a strong influence on the final morphology, as discussed earlier. Figure 2.11 shows a three-dimensional model of a footprint made by someone walking on a slick gypsum playa barefoot today. The movement of the foot on the muddy surface impacts on the track morphology. This is what a real track looks like, and not all tracks are going to have perfect anatomical form. Taphonomy comes into play. As discussed earlier, this is a posh word for all the things that happen to a fossil, in this case a track, after it is formed. The withdrawal of the foot may disturb the toe pad impressions or side walls of a track. The side walls may collapse and crumble. Water may infill the track, weakening the side walls. And all this happens before the track gets buried. Again, perfect anatomical preservation is unlikely and, if found, should make ichnologists suspicious. The formation of a footprint may also deform or displace sediment around the track margins. Little ridges may be squeezed up around the track's sides. As the sole of the foot rotates around the ball, it might push small slabs of sediment to the rear of a track, and the toes may scrape forward or flick sediment out of the track. These features are not always present, but they help in the interpretation of a track. Track morphology helps identify a print as being made by a human, but a track needs to be part of a trackway. If you are Captain Kirk or Spock, then you can materialize out of the ether, but normal folks must walk. Therefore, a given print should be part of a line of prints. In fact, the presence of a left-right-left sequence is one of the key criteria for defining a track as being human.[16] Collectively, the morphology of a track and the presence of a trackway are usually sufficient to define a track as being human.

Let us now think about the physical age of a track-maker. Were the tracks made by a youngster or an old person out for a stroll? If you have kids, you may have cast their feet in plaster when they were babies and, as they grew, bought countless pairs of expensive shoes. Our feet grow until sometime in our mid-teens, according to well-defined growth curves that transcend race, gender, and to some extent nutrition.[17] So if you find a small human footprint, you can make a reasonable guess at the age of the track-maker using one of the many empirical growth curves that plot foot size against a child's age. In fact, you can do the same for a small mammoth track by analogy with modern elephants, for which there are growth curves. (If you are interested in this, we refer you to the information in the postscript.) For the giant ground sloth, this is not so easy, since there are no living relatives that would make suitable analogues.

The human body conforms to a standard template in which the size of your feet is broadly in proportion with other body parts. Tall people tend to have bigger feet. Yes, there are always exceptions, and you may be the exception to the rule, but if you have enough data, you can make a statistical estimate of stature from foot length that filters out all the wonderful variance in body size out there. Broadly speaking, the human foot is about 15 percent of your stature, and although this varies with ethnicity, it does prove a first-order approximation.[18] How relevant these generic anthropometric guides are to Indigenous people is unclear. Aleš Hrdlička made extensive study of the Indigenous peoples of the American Southwest at the start of the twentieth century, but direct correlation of stature and feet is elusive in this work.[19] He does find that Native Americans are generally taller than those of European heritage.[20] Hrdlička was the first curator of physical anthropology at the US National Museum, now the Smithsonian Institution National Museum of Natural History. He was and remains a controversial figure and without doubt had little regard for Indigenous Americans, many of whom were the subject of his anthropological work, but there is currently little alternative work out there.

Someone running will leave footprints that are more widely spaced than someone walking, so by measuring the distance between footprints, we can estimate the speed at which they were traveling and determine if they were running. When someone dances on a beach barefoot, they make lots of prints with different shapes. In this case, the footprints tell you about motion or the biomechanics of the track-maker. When a foot contacts the ground, it applies pressure to the sediment, which either moves out of the way or compresses to make room for the void that is the footprint. The depth of a track is therefore a measure of that pressure; the more pressure, the deeper the track is.[21] Footprint studies use this substitution of pressure for depth to understand the biomechanics of the track-maker. One final inference a footprint can make is presence. It is like a flag that says someone was here.

So footprints can tell us a huge amount: They can tell us about presence, the biomechanics of the track-maker, the speed and mode of travel, the stature and even the weight of the individual, and perhaps the individual's age. To this, we must add behavior. How does one trackway of prints interact with another? Or how does a human trackway affect the behavior of another animal? This is a rich vein of information that can provide us with a snapshot into past life.

As a brief illustration of this, when paleo-tracking at White Sands, we can see how twisty sloth tracks are. We call this the tortuosity of a trackway. Left to their own devices, giant ground sloths tend to leave quite straight or gently curved trackways, some of which we can trace for miles. But as soon as a human trackway occurs in the vicinity of one made by a sloth, the tortuosity of the sloth's trackway suddenly increases (Figure 2.12). In one great example we have studied, a long, gently curving set of sloth tracks suddenly stops and revises, heading back the way it came. From above, the trackway looks like a perfect V. On excavation, we found a line of human tracks at the apex of the V. The human was probably not there at the same time as the sloth, but encountering the scent of the human was enough to cause the sloth to about-face and run. Whether giant ground sloths were just nervous animals or had grown to be wary of humans is unclear, but this example illustrates the power of footprints to give insight into the behavioral interaction of one animal with another.

What about the role of the Native tracker in this work? There are two schools of thought around the interpretation of fossil tracks. One involves the application of anatomical tools to describe tracks with empirical data. This is the approach we have described here. The alternative is to use a Native tracker, who has the experiential learning to interpret a track. This latter approach was explored in a series of papers by Andreas Pastoors and Tilman Lenssen-Erz, who took a group of experienced San Bushmen

Figure 2.13. A cast of a Folsom point. Folsom ranges from about 12,800 to about 12,200 years ago and is just younger than Clovis (about 13,400 to about 12,400 years ago). Photograph by and courtesy of Vance Holliday, from the collection of C. V. Haynes, School of Anthropology, University of Arizona.

trackers from northern Namibia to the footprint caves of Europe and asked them to interpret what they saw.[22] In the context of understanding the thought processes involved in Native tracking, this was a powerful exercise. But the approach clashes with the more empirical method because there ultimately is no way of testing an assertion about a fossil spoor made by a tracker. In the modern world, if you make a mistake in tracking an animal, you go hungry; that is the test. But in the fossil world, how can you challenge the interpretation without challenging the integrity of the tracker? Folks have the same problem in criminal courts. Do you believe the expert witness because they have worked in the field all their life, or do you want to see the data on which their conclusion is based? We have never asked Native trackers to interpret the footprints at White Sands, but perhaps we should at some point.

The two approaches are wrongly polarized as being scientific and not scientific, which is incorrect. An interesting observation from those who study Native tracking is the importance of dialogue in the tracking process, whether with oneself or within a group of trackers. The San Bushmen constantly debate while tracking; one posits a suggestion, another counters, and a third may see something different. Collectively and via debate, they decide and move on, sometimes thinking themselves into the behavior of the animal in question. This is the process of science, and Louis Liebenberg has suggested that the origins of science, or at least scientific debate, stem from Indigenous trackers.[23] It is an inductive process. You gather data, you put forward an idea, someone counters with an alternative, a test is proposed, and a decision is made on the best available evidence at that moment in the chase. The only real difference between an empirical scientist and the Native tracker is that one posits via numbers and the other by qualitative observation based on experience. In our work at White Sands, we have frequently had meaningful and extremely helpful discussions with Indigenous site monitors, who bring their traditional knowledge to a site and help us frame questions and ideas. Understanding the past should be a collaborative process based on mutual respect, understanding, and trust.

Footprints Compared to More Conventional Archaeological Evidence

Conventional archaeology tends to be about rubbish, ruined structures, discarded foods, and stone tools uncovered from the sands of time—artifacts from which human presence and behaviors are reconstructed. Most archaeologists dig for artifacts, recording the sediment layers in which they occur, but it is the artifact that counts most.

Artifacts allow a relative chronology to be established and technologies to be correlated by type in both time and space. Let us think of Coca-Cola bottles for a moment. The earliest bottles (about 1894) were cylindrical with a short neck. Between 1900 and 1915, the bottle developed the slender neck we associate with it today, and there was a brief flirtation with brown rather than clear glass at this time. Sometime in 1915, the classic hourglass shape was adopted, and this stuck until the introduction of the plastic bottle in 1994. The bottles evolved over time, and if you find a brown Coca-Cola bottle in a rubbish dump, chances are the dump was active between 1900 and 1915. You could in theory correlate—link in time—different rubbish dumps using the brown glass version, because it is both distinctive and short-lived. Stone tools are the same. The theory goes that the cruder the tool, the older it should be, since technology advances and tools that share common design elements represent technologies shared between groups.

American archaeologists are slightly obsessed with stone tools, perhaps more than with other types of evidence and certainly more than archaeologists in other countries. The delicate fluted and elongated points of the Folsom people are widely reported across North America and represent for many Folsom technology and therefore a group of people with shared culture, technology, and behaviors (Figure 2.13). This obsession obscures a more local variation in morphology. Other technologies, both earlier and later, have been recognized, and the evolution of one into the other has become much less clear in recent years. The power of stone tool typology is that it can be used a bit like an event horizon; find a Clovis point and you know your site dates from that time, even if there is nothing to date. The problem with stone tools, however, is that they are not necessarily static within a layered stratigraphy. They can move both up and down through the agency of something as simple as an earthworm, as Charles Darwin demonstrated in his garden.[24] An animal burrow can also mix sediments such that a stone tool originally deposited near the surface ends up at depth, and given that older sediment tends to occur at the bottom, the stone tool can appear older than it should. In contrast, a footprint can't move and is fixed on the bedding surface it was imprinted on. Mixing the sediment simply destroys the track. That is why in some ways tracks are superior to more conventional types of archaeological evidence, although simply saying this would be heresy to many archaeologists!

Becoming a Track Expert

How do you become an expert in fossil footprints? The answer is different for everyone. In terms of home discipline, it is probably more geology than archaeology, and certainly so if you are not studying human tracks, but zoology and conservation biology all have an interest in footprints.

David explains, "For me it was simply observation- and curiosity-driven. I am a conservation biologist by training, and before coming to White Sands I worked in forestry at the Eldorado National Forest in California. But the tracks at White Sands just burrowed away, and I love to learn and figure stuff out and over time became an expert in fossil tracks. The fun part is that I am learning all the time, which is a great thing."

Matthew adds,

> The first 10 years of my career were spent studying glaciers in the Arctic and Ice Age glacial landforms in Britain. At the start of the century, I began to work on Ice Age sediment in Mexico and on footprint projects. I am a geographer and geologist by training. My big chance came when I was invited to join the Koobi Fora field school (in Kenya) in 2007 to explore some potential tracks they had just unearthed. From there, I built a bit of a reputation for capturing tracks in three dimensions and started to study tracks in various parts of the world. I also started to translate some of the bespoke research software that I wrote with my friend and longtime collaborator Marcin Budka into forensic practice. Together, we still spend a lot of time researching and developing tools to help forensic professionals and

detectives use footprint evidence to fight crime. Every time I come out to White Sands, I learn something new about the tracks or how to study them; it's a brilliant place!

Dan remarks,

> It was the invitation to work with David and Matthew on the tracks at White Sands that really kick-started my work in this area, but I have always been something of a hunter. I worked for many years in Alaska, Canada, and Siberia on various archaeologic projects and spending time with Native hunters. Watching animals and looking at their tracks gave me a keen appreciation for what a trained observer can learn from studying tracks. And of course, living and working with bears provides an added incentive. It's always nice when spotting a track gives you a heads-up that you might have furry company.

Sharon Gloshay, an Apache anthropologist, contributes,

> I was invited first as a tribal observer and then as an excavator to work on the footprints at White Sands. The fact that Indigenous people were included in this project to lend their perspective and insight is a remarkable example of inclusivity. Being able to assist in excavation was a valuable and spiritual experience on a personal level for me. When excavating a site, some experts do not look for footprints. The fact that this site exposed human footprints and those of megafauna living together is an original discovery in the Southwest, and I am thankful to be able to add my perspective to this magnificent site.

You don't have to find fossil tracks to learn about footprints and what they can tell you. Footprints are all around you, if you know where to look: print left in a wet concrete sidewalk, like those on the main drag in Alamogordo, not far from White Sands; tracks left on grass verges as folks cut the corner; those left by animals that visit our yards or gardens in the night. Matthew recalls,

> The thing that got me through COVID-19 lockdown in the United Kingdom was the badger and fox tracks in the garden. Just before we went into lockdown and right after I had just returned from the

first big excavation at White Sands in January 2020, my wife and I spotted badgers in our back garden. We also had regular visits from a fox. I used the children's play sand and spread it in the corner of the garden where our nighttime visitors came and went. The next day, there were some beautiful tracks in the sand. While everyone else was panic-buying hand sanitizer, I was desperately trying to lay my hands on sand and plaster of Paris! Each evening, I would prepare the sand trap, and I would rush out the following morning to view the haul of tracks, casting the best in plaster. I added a trail camera to this setup, and the combination got me and the family through the grim months of lockdown.

In addition to Matthew's method, you can create a simple footprint tunnel to capture the tracks of smaller animals. Some people use large pipes. Others create triangular tunnels out of the plastic corrugated sheets used to protect floors from work boots during renovations. The diameter of the tunnel determines the size of animal that can get in. In most cases, it is best to keep it small. A pot of something tasty is left in the middle of the tunnel, with sheets of white paper taped to the floor on either side. Then, using charcoal powder, you lay down a black strip between the tunnel entrance and the paper. The idea is that small animals—mice, rats, hedgehogs, and ground squirrels—visit the tunnel, attracted by the bait. As they cross the threshold of the tunnel, their paws pick up the charcoal. As they push forward toward the bait and the reward, they leave tracks on the paper. You can get some beautiful tracks this way and explore the diversity of different track patterns left by the same animal as it moves. This approach has been used widely in some places to study nocturnal animals. Hedgehogs in the city of Reading in the United Kingdom have been studied this way.[25] Another great example is the study of geckos in New Zealand. Here, empirical information about the animal's body plan allows researchers to determine the snout length of an animal by studying its tracks.[26] Just as in human ichnology, we can estimate stature from the size of a footprint. In fact, footprints are increasingly being used to monitor endangered wildlife in Africa. Endangered rhinos are an example.[27] A game warden can simply walk the same path each day and note the animal footprints that cross the road. The warden can scrub out old tracks in the dirt as they go so they can spot new ones the following day. This is completely noninvasive; you don't need to see the animals to know they are safe or bother them with GPS collars. A growing body of wildlife conservation work now uses footprints. You can use spatial statistics to describe tracks in terms of numbers, recognize them, and tell if they were left by a male or female, for example.[28] This is also possible to some extent with human tracks.

Books such as Tom Brown's *The Science and Art of Tracking* offer additional advice on tracking (of varying value). Brown recommends that those serious about tracking should create a sandbox in their yard. His thesis is that tracks contain subtle tells—slivers of sediment—that can inform the trained eye on subtle changes in footfall pressure related to different types of movement. In sand, these slivers of sediment tell of friction between the sole of a foot and the surface of the sand. So experiment in your own sandpit to learn something about tracks and how to interpret them.

You can also use neo-ichnology. For example, folks have studied dinosaur tracks by looking at those made by birds. After all, birds are the living descendants of dinosaurs. You can do this yourself if you keep chickens. Study the range of different tracks they make and how they vary with different soil properties. Are the tracks the same when the ground is wet or dry? Can you deduce the behavior of one bird or another from its tracks? Tracks are all around us, and the potential to learn from them is huge—and more to the point, it is fun!

CHAPTER THREE

Cinematic Snapshots

Imagine you are sitting in a movie theater looking at the landscape of White Sands. The camera pans across the vast and dusty plain of Alkali Flat. The jagged outline of the San Andreas Mountains, silhouetted against a deep blue sky to the west, shimmers in the heat. The wind stirs on the far side of the flat, and a small dust devil catches your eye. You can feel the dust, the breeze, and the warmth despite the air-conditioned theater. Slowly the picture dissolves and blurs—the classic cinematic signpost for a flashback sequence. As the image refocuses, you watch elephant-size animals move across the flat, heading for the water and presumably the mud. Your eyes start to pick out groups of people in this vast landscape. On the far side of the flat, you can see a giant ground sloth being harassed by a group of hunters. Mammoths trample the mud, children splash in a puddle, a lone woman seems to be on some kind of mission, and folks are dragging wooden sleds laden with possessions. Footprints allow such stories to be told and provide evidence to underpin these landscape memories.

Hunting Sloths on the Playa

We last left David and Matthew lying on the desert floor in April 2017, having found and confirmed the first definitive human print at White Sands. This was to be an eventful trip.

Matthew remembers,

> The same day that David uncovered the first clear human print was also the day when things got a bit weird. I was working on a large

> sloth track, maybe 2 feet long and with a broad kidney-like shape. You could see where the claws curved forward. It was the first track I had excavated at White Sands, and finding the floor and sides of the track was not easy. You had to put your trust in the brush. As I brushed, I began to see another track within the outline of the first. It had a rounded heel, and that gave me confidence. In a little while, I had uncovered a perfect human footprint inside the sloth track. It was if someone had laid an insole made of sediment within the larger track.

David adds,

> From the surface, the large giant ground sloth prints looked like the prints Ellis Wright described in 1932—perhaps 22 inches long and 8 inches wide. When we brushed out the prints, we could see incredible claws, and the base of the foot was 3 to 4 inches below the surface. As I brushed out one of the sloth prints with incredible claw marks, I began to hear a strong British voice swearing with great excitement. As I walked over to see what the excitement was, I looked over Matthew's shoulder to see a human footprint placed on top of a giant ground sloth track.

Matthew continues,

> So I got up and started on the next sloth track in the trackway, and before long I had found the same thing: a human track inside that of a sloth. It was weird and had me scratching my head. The following day more sloth tracks were uncovered from this trackway, each with a perfect human foot at the bottom. The only way this made any sense geologically was if the sloth had walked first and the human had followed, placing their feet exactly within the outline of the sloth track. The sloth tracks were large and the spacing between them significant. For a human to have placed their foot so perfectly each time—it was clearly intentional, because they must have been stretching to make each step match.

Slowly and over several days, Matthew, David, and an intern named Jackson uncovered a whole trackway of sloth tracks with a human foot inside (Figure 3.1). At the end of this trackway were lots of sloth and human tracks (Figures 3.2A). Some of the sloth tracks were made by a single claw and formed a broad circle. They seemed to indicate that the sloth reared up on its hind legs and turned, swinging its arms, which grazed the surface. We called these flailing circles, because that is exactly what the animal seemed to be doing—flailing with its arms as it turned. The first such circle we saw was at the end of one of the trackways with the superimposed prints. Had the animal gotten irritated by being stalked and suddenly reared up to turn on its stalker? That is what the tracks seemed to be saying on the muddy floor of the playa. There were also human tracks of someone approaching the circle with the sloth at the center. The human tracks seemed to have been made by someone on tiptoes, since no heel was visible—only the toes. In these types of situations, you develop stories to explain the evidence—testing, rejecting, or revising the story with each new trace found. In fact, the story helps you focus on the next target to excavate. If you want to give it a bit of scientific pretension, you can talk about multiple working hypotheses, an idea developed by T. C. Chamberlain in 1897.[1] The analogy he used was that research was like parenting children; you should not favor your firstborn, but should treat your children, or in this case your stories, equally. He has a point; a researcher should not latch onto the first idea that comes into their head. Working in the field is similar. One of us will put forward an idea to explain the tracks, to be countered by another idea and replaced in time by a third as the evidence unfolds. This constant storytelling drives the inquiry and makes fieldwork fun.

Rearing on its hind legs, the giant ground sloth would have been a formidable prey for anyone, let alone humans without modern weapons. Tightly muscled, angry, and swinging its forelegs tipped with wolverine-type claws, it would have been able to defend itself effectively (Figure 3.2B). The tracks revealed in April 2017 appeared to suggest that our ancestors used misdirection to gain the upper hand in this dangerous close-quarter combat situation with a potentially deadly creature. Was the stalking of the ground sloth—the deliberate placement of the human foot in the sloth track—a game? Was it simply adolescent high spirits? Or was it aimed at irritating the animal being stalked such that it would rear and turn, allowing another person to strike a potentially killing blow while the animal was distracted? We can't be sure, but the latter seemed to be what the tracks were saying—a story of life and death, written in mud (Figure 3.3). We should add one word of caution here: We don't know the precise time gap between the formation of the sloth tracks and the formation of the human footprints. It wasn't long, for sure, since the sloth tracks had not filled in, but it may not have contemporaneous as implied by our reading described above. There is always an element of uncertainty, and one is left with the most likely or simplest scenario—what scientists like to call the most parsimonious.

Giant ground sloths were strange animals—bigger than modern cattle—and their skeletal structure suggests that they were more muscular than silverback gorillas. They belonged to a hugely successful and diverse order of animals with little relationship to modern tree-dwelling sloths and even less to Sid of the *Ice Age* film franchise. Perhaps the most distinctive feature is how they walked on the outside edges of their feet, in what scientists call a mediolateral stance, to presumably allow the development of the huge claws used to both grip and rip into trees (Figure 3.2B). The exact species that made the tracks is not known. Fossils of two species of ground sloths, and their dung,[2] have been found in New Mexico. The remains of *Paramylodon harlani* are known from sites in the northern and eastern regions, while *Nothrotheriops shastensis* is common in southern counties of the state and was a desert browser.[3]

We found more flailing circles and could clearly see, as we discussed earlier, that sloth tracks become irregular and erratic as soon as a human track is found in the vicinity. There is evidence from other sites in the Americas that giant ground sloths were hunted,[4] but you must ask: What would convince someone to engage in such a deadly game? Surely the bigger the prey, the greater the risk.[5] There is an important observation here: Small game offer little risk of injury in their capture. Yes, you need a lot of small game if there are many mouths to feed, but this food source is likely to be reliable. So why take the risk of getting hurt? Was it because a big kill could fill many stomachs without waste? Maybe it was pure human bravado. At the end of the Ice Age, the human population in the Americas was growing fast as people spread out over the prairie and plains. It was also a time of animal extinctions: More than 38 species of large animals, including the giant ground sloth, went extinct. Many paleontologists favor the argument that human overhunting drove this wave of extinction, and for some it has become an emblem of early

Figure 3.1. A reconstruction of the giant ground sloth *Nothrotheriops shastensis* as envisaged by Gabriel Ugueto. Note the mediolateral feet and the long claws.

human impact on the environment. Others argue that climate change was the true cause and that our species is innocent. It is a giant crime scene in which footprints now play a part. Our data confirm that human hunters were likely attacking megafauna and were probably practiced at it. Unfortunately, the data do not cast light on the impact of that hunting. Whether humans were the ultimate or immediate cause of extinction is still not clear. There are many variables to be considered, including rapid environmental change. But what is clear from the tracks at White Sands is that humans were then, as now, "apex predators"—at the top of the food chain. It is important to recognize, however, that megafauna and humans appear to have lived together for many thousands of years at White Sands without apparent impact.

Trampling Mammoths

If you want to study the biomechanics of an athlete, you ask them to run or walk on a treadmill with a pressure-sensitive belt. This records the pressure below the foot as it contacts the ground, first as the heel strikes and then as weight is transferred down the outside edge before it crosses via the ball of the foot to the inside edge and finally reaches a peak between the first and second toe as the foot pushes forward. The analysis is highly diagnostic and, to some extent, perhaps unique to an individual.[6] It provides important information to assist in treating foot or leg injuries. It is easy to convince a human to walk on a pressure plate, but what about an elephant?

Some patient colleagues have done exactly that, getting pressure records for both Asian and African elephants.[7] And one might expect an ancient mammoth track to show a similar pattern of depth variation. After all, the basic assumption in the biomechanical study of footprints is that pressure can be substituted for depth. Parts of a track that are deeper than others should in theory be the locations of maximum plantar pressure.[8] Our research team had just started to experiment with ground-penetrating radar, with Tommy Urban leading the work. We had captured several mammoth tracks as part of this effort, and in processing this data Tommy

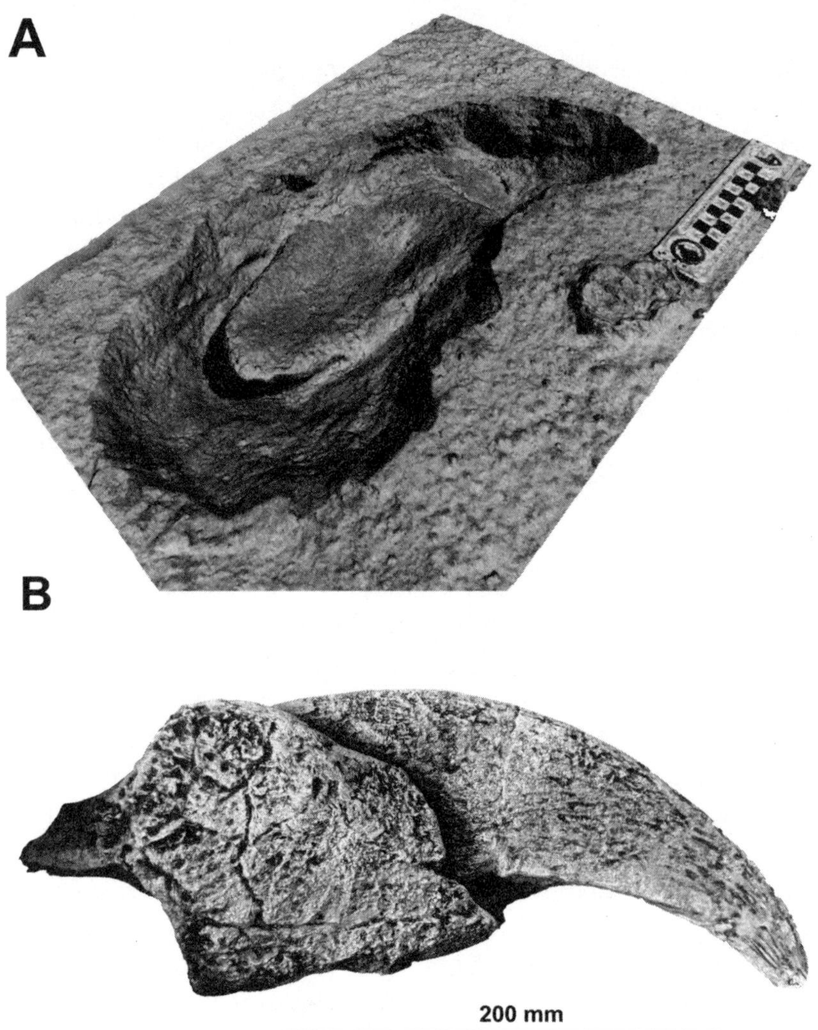

Figure 3.2. A three-dimensional model of a giant ground sloth track with a human track inside it. It is part of a trackway on the west side of Alkali Flat, in which every step has a superimposed human-on-sloth print. B: A mold of a claw from the giant ground sloth *Nothrotheriops shastensis*. Such claws were used to rip into the bark of trees and shrubs, and would have been fearsome during a defensive encounter.

Figure 3.3. A sloth hunt as envisaged by Karen Carr. Distraction was key to the hunt.

drew our attention to an interesting observation. Beneath the mammoth track was a weird three-dimensional shape in the radar data. It appeared to be caused by slightly firmer sediment.[9] In planform, this corresponds to exactly where the plantar pressure record of an African elephant reaches its peak. At that point, we were grateful for those veterinary researchers who had collected the elephant data. In fact, we were able to put that pressure data beside what we saw below the mammoth and draw a link. A big animal such as a Columbian mammoth does not just leave a surface footprint, but consolidates the ground below to leave a trace independent of the surface track.

Around this time, we were chasing down mammoth tracks to study, and we cut several in half using a chainsaw.[10] The chainsaw makes a clean cut, which would not be as easy to make with a spade or trowel since the ground is quite hard. By cutting a line across a mammoth track, we could then dig out one half and view the remaining part of the track in cross-section. What we saw was not especially surprising, but was exciting nonetheless. In most cases, the actual track was quite small, perhaps the diameter of a medium-size pizza, but around it the sediment layers had been displaced and folded (Figure 3.4). One of the reasons you can see mammoth tracks from space in satellite images (yes, really!) is not because the track is large, but because the deformation of sediment around the track makes it appear much bigger than it is.

We spent a lot of time trying to work out how to study the giant trample ground at White Sands. Here, lots of mammoth tracks are visible, etched out by the wind from the lakebed. The muds are baked and cemented firm, but the deformation below each track has set the layers up at an angle. This gives purchase for the wind, which has etched out this swirling pattern of overlapping tracks. There is evidence here for trunk traces—places where a trunk has been dragged or swirled in the sediment, leaving short, curving marks.[11] Modern elephants seek out mud and shallow water as an aid to cooling as a way of dealing with parasites, and also to potentially seek out specific salts and minerals. Columbian mammoths would likely have done the same. They were not as hairy as the European woolly mammoths but still had some hair, which would have been home to a range of parasites (Figure 3.5). These might have been deterred by a bit of mud. There is no doubt that mammoths congregated in these muddy parts of the former lake basin. It is quite hard to get a handle on just how many mammoths were present at any one time. Certainly, there was a diversity of sizes, but we are yet to do a comprehensive study—not least because the logical way to do such a study is using a drone, which is prohibited at present.

Matthew recalls, "David would always produce something unusual every time I would visit, and this day was no exception. This time, he was proudly showing off the discovery of one of his interns."

David recalls, "A few weeks earlier David Dennis, a summer intern working on trackways, had volunteered the idea rather cautiously that they had seen a head impression of a mammoth. So I had them show me and took Matthew to the site a few days later. Sure enough, there was the impression of the head of a mammoth with a trunk and eye socket (Figure 3.6A). But was it real? Would a juvenile mammoth really lie like that in the mud leaving a trace? Or was it something more sinister—the partial remains of a butchered mammoth?"

Matthew adds,

> It really did look like the print of a mammoth head and trunk. The problem is your eyes can be deceiving. You see what you want to see in the shapes before you. Like a lot of things like this, you are not sure one way or another, but we did set about documenting it, which is always a hint at one's true instinct even if you can't fully admit it to your colleagues. It was a few months later when my wife, Sally, showed me a tweeted picture of an elephant head impression made in sand at Chester Zoo in England (Figure 3.6B). The image showed a perfect impression of a young elephant's head, trunk, eye socket, and even the folds along the outer edge of the trunk. Perfect. It was one of the moments when you realize something is possible, and it put a whole new light on a fossil track!

Since this finding, the research team has speculated endlessly about whether this impression is evidence of a mammoth carcass or just a youngster lying in the mud. We currently don't have any direct evidence of mammoths being hunted at White Sands, but we have hypothesized how you might go about such a thing. One option we favor is to cause the animals to stampede while they're caught in the mud; this might lead to the elderly and the young being trampled. We have no evidence yet, and there is still a lot of work to be done on the mammoth tracks of White Sands.

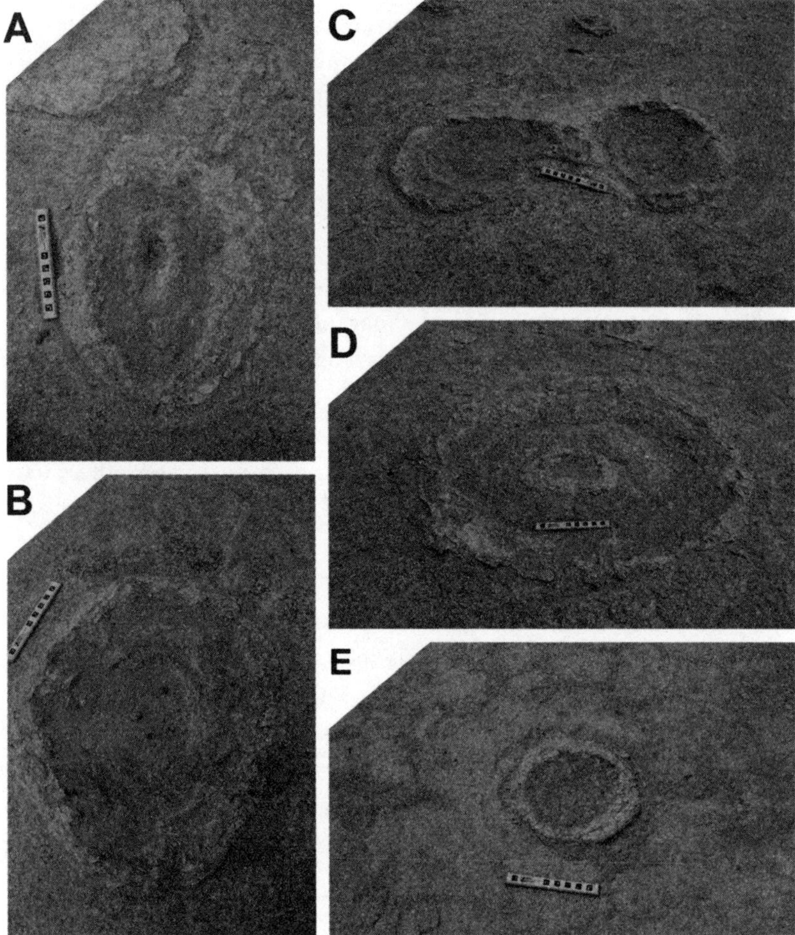

Figure 3.4. A selection of large mammoth tracks from White Sands. They are generally large, so we are certain they were made by Columbian mammoths rather than mastodons. A: A mammoth track with a human track in the middle; both have deformation rims. B: A classic mammoth track with concentric rims caused by deformation around the foot. C: Manus (front) print and pes (back) tracks just overprinting one another, forming a distinctive figure eight pattern. D: A mammoth track with large deformation rings around the print. E: A smaller mammoth track with less deformation around the actual track. The central basin is close to the size of the animal's foot.

Children of the Playa

It was April 2019, and our work had been briefly held up by the shutdown of the federal government at the start of that year. The first documentary crew to venture out to White Sands was due to arrive in a few days, and with them, Greg McDonald and Dick Mol. Greg is the foremost authority on giant ground sloths, and Dick is an expert on mammoths. They were to be filmed with the fossil tracks, with discussion in both English and German, for a European documentary. One of David's assistants, Cyrus Green, had recently discovered a beautiful collection of sloth tracks and was at work with ground-penetrating radar capturing these trackways. David and Matthew were rapidly uncovering some of the sloth tracks, which were just an inch or less below the playa floor. The film crew had sent out an articulated reproduction of the foot bones of the *Nothrotheriops shastensis* ground sloth, and we were having fun placing the bones in the tracks we uncovered. The problem was that the tracks were not quite as good as we had hoped. They were shallow and somewhat deformed. That was when we started to notice small human tracks. As we widened our surface excavation beyond the sloth tracks, we suddenly started to see lots of child-size human prints. They came at right angles to some of the sloth prints, crosscut their margins, and even trampled their bases.

Matthew recalls, "My young daughter back home was in a *Peppa Pig* phase at the time, and I could not get the tune out of my head as we worked. And it was Peppa Pig, who likes to jump in muddy puddles, that connected the dots for me. Here was a group of children playing in a puddle created by the passage of a giant ground sloth. As soon as the connection was made, the story was clear to be seen in the tracks!"

Sharon Gloshay adds,

> When I saw the child prints for the first time, I was in total awe. It brought to me the saying of my Apache people that we have always been here. The fact that youngsters were present illustrated that the time in that place was peaceful—an existence where people interacted with the natural world in a way that exhibited a balance in life. The codependence of life ensured survival, survival in a landscape that was bountiful and plentiful. Our people have always believed that

Figure 3.5. Mammoths of White Sands as envisaged by Karen Carr. Note the distant campsite. If mammoths were hunted, carcasses would have most likely been processed close by.

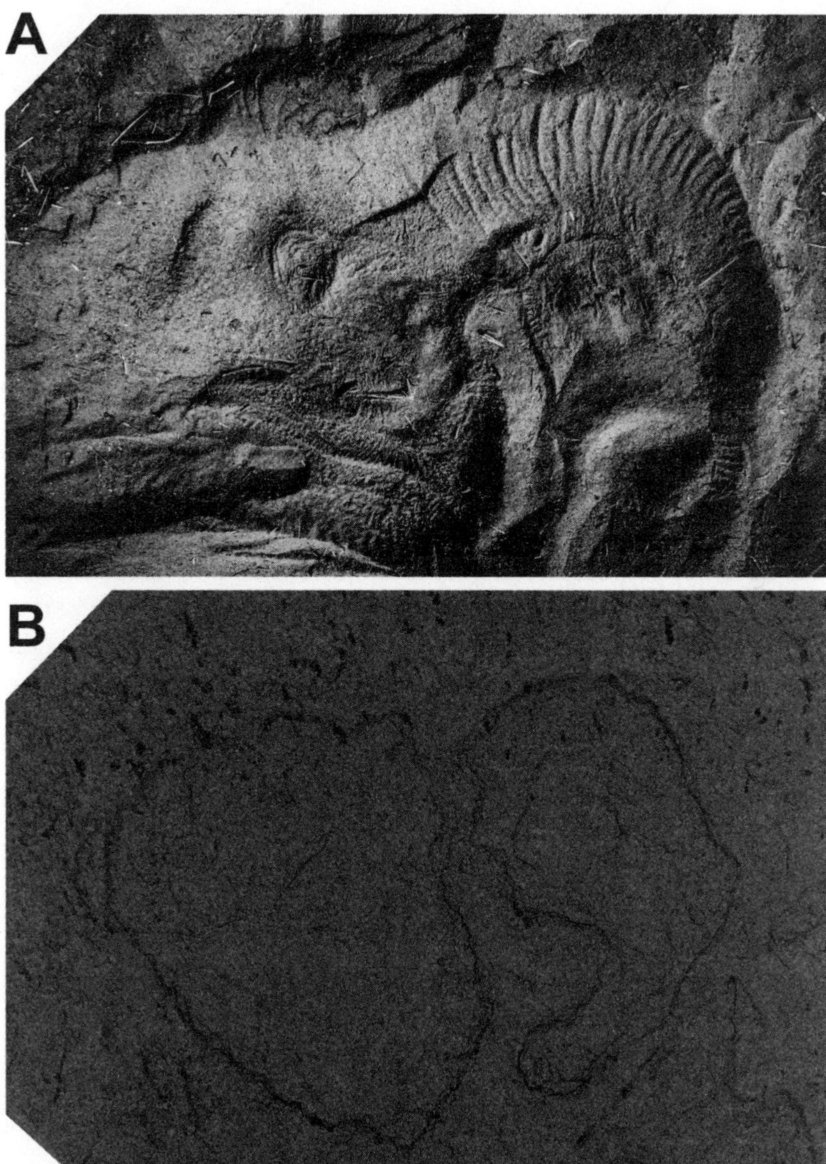

Figure 3.6. Body prints of an elephant and mammoth? A: A head impression of a juvenile elephant at Chester Zoo in the United Kingdom. B: A 3D model of a mammoth impression at White Sands. The images are remarkably similar, and the modern example shows that face impressions are possible. Photograph reproduced with permission of Chester Zoo.

one takes only what is needed, and this is done with respect. We still sing about these interactions and have prayers associated with the sacrifice of animals to provide sustenance for our people. The child prints ensured that children were provided and cared for by the adults.

Across a surface scrape of about 5 yards, there were perhaps six or seven sloth tracks, two of which had clearly been trampled by children at play (Figure 3.7). It is difficult to say how many children were playing when the sloth tracks were wet puddles—more than three, perhaps as many as five or six (Figure 3.7). This is where an ichnologist tries to perform a minimum number study. What is the smallest number of people that could have made the tracks? Finding the answer is not as easy as you might think. We explained in the previous chapter how tracks change in size with motion and that one track length doesn't really represent one individual due to this variation. To work this out, we need one child to run, walk, and jump in a puddle, and from this we can compute the variation in track size that this one child makes. If we measure the length of all the tracks around the sloth puddle, we can use the absolute range in size, smallest to biggest, and our variance estimate to work out the smallest number of folks who could have made the tracks. But no one has ever created a variance estimate for a jumping child! We have them for walking adults, but not for playing children. That would be a great study if someone wanted to get involved.

Matthew explains,

> Within the fossil human footprint record, there are quite a few examples of child-size tracks. Perhaps the best I have personally encountered are those from Namibia, where inter-dune muds deposited by flooding rivers capture lots of relatively recent footprints. At one site, there are some exquisite child-size tracks that have a playful disposition and overprint tracks left by a flock of goats and sheep.[12] It was clear that children as young as three or four were out tending the family's herds. There are also children's tracks at the famous Ileret site in northern Kenya (*Homo erectus*)[13] and more at Melka Kunture in Ethiopia (*Homo heidelbergensis*).[14]

It is true that child-size tracks capture the imagination and bring out maternal and paternal feelings. And the work at White Sands shows that children's footprints are not rare, but are the commonest type in terms of size. If you stop a moment and think about this, it makes good sense. Imagine you are taking a walk down a beach and you have five children with you. As you walk, trying to find a moment of peace in the chaos, the children will walk and run around you as they play and chase one another. For every step you take, the children will take several more, not just because of their shorter legs, but because they are energetic and having fun. Why should White Sands be any different? There is no kindergarten or nursery to park your children in during the day, so they come to work with you out on the playa as you forage and hunt for food. The tracks at Melka Kunture tell a similar story about a child of perhaps just one or two years old standing in mud beside an adult butchering a hippo carcass. Children today have a much more sheltered life than those in the past, when school and learning involved observing your elders at work and your playground was anything you could find, including the delight of a water-filled sloth track.

More recently, we found another beautiful example of kids at play—this time in an elongated mammoth track, the base of which was covered in small, superimposed child-size tracks. An even better example of children at play was found by David in January 2023. He says,

> We started work in September 2022 on a natural cliff exposure on the west side of Alkali Flat. Floodwaters had carved the gully, and we were at work cleaning the face for Jeff Pigati and Kathleen Springer of the US Geological Service (USGS) to describe. Matthew joined us in January 2023, and I was at work cleaning one of the benches in the face formed by a hard layer of gypsum. That is when I saw the first handprint, and a small one at that! Carefully, I worked the loose material out of the hard surface and grew in confidence at the discovery as I noticed a second handprint beyond.

Matthew adds,

> We often play tag in uncovering tracks. It helps to get different perspectives, and David is always in demand. I think he had gone to take a conference call and could be seen pacing out on the salt flat. In fact, he has discovered more footprints while on such calls

Figure 3.7. Children playing in footprint puddles at White Sands as envisaged by Karen Carr.

> than at other times. Anyway, I had taken over the handprints and was hard at work with a soft wooden probe and a brush. I noticed a fist-shaped lump that was grooved by finger marks. In time, I would find another and a few other divots, forming an arc centered on two round impressions. They were separate from the handprints that David had found.

The final story that emerged from this work was of a small child kneeling on the ground, grabbing fistfuls of sand around the arc of their reach (Figure 3.8). The fists of sand had yet to be picked up, but the arc of play was clear. Just behind, an even smaller child was crawling, perhaps moving to look over the shoulder of the first child (Figure 3.9). Matthew recalls,

> We were trying to explain the relationship of the children to each other so that the paleo-artist Karen Carr could bring the scene to life. We always have artwork in mind and on the go—not only for the popular versions of our scientific papers, but ultimately for the visitor's center at the park. Words sometimes are not enough, so in desperation one evening I roped in my children to enact the scene on our kitchen floor. Alex, my stepson, played the part of the older boy, and Zoë was the younger child. We videoed them crawling about on the floor and sent it to David for onward transmission to Karen!

A Lonely Journey

Every parent knows the feeling. You are hurrying along when your child starts crying. You pick them up to comfort them and move faster, but your arms begin to tire. Add to this a slick mud surface and a range of hungry predators around you (Figure 3.10), and that is the story the longest trackway of fossil footprints in the world tells us.[15]

Part of this trackway was spotted originally by David. Remember those cowboy boots? And it featured in the initial January 2017 find. We started to look at this trackway again, and in fact, it was two trackways a yard or so apart, with one heading north and the other south. Judging by the size of the tracks, both trackways were made by the same person, and they were in a hurry. Neither trackway shows any deviation, although the individual tracks were varied in morphology. Together these things suggested that the individual was in a hurry, a fact confirmed by the spacing of the tracks. The individual was moving fast across the mud, and as they did so, their feet slipped, elongating the toes and compressing the mid-foot and heel. Some of the tracks had curved, appearing banana-shaped when viewed from above (Figure 3.11). This slippage makes determining the actual size of the tracks difficult, but using examples with little slip, we got a size of about 8 inches, which is quite small—about a US size 5 shoe for woman or size 3.5 for a man. Today, the average woman's shoe is about 9 inches in length. We can deduce that the track was made by a young woman or perhaps an adolescent male. Compared to many other footprint trackways around the world, this one is remarkable for its length, being at least 2 miles long and probably much longer. This individual did not deviate from their course. But what is even more remarkable is that they followed their own trackway home again a few hours later (Figure 3.11).

Each track tells a story: a slip here, a stretch there to avoid a puddle. The ground was wet and slick with mud, and they were walking at speed, which would have been exhausting. We estimate that they were walking almost 4 miles an hour. For comparison, a comfortable walking speed is about 2.5 to 3 miles per hour on a flat dry surface. At several places on the outward journey, there are a series of small child tracks, made when the carrier set the child down, perhaps to adjust them from hip to hip or for a moment of rest. Judging by the size of the child tracks, they were made by a toddler, around two years old or slightly younger. The child was carried outward, but not on the return. The outward tracks are broader due to the load and more varied in morphology caused by outward rotation of the foot (Figure 3.12). The tracks of the homeward journey are less varied in shape and have a narrower form. We might even tentatively suggest that the surface had dried a little between the two journeys.

David recalls, "Vince Santucci, the Park Service's senior paleontologist, was out and watching us excavate tracks from the double trackway, but was not yet participating. After a while, he decided that he felt comfortable enough with what was going on to try it himself, and quickly after he started excavating, he said, 'I think I have a little kid.' We were all a little

Figure 3.8. Handprints on one of the upper benches in the section shown in the previous image. The wooden stick and the makeup brush are tools of the ichnologist.

bit surprised—since toddler-size prints were rare at this point—until we looked, and sure enough, right next to the main trackway was this tiny little track. Beginner's luck!

Matthew adds,

> The double trackway holds a special place in my heart. I was out there in January 2018 and had just learned that my wife, Sally, was pregnant. It was big news. I had two boys with my first wife, then in their late teens, and the thought of being a dad again was something of a shock! David and I were working on the double trackway and had just found the tiny child prints when my phone pinged. Sally was trying to send me a picture of our first baby scan from the UK. Cell reception is poor out on Alkali Flat, and come what may, I could not get the message to download. David came to the rescue, and I saw the picture of my daughter on his phone while lying aside the trackway. It was a moment I will never forget. It connected me to the trackway; Sally and I would name our daughter Zoë Olwyn in due course—Olwyn being a Welsh name meaning "white foot."

The trackway was long, very long in fact, and was crossed by several different Ice Age animals. A mammoth seemed to take little heed of the human trackway. At one point, we can see how the outward human tracks were deformed and partially closed by the passage of the mammoth. As the animal put its foot down onto the soft mud, it caused the mud to liquify and flow forward, closing the human track in front. We know therefore that the human passed first; their tracks were deformed when the mammoth passed by later. But what is neat is that on the return journey, the human steps into the middle of the mammoth track. The mammoth passed between the two journeys.

Figure 3.9 (*opposite page, above*). Children crawling in the mud at White Sands as envisaged by Karen Carr.

Figure 3.10 (*opposite page, below*). The double trackway journey as envisaged by Karen Carr. The artwork shows a woman, but we don't know for sure that the individual wasn't an adolescent male. One has to be careful with gender stereotypes, even in the past.

At another site, we traced a ground sloth across the human trackway. Here, the animal behaved differently. In fact, the ground sloth appears to have done a little dance! The sloth tracks crosscut the outward human journey and are in turn crosscut by the return journey. But as the sloth encountered the first set of tracks, it appears to have risen, perhaps on its hind legs, and presumably in response to the human scent. Perhaps it was wondering whether the human was still close. We can see from the tracks that it began to turn through a complete circle while upright. We can see the claws of the front feet turn and the rear feet make a shuffle. Having performed this pirouette, the sloth appears to have returned to its normal gait and proceeded on its way. The behavior fits with what we know from sloth tracks at other locations on the flats: The animals change direction and are clearly skittish when humans are scented. An aspect of these encounters is just how securely they date the human tracks to the late Pleistocene, to a time before both the mammoths and giant ground sloths went extinct.

The trackway tells a remarkable story. What was this individual doing alone and with a child out on the playa, moving with haste? Clearly, it speaks to social organization. They knew their destination and were assured of a friendly reception. Was the child sick? Was it being returned to its mother? Did a rainstorm quickly come in, catching a mother and child off guard? We have no way of knowing, and it is easy to give way to speculation for which we have little evidence. What we can say is that the individual was likely uncomfortable on that hostile landscape, but was prepared to make the journey anyway. So the next time you are rushing around in the supermarket with a tired child in your arms, remember that even prehistoric parents shared your emotions.

Transport on the Playa

Straight traces—lines, to be specific—don't feature often in the ichnologist's playbook, and they look artificial in a world of curves. Clay swells with water and contracts when it dries. So as a lakebed dries, the clay on its surface also contracts and cracks to form crude polygonal patterns. The diameter of these polygons varies, and several sets of polygons may be

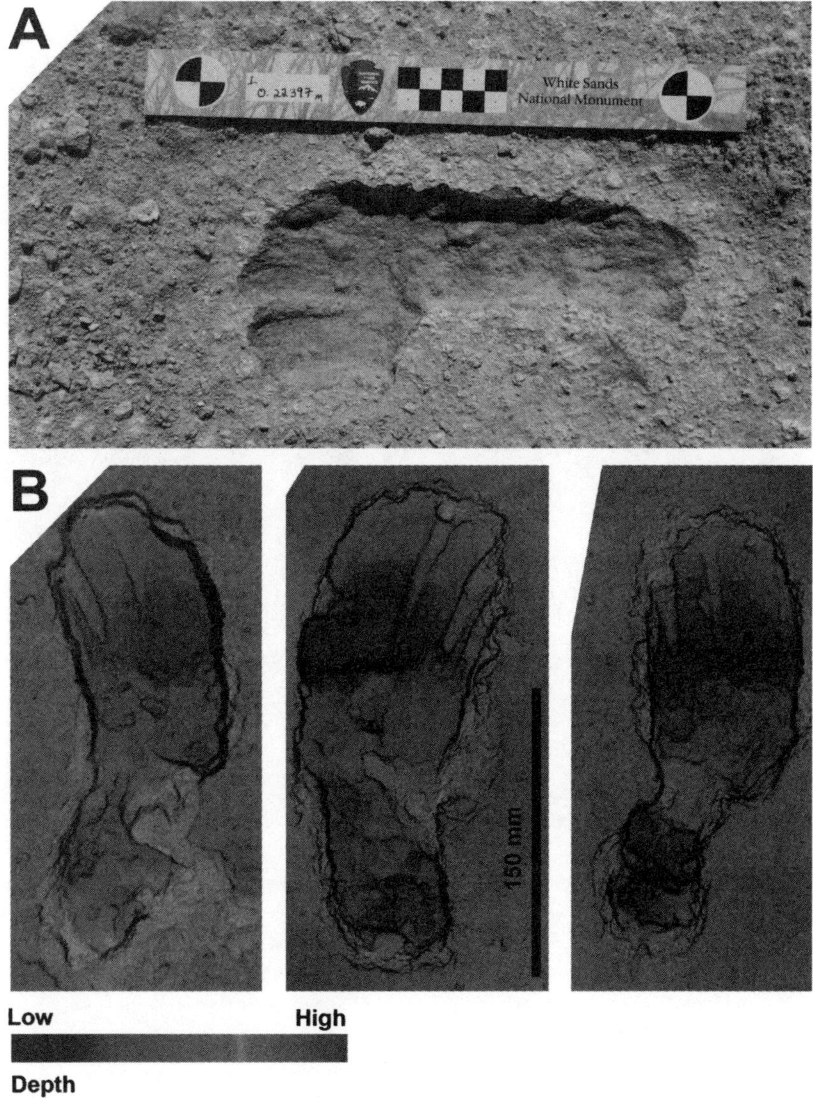

Figure 3.11. A: One of the undisturbed human tracks from the double trackway. Most of the tracks show evidence of slippage and are therefore elongated, but this track gives a true estimate of the size of the human foot that made the prints. B: A series of three-dimensional false-color models of tracks from the double trackway, showing deformation and slippage. Note the elongated toes and compare these with the modern example from a similar playa shown in Figure 2.11.

Figure 3.12. The double trackway at White Sands is remarkable for its length and just how straight both the outward and return journeys were. Here, the two trackways are viewed looking north. The skyline has been amended, since the area overlooks the White Sands Missile Range.

nested one into the other. You will see the same sort of thing, but usually much smaller, in dried puddles. On the playa, lines made by this process are quite jagged and form a clear network. But there are much straighter and longer lines out on Alkali Flat and around its margins (Figure 3.13). Matthew recalls,

> I saw these on my first visit to White Sands and was intrigued, but I also dismissed them as the imprints of branches or root traces. The ones I saw then were quite short and broken. It was Tommy Urban who set us thinking about them. He saw several linear lines, and perhaps parallel lines, in some of his ground-penetrating radar surveys. At the time, he was conducting tests with different size antennas, and these were small areas—they didn't quite extend far enough—but the lines were there. In a three-way conversation via email, Tommy, Sally Reynolds, and I came up with the idea that they may have been created by some form of sled or travois. That idea took root, but slowly.

David adds,

> I remembered seeing linear lines out in the mammoth trample area and around the eastern edge of the flats. As the idea of them being travois took hold, I started to point these out to Matthew and Tommy. The ever-present fear out on the flats is that some of these structures are relict jeep tracks or the scars of past missile crashes. But the linear structures as we began to call them were too fine for this, often just a few inches wide and way too small to be jeep tracks.
>
> The liner structure can extend for several hundred yards, crossing over and beneath mammoth prints along the way. The most interesting set of linear lines is a place on the mammoth trample ground where there is a scatter of lithics (stone flakes) that appear to be at the center of a series of converging linear structures. From above they look like the spokes of a wheel. It is here that the potential body and trunk print described earlier in this chapter was found. Were the linear structures evidence of folks moving meat and body parts from a mammoth kill?"

Figure 3.13. A linear structure found at White Sands. Note how it contrasts with tire marks made by the UTVs.

What is a travois? It is a simple sled, or wheelless barrow, made from one or more poles. Two branches lashed together form the sled. Sometimes, the flexible end of the branches may be in contact with the ground, and at other times it may be the lashed apex. The flex in the branches helps the sled move and adds a dynamic bounce that stops the poles digging into the ground. The ethnographic literature of Indigenous Americans is full of examples of this type of vehicle, from small versions pulled by dogs to larger versions pulled by horses. They can also be pulled by humans. Whereas a wheelbarrow is a conserved artifact, something you keep in the garden shed, a travois can be crafted as needs require—maybe from firewood, tent poles, or whatever is near to hand. After all, need is the best stimuli for innovation.

We started to really get to grips with trying to explain these features when we started to work at the site WHSA Locality 2, which is where we would eventually date the tracks. Here, we found three main types of linear structures. The simplest was just a linear groove, which sometimes presented as several intertwined grooves. It looks exactly like the mark a stick would make if dragged along the ground...and to be honest, that is probably what happened. There are human footprints of varying sizes alongside, and some of these are clearly truncated (crosscut) longitudinally by the groove—the exact same pattern that would occur if someone dragged a stick behind them. The footprint comes first, and sometimes the stick scores away part of the track along its length. In a couple of cases, you can see how the stick bounced along the surface, making a series of transverse ridges in the groove, like a pecked line along the base. There is no doubt about such a simple linear feature. Whether it was created by a spear being dragged or a single branch of firewood is not clear, but the association between people and the groove is there.

The second type of linear structure involves two parallel grooves that are equidistant from one another—exactly what would happen if you lashed two poles or sticks together close to one end, forming a triangle. Footprints occur between the two grooves and in some cases are truncated by them, as with the previous type. This is the pattern that would be left by the simplest form of travois. The third type is similar, but has a broader runnel between the two parallel grooves as if something has been dragged along, with a contact area wider than just a pole. This could be caused by a load slung between two poles dragging along the surface or something wrapped around the apex of the travois, perhaps to reduce drag. There is no real record of the apex of a travois being wrapped in the ethnographic literature. But on mud, there is a mechanical advantage to doing so. On a hard surface, friction is reduced by the flexibility of the poles; they bounce along the surface. On a muddy surface, they would dig into the mud, so creating a pad for the poles to ride on reduces friction. This is where modern-day experiments can help. The posh name for this is neo-ichnology. Matthew explains,

> It started like most things, with a madcap scheme one weekend. I live close to Poole Harbor in the UK, which at low tide has lots of exposed mudflats. Where better to try some experiments? So I crafted a couple of simple travois out of modern materials from the local DIY store. The aim was not to replicate what was used at White Sands, but simply to see what traces would result. The Sandbanks neighborhood is a spit of sand with million-dollar houses on it. Per square meter, the land prices rival those in Manhattan. It is the playground of footballers, celebrities, and the rich, but on a Sunday at low tide, the mudflats are alive with people kite surfing, kayaking, and paddleboarding, as well as mad geology professors trying out their travois. My young daughter acted as the controlled load and my son as videographer. We tried to measure the force it took to move a travois using a simple strain gauge. The single pole moved with the least resistance, then the travois with the apex on the ground, followed by the travois with two points of contact. But the revelation was how much easier it was to move the travois when a cloth bag was wrapped around the points of contact. This simple option stopped the poles from digging into the mud and created a film of water and sand on which the poles slid. This was never intended to be a precise archaeological experiment, but aside from being fun for the kids, it gave some basic insight into what sort of tracks could be created, and their similarity to the range of traces found at White Sands was striking. There was one other observation from these experiments. At one point, we watched a group of children and young adults haul their kayaks over the mud to the water's edge. They moved as an untidy group, one or more of them dragging each hard plastic kayak along. After they had moved away, we went and looked at the traces, and I was struck by just how similar the assemblage of traces was to what we see in White Sands.

Our explanation for these linear traces seems obvious to our research team. We have studied them, lived with the ideas, and had vigorous debates about them in the field. And crucially, we have listened to our Indigenous site monitors, who are clear about what these traces are and have added much to the debate. But this is far from what is needed to convince our peers, skeptical scientists who don't like the idea that we have potentially found a record of the oldest (as we discuss in the next chapter) use of transport technology in the world. Such a claim is a big claim, but it is potentially true. For the record, the earliest documented use of the wheel is currently found in Mesopotamia and dates from only the fourth century BC. The lack of other evidence of transport technology reflects the fact that the wood, bone, and fibers from which it would be made are not easily preserved. At White Sands, it is not the technology, but rather the marks left by that technology, that are preserved. Our species (*Homo sapiens*) left Africa sometime between 60,000 and 90,000 years ago. It was an epic journey; people did not stop until they had reached all earth's continents, even Antarctica, although not until John Davis landed there in 1821. As our ancestors moved, they hunted and gathered produce, constantly moving as most migrants do. Move house often enough and you end up with few possessions, but you will always have something to carry. Even the hero of the eponymous popular literature series *Jack Reacher* carries a toothbrush in his pocket! As you move, you will have stone tools, bowls, food stocks, tents, and tent poles to carry. If you take down a large animal, you will have meat to carry back to camp to process and preserve. And for those big sea and river crossings, you are going to need a boat.

It is always important to consider what else could form the linear traces. The obvious one is the transport of firewood. The dragging of single poles or logs of firewood would leave traces that might look like the first type of trace we described above, and this can't be ruled out. The ethnographic literature suggests, however, that most firewood is broken down into bundles, which are carried as bundles using headbands or shoulder straps known as tumplines. We can't rule out the dragging of firewood as a cause of some of these traces, but the options are not mutually exclusive. You can carry firewood on an improvised travois and then burn the travois!

Some folks have suggested that the linear structures might be animal traces, and it is true that animals can leave marks that are linear in nature. For example, modern-day beavers drag wood into the water to build their dams and lodges, leaving traces on the banks of lakes and rivers. During the Ice Age, giant beavers (genus *Castoroides*), perhaps shoulder high on a human, were widespread in North America. But their reported range does not extend into the American Southwest, and such explanation fails to account for the associated human footprints. Modern elephants are known to leave a range of traces associated with trunk movements, and potential drag marks have been identified in the fossil record. In general, these are short, broad, and usually gently curving traces that occur in direct association with elephant tracks. While mammoth tracks do occur at WHSA Locality 2, the linear features are longer and more varied than any mammoth/elephant trunk trace previously reported. Tail drags from giant sloths are hypothetically possible, but would be associated with sloth tracks unless the animals were levitating! The linear features at White Sands are not associated with sloth tracks. Given that the footprints occur on the edge of a wetland, could the features be the keel marks of boats? The traces seem inconsistent with the boats recorded in ethnographic literature and the oral traditions of the First Nations. For example, tule boats have broad keels formed by rush bundles, as do umiaks, while skin-covered bull boats (coracles) tend to leave broader, shallow impressions. Dugout or bark canoes could potentially leave deeper, more prominent keel marks. In science, there is often no absolute answer to questions like this—just the balance of probability—and we should always be guided by the simplest explanation (Figure 3.14). Strong support for our interpretation comes from our Indigenous colleagues who have seen these traces. They interpret and recognize similar behaviors and transport systems in their oral histories.

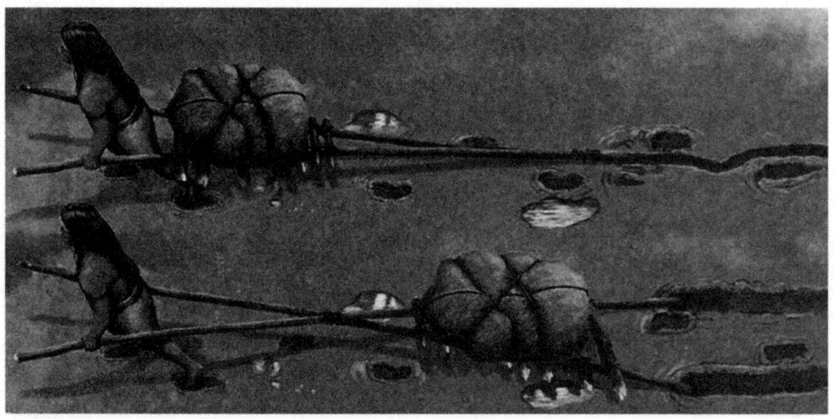

Figure 3.14. Different types of travois in use at White Sands as envisioned by Gabriel Ugueto.

Life on the Playa

As the audience grows restless in the theater, the image becomes blurred again as the film returns to the present day. The wind is picking up and you can almost taste the dust in the air. What a barren yet beautiful place. "Who would live there?" wonder the audience members as the lights go on and they begin to file out of the theater into the evening. It is hard to equate the rich, diverse life of the former lakebed with the salt flats of today. That is the power of water in the form of a large lake (or at least a seasonal wetland). Water brings resources—animals to hunt—and not just the big Ice Age beasts, but the small rabbits, hares, and birds that provide a staple for many hunter-gathering societies. There may have been shrimp in the water. Ditch grass, which we know was abundant, was eaten in some communities. Reeds provided cordage for making things. Dried lakebeds may have been social hubs on migratory roots for mammoths and places where people came together to mingle, gossip, pass on the news, and learn about the landscape in which they lived. Sharon Gloshay remarks, "Our Indigenous people have origin stories that cite monsters, and the mammoth tracks at White Sands show that these large animals lived alongside people. Our people were migratory and followed the water, food, and plants. They lived in the seasons, migrating with them. White Sands once held a lake abundant with life, life to sustain a people, allowing them to develop their songs and prayers to immortalize that experience. Life at White Sands was peaceful and plentiful, in my opinion."

We have no idea what the social structure or density of the population was at this time. All we can say is this: There are lots of footprints, and they give us insight into past lifeways on the margins of a lake or wetland like that which occupied the Tularosa Basin at the end of the Ice Age. In the traces, we can see family groups of the great megafauna and humans, both juvenile and adult, on the same landscape at the same time, but exactly when these traces were made is another story, and one for the next chapter.

CHAPTER FOUR

How Old Is a Footprint?

Although it's sometimes a delicate question, it is easy enough to ask a person their age. But a fossil footprint can't talk—so what then? If a print is a few days old, an expert tracker will be able to take a guess at its age. The track may have puddled water from the previous night's rain, or it may have begun to dry out, with the surface starting to crack. Leaf debris may have fallen into the track, or a beetle may have left a trail across it. There are many such "tells" for the observant, but if a track is more than a few days old, the chances of accurately working out its age become harder. You must rely on stratigraphy and geological context for anything old (Figure 4.1). Is the track buried by organic soil or inorganic sediments? Has that sediment been turned into rock or hardened in some other way? How much sediment lies above the track? These are the sorts of questions geologists ask when trying to work out the age of a track. The best place to start is by finding, or creating, exposure through the in situ sediment layers that contain the footprint. An exposure is simply a small section that has been freshly eroded or dug. Digging a pit with steep sides creates an exposure through the sediment, or you might find a natural cliff where a stream has eroded its banks (Figure 4.2). In situ means that the sediments and soils have not been disturbed or reworked since they were deposited.

Let us create a simple scenario involving a child walking on a lakeshore with their parents. Tracks of three individuals are left in the mud of the shore. If that mud dries in the sun, the tracks may be preserved. There is a risk that they won't be, of course. For example, if a herd of bison comes to drink, the prints may be trampled away. If it rains and the tracks fill with water, the sides may slump. But let us stick with the idea that the tracks bake hard. The damp recesses of the tracks are ideal for algal growth, and this might help bind the sediment grains and strengthen the sides of the track. A few days later, perhaps, the lake rises just a few inches. Maybe it rains in the mountains that feed the streams that flow into the lake. As the muddy waters rise, they gently fill the tracks. Over time, silts and clays settle out from the water. The tracks become buried. Again, we must rely on luck to prevent our embryonic fossil tracks from being destroyed by further trampling or erosion. That herd of thirsty bison can still destroy a buried track if it is just a few inches below the surface.

But let us assume that it is a lucky set of tracks, and over time, with shifts in drainage and climate, they become buried by further layers of sand and silt to the point where they are well and truly hidden. Each layer of sediment adds a load to the one beneath, which helps compact the sand and drives out water. Evaporation of water on the surface may draw water upward, and as it evaporates, precipitated cements can help bind the sediment. Limescale, which is common in areas that derive their water from limestone-rich ground, is an example of such cement. Bacteria can also help precipitate cement. In Namibia's coastal dunes, sea fogs roll in from the sea and salt gets left on the surface of the sand and mud. Here, ancient footprints are cemented by common sea salt. Cementation of sediment, by whatever means, is usually a slow process, and over geological time, our sediment will turn to stone, a process geologists call lithification (*lĭ́thos* means "rock"). But we don't need to run the process to its end. Let us stop while the sediment is firm and partly glued, but still able to be dug by a shovel.

Sticking with our original scenario, of a set of tracks made by a child and their parents, the next stage is for the wind to erode the former lakebed, cutting deeper in the center, thereby leaving a low cliff around the margins. Geologists come along with their picks and spades and clean one of these bluffs to create a vertical exposure. If they are lucky, and observant too, they may notice the dried lakeshore as a distinctive layer in the small cliff. Then they carefully excavate the bluff to reveal the former lakeshore with its three sets of footprints. "Hooray," they shout. Then they scratch their heads; how old are these tracks?

Some basic geological principles will help. A footprint at the base of a pile of undisturbed sediment layers will logically be older than one at the top, just as the first line of bricks in a house must have been laid down before the ones closest to the roof. Geologists call this the principle of superposition, and provided things are in situ (and have not been turned upside down by mountain building!), the layers at the bottom should be older than those at the top. Geologists can also guess at sedimentation rates, or how quickly sediments are laid down. Take a lump of soil from your backyard, place it in a bottle full of water, and shake. The water will turn

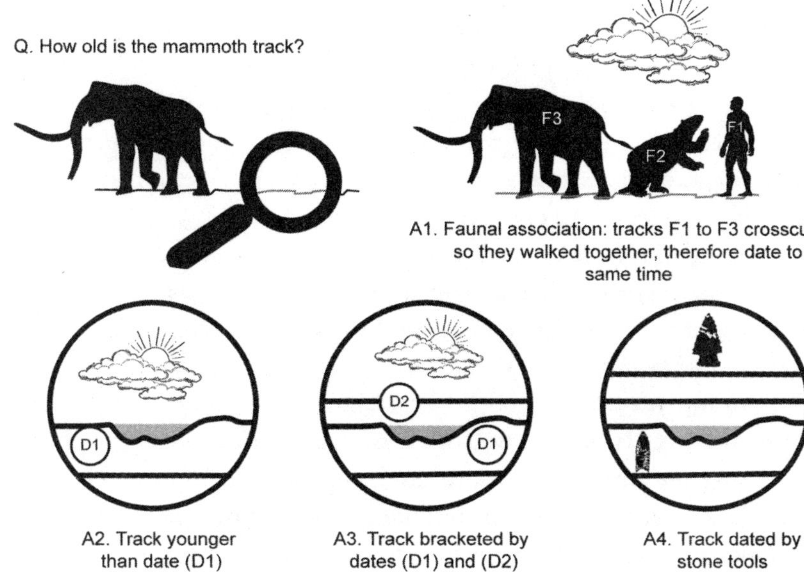

Figure 4.1. How is a footprint dated? Answer 1 involves biostratigraphy. If a set of animals left footprints at the same time, determined by how they crosscut one another, then you know the tracks were made when they all lived. If some of those animals became extinct at the end of the Ice Age, the tracks must date before then. Answer 2 involves finding something to date below the track. You know the track is younger than what has been dated, but not how much younger. Answer 3 is the ideal solution, with a date above and a date below the footprint to age bracket it. Answer 4 is included for completeness. In theory, you can bracket the age of a footprint between two stone tool cultures, the one beneath being older than the one above. This method does not currently apply at White Sands, however.

brown as the soil disperses, but as soon as you let it stand for a moment, the big particles will settle to the bottom. After half an hour, there will be a layer of sediment at the bottom, and the muddy waters above will have cleared slightly. Large grains of sand settle faster than smaller ones; this is referred to as Stokes' law. Fine particles, especially those made of clay, are very small and consequently take a long time to settle out. The clay in our bottle may take up to 15 hours to settle out. Not only are clay particles (platelets) very small, but they have tiny electrical charges that repel one another, and this all hinders settling. Let us translate this to our geological scenario. If all the sediment layers above the footprints are composed of sand, then the sedimentation rates may have been quick and the tracks quite young. But if there are lots of clay layers above, the sedimentation rates may have been slower. How dirty the water from which the sediment settles also comes into play; we call this the transport load. So the type of sediment gives the geologist a clue as to the age, as does the thickness of the layers, but only in the crudest of terms. We call this determination relative age; footprints on a layer at the bottom of the sediment pile must be older relative to the ones on a layer at the top.

The other way we can deduce relative age is by looking for crosscutting relationships. We mentioned these in an earlier chapter, but they are worth a quick recap. Think of a beach, and let us imagine a line of human tracks and a line of bear prints beside it. Our imagination leads us to believe that the two animals were not on the beach at the same time, since bears and humans don't get on that well. On closer inspection, we notice that the trackways converge at one point; the bear prints are imprinted on top of the human tracks. Perhaps the outline of a bear print cuts across the edge of a human track. We know, therefore, that the bear came second. Maybe it was stalking the human, but in truth, we don't know. There may have been hours between the two events. If the trackways don't crosscut, then we have no way of working out the chronology of events. For all we know, the human and the bear may have been walking hand in hand down the beach!

Tracks that do crosscut one another provide a powerful tool for working out the sequence of events. We have used this tool extensively at White Sands to show that barefoot human tracks are contemporaneous with those of extinct Ice Age animals, such as giant ground sloths and mammoths. Where a mammoth or sloth track crosscuts a human footprint, you know that the human walked first, and vice versa. In the absence of other evidence, this places human tracks like those at White Sands to at least the end of the Ice Age—what geologists call the terminal Pleistocene. The tracks could be older, but we know that they can't be younger (Figure 4.1).

Dating tracks at White Sands is complicated by the fact that many of the footprints are located right on the surface of the former lakebed, with no overlying layers. The tracks are infilled by sediment, but it is hard to be sure that this fill is in situ. It is therefore difficult to date them. Have they always been so close to the surface? Well, yes and no is the answer. In a large lake, most of the sediment is deposited near the shore, where streams run into the lake. Here, the standing body of water checks the velocity of the inflowing water, and since sediment transport depends on water velocity, most of it is deposited close to the shore. The fine clays get washed into

Figure 4.2. Different types of excavation. A: A natural section cleaned off for study. B: A trench dug at WHSA Locality 2. David Bustos is at work excavating a footprint on the floor of the trench.

the center and settle out. A layer of sediment deposited over time will vary in thickness—thin at the basin center and thickening to the lake margins. In the basin center, the layers are condensed and thin compared to those at the margin, so there is less to remove. Deep and therefore old sediment layers will be closer to the surface than the margins. There is also another explanation at work: Once the surface becomes stable, it has the potential to remain the same for a long time. Stability might be achieved by being closer to the water table, for example. The natural playa cycle also serves as protection. When it rains, standing water collects in low points of the playa. Slowly, this water evaporates, and this draws gypsum salts toward the surface. The surface puffs up with the growth of gypsum crystals. This crust is then eroded by the wind to feed the gypsum dunes. The crust acts as a disposable and protective layer for the surface beneath it. The water regime is critical here, involving just enough rainfall to cause gypsum to bloom and just enough wind to remove it, but not to the point where the surface beneath will erode. It is a delicate climate-directed balance, which is upset by human-induced climate change and/or changes to the underlying water table. So, yes, things can survive near the surface for a long time. If you live in a temperate, rainfall-rich region, it is hard to imagine a landscape that could potentially be stable for thousands of years, but this is not the situation at a place like White Sands.

Dating the Tracks at White Sands

Enough with the background. Let us turn our attention to how the tracks at White Sands have been dated. Back in 2017, at the big meeting to discuss the tracks, their age was on everyone's mind, since seeds (Figure 4.3) taken from trenches cut on the missile range had yielded dates older than 20,000 years using radiocarbon dating. The problem was that, at the time, no one had linked the tracks to these dates effectively and had not even established that there were human tracks present at all.

Matthew recalls,

> When I started to work at White Sands, I tried hard to steer folks away from questions of age. I was not convinced that they could be easily addressed, and the fact that the tracks were at least as old as the end of the Pleistocene (Ice Age) was clear from the crosscutting relationships between fauna that died out at that time and the human tracks. Obsessing about the age detracted, in my view at least, from the true potential of the site, which was to provide insight into the behavior of the different animals, including humans, on the playa. I was all about behavioral ecology and drawing out stories from the tracks. This, in my view, would make the site come alive for folks. In fact, between 2017 and 2019 I succeeded in this, but on a fateful day in September 2019, this changed.

David continues,

> I had taken Matthew to what would become WHSA Locality 2 on several occasions. In fact, it was one of the first stops during the field meeting of January 2017. While certain I had seen humanlike tracks at the site in the past, conditions worked against me. Things must be just right at White Sands to see track traces. Matthew was over for a short visit in September 2019, and we had been working out on the mammoth trample-ground. There was a hint there of a layer of seeds below a human track, and this got us on to the question of dates. So I took Matthew back to the original site, and conditions for the first time during one of his visits were just right to see tracks at this site: not too wet and not too dry, and the surface had been both washed and blown free of debris.

Matthew remembers,

> We started to look at the surface. Imagine a stack of playing cards, each representing a layer of sediment. Push the top half of the stack back and you get a set of card steps, some with wider treads than others. At the bottom there are wider treads, and toward the top they get narrower or are absent all together. That is exactly what the bluff looked like, but it was only a meter or so tall. It was on these lower surfaces that we began to see tracks, first one and then another, leading into the face. The tracks were subtle, picked out by differences in sediment color, but they were clear enough, and we started to brush them out. Soon, we had a short trackway of two or three steps that disappeared into the slope where one layer of sediment blended into another. We cut the overlying layer back a little, and sure enough, the next track in the sequence became visible. The line of footprints we had been tracing led into the bluff and under a layer of sediment that was clearly in situ.

David adds,

> As we worked at this line of tracks, I began to see seeds of *Ruppia* sp. (Figure 4.3). This is better known as common ditch grass, and its seeds are distinctive. At the center is a tiny drop-like core from which little spicules stick out. Imagine a cartoon featuring a mine floating in the water. It has a round body from which spikes protrude. That is exactly, in miniature, what one of these seeds looks like. I knew that these seeds were old, both from original dating prior to 2017, but also because Jeff Pigati and Kathleen Springer from the USGS had been out to do some preliminary dating in April 2019. They had confirmed that the seeds were old. We suddenly had tracks sandwiched between seed layers that could be dated.

Matthew recalls, "I have been asked many times by reporters how I felt when we realized the tracks were likely to be old. They expect me to say something about being excited or amazed, but in truth my heart sank. Pushing back the antiquity of human occupation in the Americas is not something for the faint-hearted, and the prospect of a seriously old site was not something I relished. It would take the fun out of the work, and in many ways, it has, for me at least."

Figure 4.3. *Ruppia* (common ditch grass) seeds, with their distinctive shape, used to date the footprints at White Sands.

In the fall of 2019, the elements that would become our research team began to plan and seek permission to dig a trench focused on September's discovery. Getting permission to disturb the ground in this way is not simple. There are archaeological permits to acquire, and the Indigenous people affiliated to White Sands must be consulted and agree. There are also logistics to plan and organize. In those early days, we didn't know each other well. Jeff Pigati and Kath Springer had been at the original meeting in January 2017 and recalled Matthew's outspoken comments, but he in turn did not remember them. To add to the tension, a TV company wanted to join us in the field and follow our work (Figure 4.4).

Matthew remembers,

> To a backdrop of worrying stories about a mystery virus emerging from China, we assembled in January 2020 for our first big excavation. There were a lot of moving parts, including a film crew who tried (and often failed) to be as unobtrusive as possible. We marked out a huge area for survey—way too large to be practical—and

> promptly ignored this huge grid as we began to focus on the labor of digging a trench. *Digging* is perhaps the wrong word. The ground is compact in places, in other areas softer; it is best described as a layer cake of alternating layers of indurated sand and softer brown silt, all of which sits above blue clay at depth. The clays represent the lake. You need deep still water to deposit clay, while the sands above were deposited by the interplay of blown gypsum sand from the eroding lakebed and sediment washed down the slope. Kick the sediment with your boot and your toe comes off worse. Yes, you can make progress with a pick, but we needed something more effective.

David adds, "We had cut a few shallow soil pits for Matthew and others in the past using a chainsaw. It cut easily through the sediment, and while this blunted the blade, the absence of pebbles or larger stones ensured that the cuts remained clean and sharp. But our safety officer put a stop to this when biological technician Patrick Martinez shared a video of the chainsaw in use on social media. So we got a larger, heavier, dirt-rated saw designed for trenching and laying cables. This is what we planned to use to cut the sides of the trench.

Matthew continues,

> It was stressful watching the dirt saw. It was heavy and powerful and, in some ways therefore more destructive and difficult to use than the original chainsaw. And boy, was it temperamental; the chain got clogged repeatedly with clay. We managed to cut one line the length of the proposed trench and then a second one parallel to it about half a meter to the side. In this way, we had two parallel incisions. Cuts at right angles created blocks between these two lines that, in theory, we could lift out of the trench and set to one side. These blocks were heavy. It took us several days to get a passable trench, maybe three-quarters of a meter high dropping down to a few inches deep in other places. The scale of the task weighed heavily. Jeff and Kath were due in a few days to start their geological survey in the trench, as were the film crew. Every time the dirt saw stuttered to a stop, the tension rose. It is hard not to let your impatience and stress show when folks are working flat out to fix a recalcitrant bit of machinery upon which it became clear we were relying.

Figure 4.4. Jeff Pigati and Kathleen Springer try to work while being filmed in the trench dug at WHSA Locality 2 in January 2020. This trench was extended during fieldwork in January 2022. Note that the skyline in the photograph has been altered.

Dan says,

> All archaeological excavation is destructive, and so we always try to balance what might be learned through excavation against what will be lost. The Park Service's mission focuses on preservation, and often leaving an archaeological site unexcavated is the best way to preserve it. In this case, there was an important additional consideration: David had documented how quickly parts of the area were eroding, and I was dismayed to see just how much had been lost since my previous visit. Knowing that climate-driven erosion is gradually destroying these deposits lent our work urgency. We knew this part of the story at White Sands would eventually be lost forever if we did nothing. As I watched David and Patrick guide the blade of the saw into the track-bearing sediment, it was this knowledge that made me feel like we were doing the right thing. I knew that the

only way to preserve what was there was to study and document it. Understanding the layers and the relationships between them would be critical to understanding the tracks we were seeing and to preserving and sharing their story.

Those first hours and days of removing the blocks from the trench were some of the most exciting of my professional career. I wasn't cleared to run the dirt saw, so I focused on breaking the blocks loose from their base to remove them from the trench so that Jeff and Kath could study the trench wall. The best way to do this was to work from the downhill end of the trench and pound an iron bar horizontally into the face of the block to split it along the line between layers of sediment. Doing this allowed us to work our way along the trench. We quickly discovered that the surfaces we exposed in this way often had very well-defined tracks on them, including tracks that were clearly human. Some had hundreds of *Ruppia* seeds with their delicate stems still attached. Others showed mammoth tracks bisected by the saw cut, the other half still visible in the profile of the trench wall. I remember lying awake at night, my body exhausted by the day's hard physical labor but my mind just buzzing with awe at what we were seeing.

Matthew continues,

After about a week of hard labor, we had a trench through the high parts of the layer cake. We could trace the footprint surfaces we had explored in September 2019 into the trench, and the cross section of mammoth and human tracks was visible in the walls of the trench. Jeff and Kath had arrived and set to work making a perfect scale drawing of the layers in the trench and describing each in detail. We were already cursing under our breaths the demands of the film crew, who had a documentary to make and whose work kept disrupting ours. Big excavations with lots of moving parts are never as much fun as working with just a few people and no hassle!

Dan adds,

As the work progressed, we quickly realized that this was going to be a much bigger task than we anticipated, for the simple reason that the track-bearing layers just kept coming. Soon we realized we were going to have to make another pass with the saw within the trench we had started because we needed to go deeper. I think we all began to feel a tension between wanting to accommodate the film crew and wanting to get on with the work that had brought us there in the first place. Having to "dig more quietly" and to work without speaking while they filmed was maddening, particularly as the days we had left quickly wound down.

I remember walking over to ask Kath and Jeff how much deeper they needed us to go as they carefully mapped and described the layers in the trench wall. Jeff was wearing a magnification headband that looked like something from *Back to the Future* to help him see what he was looking at in greater detail. We started calling these Jeff's Way Back Glasses because we realized they did let him peer into the past. In response to my question, they both uttered what has since become a familiar refrain. "Deeper," they said in unison. "We need to go deeper."

When the excavation came to an end, the team separated. It is worth pausing at this point to focus on what the trench looked like. Figure 4.5 shows a montage of one of the trench walls, with the footprint surface indicated on it. The sequence splits into two elements vertically. At the base is a blue clay, interpreted as being deposited in a lake. Footprints occur on the top surface of this clay, imprinted as the lake shallowed. Above this was a succession of thin layers of sediment alternating between white gypsum-rich sands and brown silts. The gypsum was likely blown in from the exposed lakebed, while the brown silts appear to have been washed down the slope. The layers at the interface between these two environments were often cemented hard by a mineral called dolomite (Figure 4.6). Dolomite is a type of calcium carbonate in which the calcium is replaced by magnesium. It can occur where ground waters with different salinity mix and in an environment of regular wetting and drying. It is worth emphasizing that human footprints are to be found throughout the section, and particularly prized by the team where those found in the base of the trench. Between the different layers of sediment, distinct horizons of *Ruppia* seeds were recovered. This common ditch grass had clearly bloomed periodically at the site, leaving thick layers. The seed samples went to Denver and the USGS radiocarbon lab where Jeff is based (Figure 4.3). What followed was a period of waiting amid the worsening pandemic and growing fear of what it would mean to our loved ones. It was an unsettling time as societal lockdowns came into force in various parts of the world. Gone was any chance of more fieldwork in April. In late March, the day that we had all been waiting for came: the first radiocarbon dates and a first real sense of how old the footprints would be. But perhaps we should first introduce radiocarbon dating.

Radiocarbon Dating

Radiocarbon dating is the workhorse of modern archaeology and is great at dating things within the last 50,000 years. It starts with cosmic rays. Yes, it sounds like something out of science fiction, but exploding supernovae in galaxies far, far away produced streams of ions that impact our atmosphere. They bombard nitrogen, one of the most common gases in the atmosphere (Figure 4.7). When bombarded, it gets converted to carbon-14, which is a radioactive version of carbon-12. It is an isotope, and some isotopes are unstable and decay over time by releasing radioactive particles. In this way, carbon-14 slowly turns back into carbon-12, which is stable, and this radioactive decay occurs in an exponential fashion. In fact, it takes 5,730 years for carbon-14 to decay by half its mass, another 5,730 to decay by another half, and so on, which is why the magic number of 5,730 is referred to as its half-life (Figure 4.7). The ratio of carbon-14 to carbon-12 is fixed in the atmosphere at a point in time, and therefore it is fixed in all living matter, including you, while you remain breathing. If the ratio changes in the atmosphere, with a few breaths, the ratio in your body will adjust to match. But once you are dead, it won't. The carbon-14 will no longer be replenished in your body, and it will slowly decay. We know the half-life, and if we determine the amount of carbon-14 left in your body, then we know how long you have been dead. That, in essence, is radiocarbon dating; it dates dead things. The rate of decay is quite fast, so you can't date things much older than about 50,000 years, but it works well for young things. Willard Libby (1908–1980) pioneered this process, winning a Nobel Prize in 1960 along the way, and you can trace the origins of his research back to the Manhattan Project and the first Trinity test at White Sands. As radiocarbon dating became increasingly

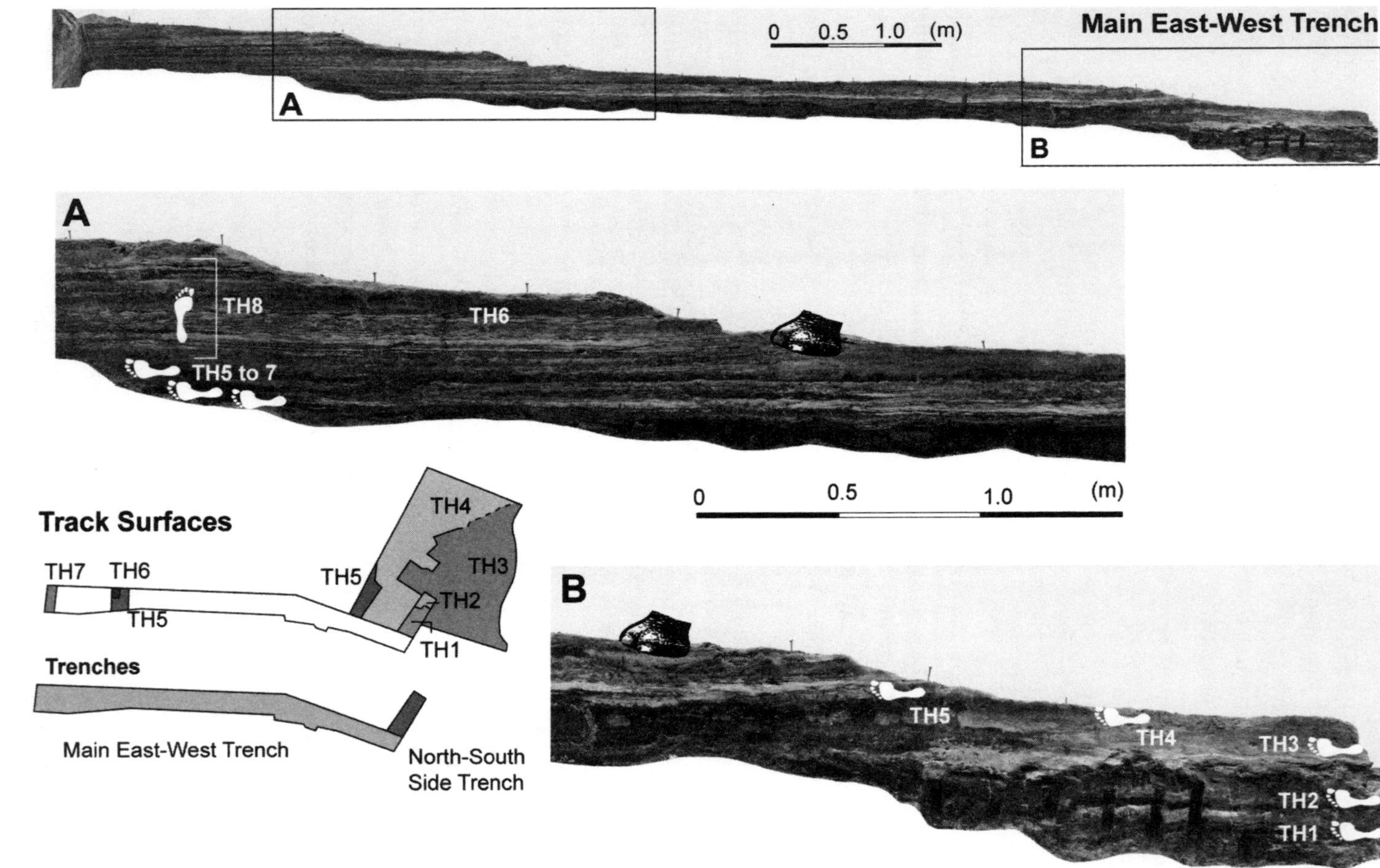
Main East-West Trench
0 0.5 1.0 (m)
A
B
TH8
TH6
TH5 to 7
0 0.5 1.0 (m)
Track Surfaces
TH7
TH6
TH5
TH5
TH4
TH3
TH2
TH1
Trenches
Main East-West Trench
North-South
Side Trench
TH5
TH4
TH3
TH2
TH1

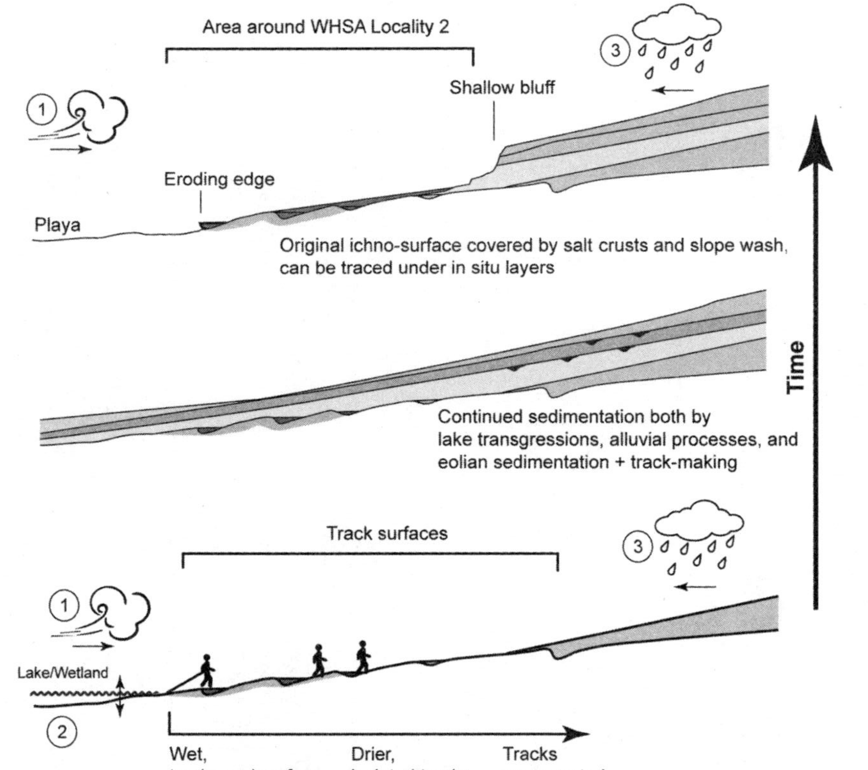

Figure 4.5 (*opposite page*). The side wall of the main trench at WHSA Locality 2, White Sands. The locations of mammoth tracks and human track layers are shown.

Figure 4.6 (*left*). An illustration of the formation of some of the natural footprint surfaces in the vicinity of WHSA Locality 2. It shows the interplay between gypsum sands blown in from the lakebed and slope-washed material, both of which overlie lake sediments. The exposed sediment surfaces are subject to wetting and drying cycles, which promote cementation by dolomite.

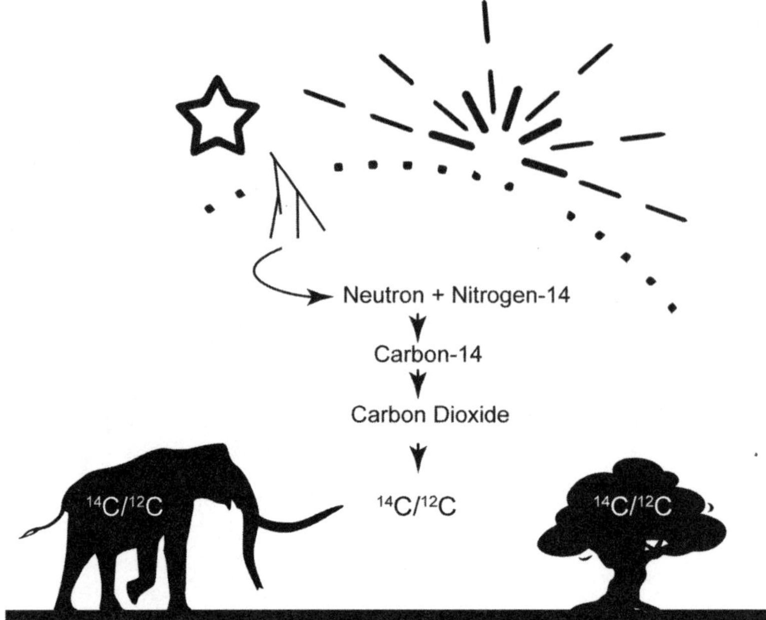

On death the $^{14}C/^{12}C$ ratio is no longer synced by respiration with the atmosphere so every 5,730 years half the ^{14}C decays

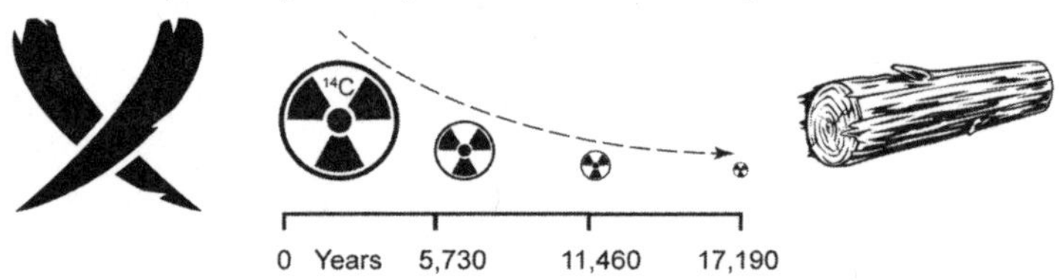

Figure 4.7 (*above*). The principles of radiocarbon. The upper panel shows how carbon-14 is created and incorporated into living organisms. The lower panel shows how this carbon decays radioactively over time in an exponential fashion based on the material's half-life. This process starts at death.

Figure 4.8 (*opposite page, above*). The calibration of radiocarbon dates. The upper illustrations show how you can create a chronology (dendrochronology) by looking at the distinctive pattern of tree rings. Wide rings correspond to good growing seasons and will be common to trees in the region. You can match wood samples of various ages to create a calendar and count rings to get the age. If you know the date of specific tree rings (lower right illustration), you can compare the radiocarbon age with the calendar age to create a calibration curve, as shown in the graph on the left.

Figure 4.9 (*opposite page, below*). A sample calibration curve. On the vertical axis are the carbon-14 values obtained from the dating process; these follow a normal distribution, as shown. The dotted horizontal lines extend to the calibration curve and down to the calendar age. Note that in this case, the potential age falls in two distributions with different probabilities: There is a 76 percent chance that the age is between 21,100 and 21,500 years BC, but also a small chance (18.7 percent) that it is older.

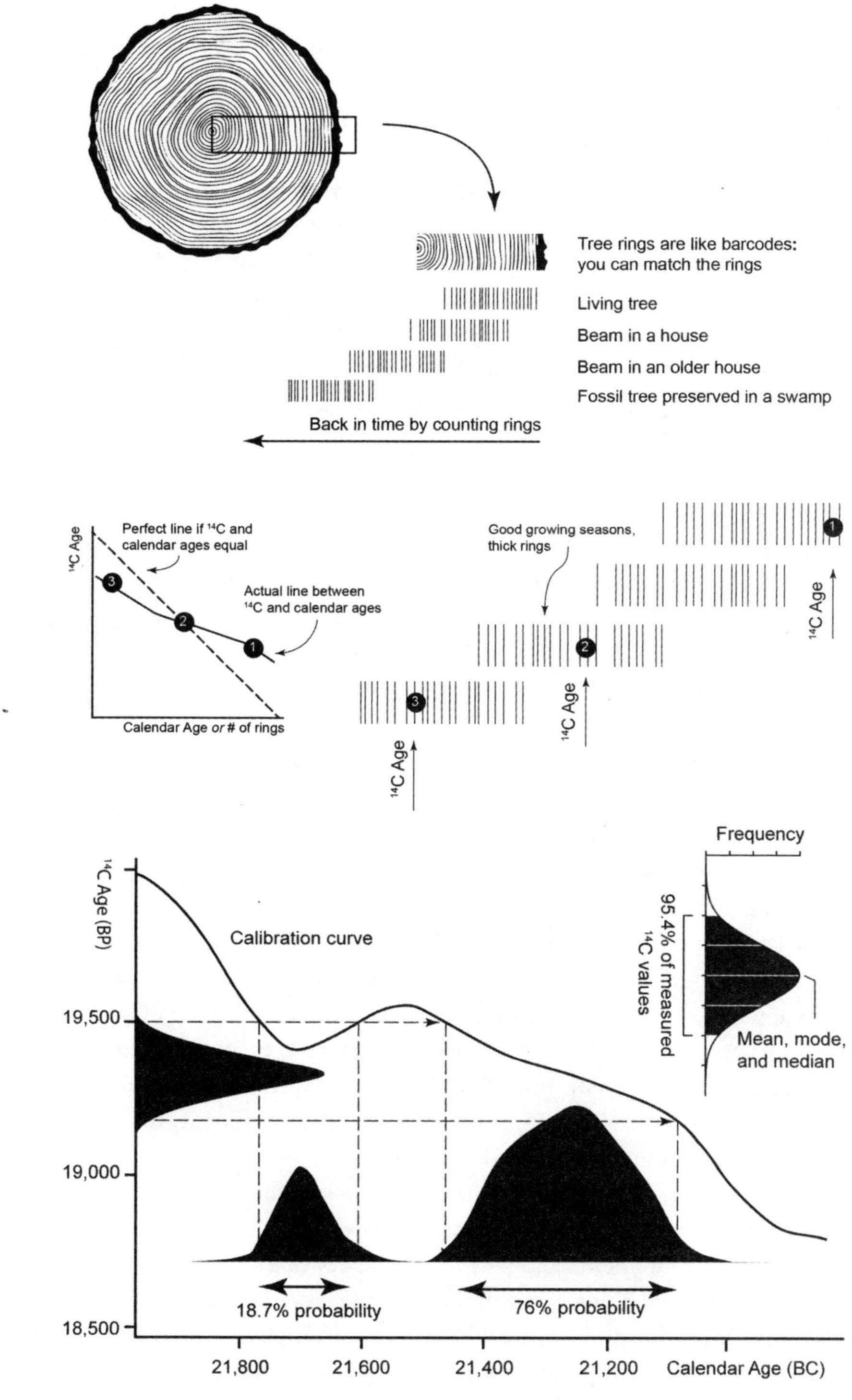

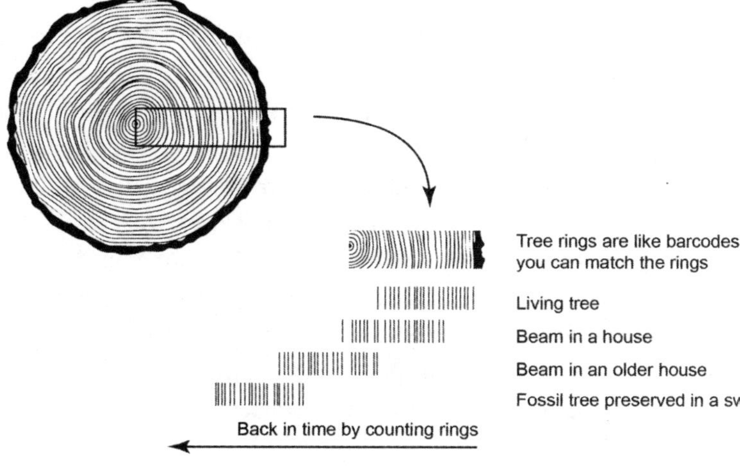
Tree rings are like barcodes:
you can match the rings
Living tree
Beam in a house
Beam in an older house
Fossil tree preserved in a swamp
Back in time by counting rings

^{14}C Age
Perfect line if ^{14}C and calendar ages equal
Actual line between ^{14}C and calendar ages
Calendar Age *or* # of rings
Good growing seasons, thick rings
^{14}C Age
^{14}C Age
^{14}C Age

^{14}C Age (BP)
Calibration curve
Frequency
95.4% of measured ^{14}C values
Mean, mode, and median
19,500
19,000
18,500
18.7% probability
76% probability
21,800
21,600
21,400
21,200
Calendar Age (BC)

available and routine, it had a big impact on both archaeology and geology. But it is not without its limitations.

In the early 1980s, it became clear that the ratio of carbon-14 to carbon-12 in the atmosphere was not constant. This should not have been a surprise, since Willard Libby recognized this from the start. The flux of cosmic rays changes over time with lots of variables, not least of which is the strength of the sun's surface activity. The result is not a fixed amount of carbon-14 in living things, but instead an amount that varies over time. Some form of calibration or correction was needed, and this starts with the humble tree ring (Figure 4.8). Tree rings are annual productions. A ring consists of two parts: a thicker layer associated with fast growth and a thinner layer associated with little or no growth. In a good year, a tree ring will be thick. In a dry or cold year, the ring will be thinner. It is like a barcode that literally reflects climate over the life cycle of the tree. We can use this barcode to make a tree ring chronology. Chop a tree down and count the rings while also documenting the thickness of each ring. Find a tree used as a beam in an old house and take a wood core from it. Again, count the rings and note their thickness. You now have two barcodes, one from the tree and one from the beam. If part of the barcodes match, both trees lived through the same sequence of warm and cold summers. Therefore, you can join the two parts into one chronology. So by finding older bits of wood and matching the barcodes in each, you can build up what is known as a dendrochronology ("tree time"), which, with luck, can extend back several thousand years. Count back a thousand years using this chronology and take a sample of wood from a layer of known age. You know its calendar age by counting the rings. In theory, the radiocarbon age should match, but because of variation in the cosmic ray flux, it won't. With lots of tree rings of different ages, we can build up a calibration curve that shows the departure between calendar ages and radiocarbon ages (Figure 4.9). Crucially, this allows you to calibrate a radiocarbon date and convert it to a calendar age. By international agreement, there is a standard calibration curve for radiocarbon ages.

When the carbon-14 is measured, you take multiple observations, and these give a range of values around an average or mean value. If we take lots of measurements and plot the frequency of each value, the most common values will occur in the middle and the less frequent ones to each side. The shape of this plot should look like a bell: high in the middle and tapering to each side. We call this a normal probability distribution. The most frequent value (mode), the average observation (mean), and the one halfway from each extreme (median) should in theory all plot in the middle. The steeper and pointier this curve, the less the error around the mean. By contrast, a flat curve has much larger errors. When we measure carbon-14, we take lots of observations, and they describe a probability distribution. In reporting the value, we use the average and the error around that average. These will be larger for a flat curve and less for a steep curve. Therefore, a radiocarbon date is reported like this: 19,328 ± 60 years. This simply means that the date falls between 19,388 and 19,268 years. The errors are reported at two standard deviations, or 95 percent, of the mean—that is, 95 percent of the area of the bell curve. The other thing to note is that all radiocarbon dates are worked out relative to 1950, with the designation "before present" (BP for short). When we calibrate an age, we give the lower and upper ages in calendar ages (Figure 4.9). This is how the *Ruppia* seeds at White Sands were dated.

A Period of Uncertainty

COVID-19 created a period of extreme uncertainty, and many of us lost friends and family. It was against the backdrop of being locked down and unable to leave the house that the first dates from our excavation arrived in January 2020. In those days, the research team had not spent much time in each other's company. Consequently, we did not have the level of trust that we would develop in the years since. Matthew recounts,

> I don't really recall the day the first set of dates slipped into my inbox from Jeff and Kath at the USGS, but I do recall being disappointed. They were old, as we had suspected, but there were only half a dozen dates, and I was expecting more. I would come to value just how surgical and precise Jeff and Kath are in time, but initially, I must admit to being a bit underwhelmed. There was one date slightly out of order, but the rest formed a neat sequence, with the youngest at the top and the oldest at the bottom. But some of the samples from deeper in the stratigraphy had not worked. I don't know what I was expecting, to be honest, apart from volume, and the unease was made worse by the thought that we could not jump on a plane to get more samples. Emails flew and a meeting was scheduled.

Dan recalls,

> I remember once being asked what advice I would give a graduate student if they found an archaeological site that was older than Clovis. This was back when most archaeologists still believed Clovis was the oldest evidence for humans in North America. I responded that they should buckle up and get ready for a rough ride. Few topics in archaeology have evoked as much passion as when humans first arrived in the Americas, and I came of age in the field watching senior colleagues savaging one another, sometimes in unpleasant ways. Those thoughts were very much with me when the first dates came in from Jeff and Kath. When we finally jumped on a video call, I asked a lot of questions aimed at trying to figure out what might cause the dates to be in error. Were there other lines of evidence we could use to evaluate them? At the same time, I knew what I had seen as we excavated the trench. Layer upon layer upon layer, the tracks of mammoths often higher up in the section and therefore younger than the tracks of human beings. As we talked, I gained greater appreciation for just how rigorous Jeff and Kath were in their approach to collecting samples in the field and selecting them for analysis. I knew that what we were finding would receive a lot of scrutiny, but I also had confidence that we had the right people doing this work.

Matthew concludes, "Talking things out always helps. As the video call progressed, folks, including myself, began to understand the dating strategy that Jeff and Kath had applied. There was no need for multiple dates where one quality date would serve, in their view, and they had bracketed in age several of the footprint layers. The lowest footprint layer was not well constrained due to the failure of a sample, and that nagged at us all. We didn't quite have the story neatly tied up in a bow, but we had a story. And boy, was it a story!

As the summer of 2020 progressed, lockdowns were eased and then reimposed as COVID variants circulated the globe. We had regular video calls, always hoping that international travel would become possible, or even national travel within the United States, to allow part or all of the field team to reassemble and sample some more. There were crazy schemes, like sending David into the field while we watched via a video call to guide the resampling. And David did go back into the field at various points that summer and fall to collect more samples. As it became clear that travel probably would not be possible in January 2021, we started to rethink our strategy. Could we publish just the upper part of the stratigraphy and leave the rest for another day? This would allow us to proceed without waiting for more samples. We finally decided that was the best course of action and started to prepare a manuscript for the journal *Science*. Academic journals are ranked by the impact that they have and by professional prestige. For multidisciplinary research like ours, the top two journals are *Science* and *Nature*, one being American and the other European. To publish in either can be career defining, and the competition to grace the pages of these journals is intense. In theory, although not always in practice, only the best and most important discoveries get published in these two journals. It is a tough, competitive world. We chose *Science* and started to prepare our manuscript, which according to the journal rules had to be brief, so every word counted. Our work was making the big claim that people visited White Sands some 7,000 years earlier than previously thought, at the height of the last glacial maximum. That claim would cause a stir, and many would oppose the ideas on principle. The paper needed to be perfect, and in February 2021 we were ready to submit.

When you submit a manuscript that you have worked on night and day for several weeks, there is a sense of loss, a gaping hole in your itinerary into which all the work you had pushed aside flows back to leave you swamped. Scientific papers are sent out to review, a process by which the editor picks a range of colleagues in the field to read your draft and try to find fault. It can be a harsh business, and people are often unkind in their comments, especially if they don't like your work. Peer review, as it is called, is not as objective as you might hope! The weeks passed. Three weeks slipped into four, and then five. High-end journals tend to be quick with their reviews, and as time passed, we began to think the worst. Then, one day in May, there was an email from *Science*. The editors were interested in publishing our work if we could address some of the comments made in the reviews. The reviews were good, some expressing real support for the work and congratulating the team, but at least one was critical of our dating, making comments that would foretell the response after we published. The editors wanted us to address something called a hardwater effect, which we discuss in the next section, and also to use another dating method to corroborate our dates. The obvious tool was something called optical stimulated luminescence (OSL), which is also discussed

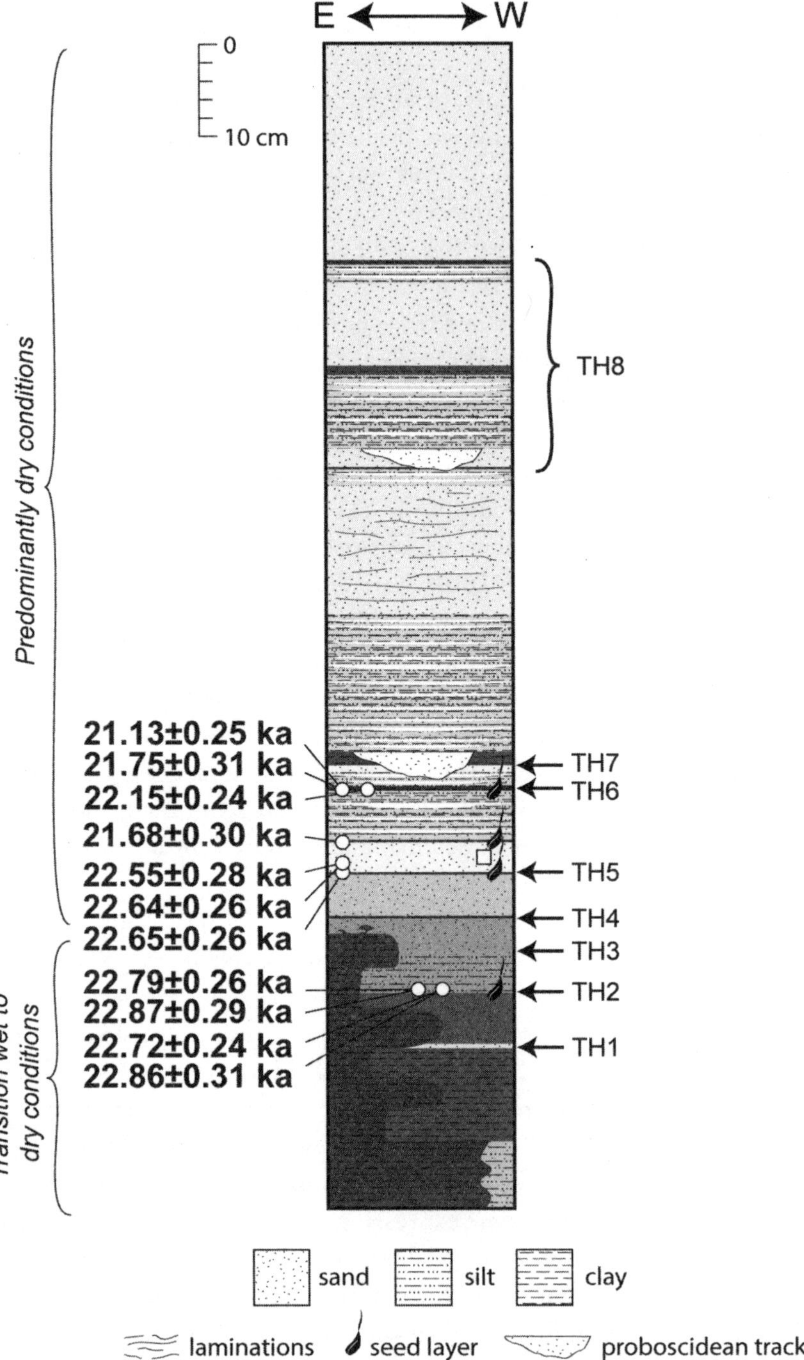

Figure 4.10. Stratigraphic log with radiocarbon dates for part of the WHSA Locality 2 trench at White Sands (Bennett et al., "Evidence of Humans in North America"). The footprint horizons are labeled TH1 to TH8. TH stands for "track horizons."

in the next section. But our colleagues Jeff and Kath were not keen and proposed an alternative corroborative method, namely to try and date the gypsum directly. Fieldwork was possible for those in the United States, although international travel was still prohibited. Jeff and Kath raced to White Sands to try and date a gypsum layer and take more samples for radiocarbon dating. The approach, a dating technique based around pure gypsum, had been successfully used in the Estancia Basin, to the north of the Tularosa Basin.[1] If it worked at Estancia, it should work at White Sands—so the logic ran.

Dating gypsum is based on the radioactive decay of uranium. Uranium-238 decays slowly to uranium-234 by releasing radioactive particles parent to daughter. In turn, uranium-234 gives thorium-230, which decays quite quickly to radium-226 and finally to lead-206. As water washes through rock or sediment, it dissolves the uranium, but not the thorium, as thorium is insoluble in water. When this water evaporates to leave gypsum with traces of uranium in it, thorium should be absent, so the radioactive clock is set to zero. Over time, a new supply of thorium will build up in the gypsum, depending on the rate at which uranium-234 decays to thorium-230. In this way, the ratio of thorium-230 to uranium gives us a potential age. This is exactly what researchers had done in the Estancia Basin and what we hoped to do at White Sands. Our colleagues in the USGS worked hard to date the gypsum, and while they gave broadly supportive results, there were simply too many methodological questions that needed further work to reliably corroborate the radiocarbon ages. Instead, we used data from outside White Sands to argue against hardwater effects, and in time, the editors at *Science* said yes! Matthew recalls,

> It was a tense few weeks as we waited for *Science* to give their final verdict on our work. We had the TV crew who filmed with us back in January 2020 breathing down our necks as they tried to finish their documentary for Nova and PBS, which had also been delayed by COVID-19. The production company was British, and international travel was still not open, but they had special permission from the US Embassy to travel to get their final shots. But of course, we did not want them to disclose our work before it was published, and for a while the pressure was intense as we tried and failed to keep all our stakeholders happy, from the film crew to the increasingly nervous National Park Service. These are the low points in doing science and

are far removed from the fun of discovery that starts the process. It was a tough few weeks.

On September 23, 2021,[2] the paper dating the White Sands tracks finally appeared. We had added more than 7,000 years to the history of humans in the Americas, and our work was reported all over the world (Figures 4.10 and 4.11).

Pushback

The ink had barely dried on the paper before people were sharpening their pencils to reply.[3] They seemed to accept the footprints as human but took exception to our dates—"too old!" they cried. If you ask an Indigenous American when their ancestors first arrived, they will say something along the lines of "Well, we have always lived in these lands." To many Indigenous people, it seems strange for scientists to be arguing about what they simply know and believe (a theme we will return to as we provide context for why the peopling of the Americas is such a contentious topic). As the replies and criticism came in, one had to be philosophical to some extent, but it did hurt. It is easy to dash off a few lines of criticism, but much harder to follow a research journey of more than five years, and much longer in the case of our story's hero, David Bustos.

Science advances to some extent by claim and counterclaim, and by rigorous debate that stimulates more questions. In *The Knowledge Machine*,[4] Michael Strevens eloquently discusses how science is supposed to work versus how it really works. He refers to what he calls the Iron Rule of Explanation, by which scientists phrase their criticism of others politely (or not!) in terms of questions that need to be asked and what data need to be collected to answer them. And that is exactly what the best of our critics did. They wanted us to address the question of hardwater and use a corroborative technique. Jeff and Kath set about doing exactly that. Rather than focusing on defending our work to every critic, they went on to innovate solutions to the problems posed and acquire new data. But it would take time, because good science can't be rushed.

It is time to explain the hardwater effect. Radiocarbon dating relies on the idea that when you take a breath, the radioactive carbon-14 is replenished and is in equilibrium with that in the atmosphere. If the flux of cosmic rays increases and therefore the production of carbon-14 in the atmosphere, within a reasonable amount of time, the amount of carbon-14 in a living plant or animal will increase to match it. But if this exchange with the atmosphere is delayed or prevented, there is a problem. As rain falls, it dissolves carbon dioxide from the atmosphere and even more as it percolates through soil. If that water ends up deep underground, far away from the atmosphere, the carbon-14 within it will begin to decay and not be refreshed. The same is true of deep ocean waters. These waters begin to age, and you can date groundwater in this way. If you have a land plant like a pine tree, then the new needles will be in equilibrium with the atmosphere, but a plant that grows in water might be affected by groundwater that is already "old." And this would make radiocarbon dates based on aquatic plants appear older than they should be. That is the essence of the hardwater problem, and of course we used the seeds of *Ruppia*, which lives in water. If there had been a hardwater effect, our dates are unlikely to have formed such a neat order, with the oldest at the bottom and the youngest at the top. This would require the supply of "old water" to be constant, and while the paleolake was clearly highly saline, its ephemeral nature and lack of deep water make the presence of old water unlikely. Nonetheless, according to our critics, we had failed to demonstrate the absence of this potential problem. If your site has been displaced as the oldest site, then attacking some else's dates as being too old is a good place to start. While scientists should aspire to be objective, they rarely are!

In January 2022, the team was back together and digging at White Sands. It was amazing to be able to travel again and to share our respective COVID stories. The plan was to extend the original trench to capture the complete sequence, work originally planned for April 2020. We had lost two years, but some folks had lost much more. Everything was to be resampled and redated. We had the first tentative discussion about the idea of dating pollen (Figure 4.12), because to our surprise, all our samples were full of it. If we could concentrate enough pine pollen, a terrestrial plant free of hardwater, then we could date it using radiocarbon. It is easy to write such a sentence. The practice is much harder, however, and at the current limits of innovation in the field of radiocarbon dating.

Plants produce pollen, which is the bane of those with seasonal allergies. Pollen is one of the earliest proxies ever used to reconstruct past climates, and the idea was first suggested by Lennart von Post (1884–1951) back in

Figure 4.11. The number of tracks excavated at each track horizon and the basic inferences about stature, track-maker age, and walking speed. MNT stands for "minimum number of track-makers."

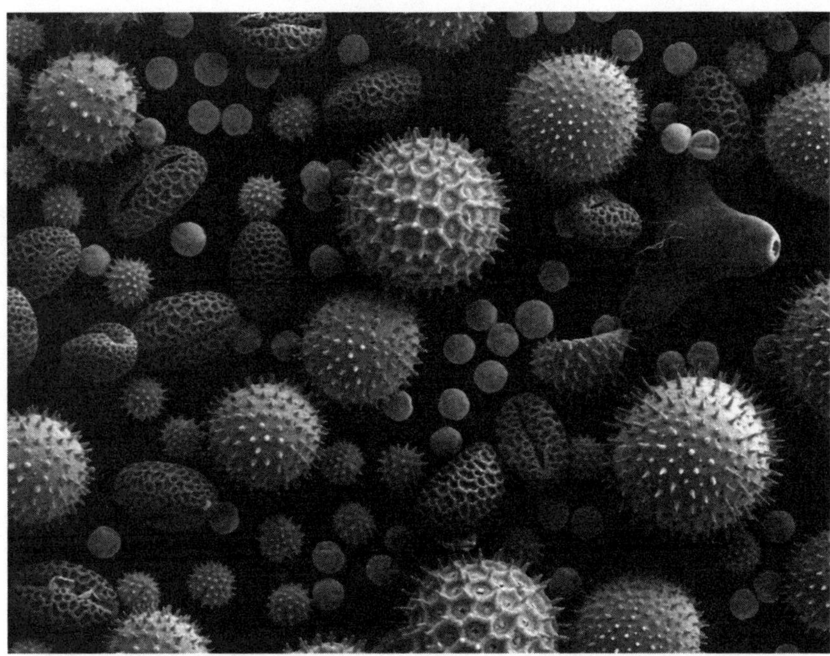

Figure 4.12. Colorized scanning electron microscope image of pollen grains from a variety of common plants: sunflower (*Helianthus annuus*), morning glory (*Ipomoea purpurea*), prairie hollyhock (*Sidalcea malviflora*), oriental lily (*Lilium auratum*), evening primrose (*Oenothera fruticosa*), and castor bean (*Ricinus communis*). Courtesy of Dartmouth Electron Microscope Facility, Dartmouth College.

1916. Pollen accumulates all around us and is a component of dust. On a dusty bookshelf, it does not stand a chance from the occasional brush with a feather duster, but in a lake or wetland, it can accumulate quite nicely. Each layer of sediment contains a snapshot of the pollen present during its deposition, and as the layers build up, they record changes in the types of pollen falling. Under a microscope, pollen is amazing, with different shapes corresponding to different plants. Not quite a plant fingerprint but close, it is also relatively easy to separate from loose sediment and other types of organic matter. Some plants distribute their pollen locally via insects, while other plants have evolved to disperse their pollen via the wind. Notwithstanding the interplay of local and regional floral inputs, you can take a stab at reconstructing the plant communities around a site from a sample of pollen. If the pollen changes in each layer, you have a record of changing vegetation, which reflects human agriculture, land use, and ultimately climate change. Pollen allows you to go a little further. Plants have natural climatic ranges—temperature and moisture ranges necessary for them to grow. If two plants have different biotic ranges, but are found in the same sample, then the climate at that time must have been within the overlap of those ranges. This idea of mutual climate ranges was first applied by Johannes Iversen (1904–1971), who used the coexistence of holly, ivy, and mistletoe pollen in wetland samples to reconstruct the temperature in northern Europe.[5]

How does the presence of pollen help with the dating of the footprints at White Sands? The first point is that if the footprints date from the last glacial maximum, climates would have been different from those at present—probably colder and more seasonal. The pollen spectrum from these deposits should reflect this and show change up the sedimentary sequence as conditions warmed as the Ice Age waned. Jeff and Kath were after something much bigger than this simple corroborative evidence. They wanted to date pollen. The average size of allergy-producing pollen is about 25 microns, although some grains are as small as 2.5 microns. A micron is one-thousandth of a millimeter (0.000039 inches) in diameter, which is basically microscopic. An individual pollen grain varies in weight, from 0.000002 to 0.000006 mg, and to have success with a radiocarbon date, you need about 0.5 to 1 mg, so between 70,000 and 100,000 grains should do it. Your eyes are probably itching just at the thought of this amount of pollen. Dating pollen has been a dream of many researchers for a while, but it was not practical till the advent of an amazing bit of kit used for the most part in pathology labs for counting blood cells.

Traditionally, a pathologist would count cells by making a slide, perhaps staining the cells with dye, and sitting there and counting them. Flow cytometry was developed to speed this process up. Different cells have different optical properties when lit by a laser. Some fluoresce; others go dark. This lies at the heart of flow cytometry. The cells are suspended in an inert fluid and concentrated into a fine flow only one cell thick. As a cell passes, a laser lights it up. A light detector picks up the response and counts the cell. The clever bit is that the stream is so thin that it begins to break up into individual drops, each with a cell in it, and the application of small electrical charges can deflect a drop into a specific container. In this way, the system can both count and separate cells. Pollen grains fluoresce when hit by a laser, so they can be counted and concentrated by flow cytometry. The process starts in the lab. A sample is washed, and the pollen floats away from heavier sediment. The pollen is concentrated even further by visual picking under a microscope, and when it is sufficiently concentrated, flow cytometry takes over. It is slow, time-consuming, and expensive in terms of machine and human time. But it does work, and with care you can concentrate more than 70,000 pollen grains. In our case, we didn't want just any old pollen grains. We wanted pine pollen, to be sure there was no hardwater influence.

Working with a bunch of colleagues across the United States, Jeff and Kath obtained carbon-14 dates based on pine pollen for each of the layers for which they had a carbon date on *Ruppia* seeds. And you couldn't ask for a better result: The pollen dates corresponded perfectly to the *Ruppia* dates (Figure 4.13).[6] There was no hardwater effect at work on this part of the section.

We went further to address our critics by doing exactly what they asked and also using an independent corroborative dating technique. Kath and Jeff switched their attention from thorium–uranium dating to OSL. In desert environments, OSL is widely used. The ground is radioactive, since radioactive minerals occur in many rocks. This background radiation is not harmful to animals and barely registers. But certain minerals, namely quartz, can accumulate this energy in their atomic structure. An atom has a nucleus with protons and neutrons, around which electrons orbit. The energy gets trapped by the orbiting electrons. The accumulation of this energy is time dependent; the longer the time, the more energy there is, and if you know the rate at which it accumulates and the amount, you can estimate time. The crucial part of this is that exposure to intense light releases this energy, essentially resetting the clock back to zero. Imagine sand blowing in the wind. Each grain of sand is made up of a quartz crystal turning in the bright light. Any energy stored is released. If a sand grain becomes buried and trapped in a layer of sediment, the lights go out and the energy starts to accumulate. If a geologist can sample this grain of sand without exposing it to light, they can take it back to the lab and measure the energy released when it is exposed to light in controlled conditions. From this, you can determine an age. It is a cool technique and can date things back to 150,000 years if all goes well.

The challenge is how to get the sample without exposing it to any light. To do this, you pound into a section of sediment a metal or plastic tube perhaps an inch in diameter and 6 inches in length. Once it's inserted, you cap the end and carefully dig the tube out, placing another cap on the open end. The sediment at each end of the tube will have been exposed to light, but the bit in the middle won't. Back in the lab, in a darkroom, you extract the sediment and pick out some grains from the middle of the tube. These are the grains you sample and expose to light in a controlled way. This has become a well-established technique, but the challenge at White Sands is that there is not much quartz, because most of the blown sand is gypsum. You also must be certain that the sediment has not been reworked or exposed to stray light rays via cracks in the soil. Despite White Sands being a beautiful desert, it is not a perfect environment for this technique, but it was worth a try. Our OSL dates confirmed our pollen dates, which in turn confirmed our original *Ruppia* dates. People really were in the Americas at the height of the last ice age. We published our new results in *Science* in October 2023,[6] and the results were again widely reported. The pollen also confirmed that the vegetation at the time the footprints were imprinted was typical of the last glacial maximum in New Mexico. Our work silenced many of the critics.

The debate continues, however. It currently centers around several issues,[7] which can be broken down into (1) hardwater, (2) stratigraphy and OSL, and (3) reworking of pollen. The first is the basic counterargument that the dating of *Ruppia* seeds gives ages that are too old due to the influence of groundwater that already has an "age"—essentially the hardwater effect. Some researchers have tried to construct hardwater corrections for our dates by dating modern *Ruppia* seeds in different parts of the Tularosa Basin.[8] They have shown that some modern seeds have an age consistent with a potential hardwater effect. The counter here is that these locations are not necessarily like those that prevailed at WHSA Locality 2 during the Pleistocene, and Jeff Pigati, an expert in radiocarbon dating, believes that the scientific reasoning used in these studies is flawed.[9] Critics have also focused on the presence of seed balls. Seed balls do occur in the sediments at White Sands and consist of clumps of seeds about the size of a golf ball. They look like dung balls, although they don't appear to have been formed in this way. Some folks have suggested that they are created by waves on lakes reworking the seeds into balls.[10] After sampling different seeds from these balls, some researchers have suggested that they contain seeds of different ages. They suggest that by analogy, our seed dates must come from seeds of mixed ages. The fundamental problem with this is that we did not date seed balls but instead dated distinct and continuous layers of seeds. Moreover, our seed dates are based on large seed samples.

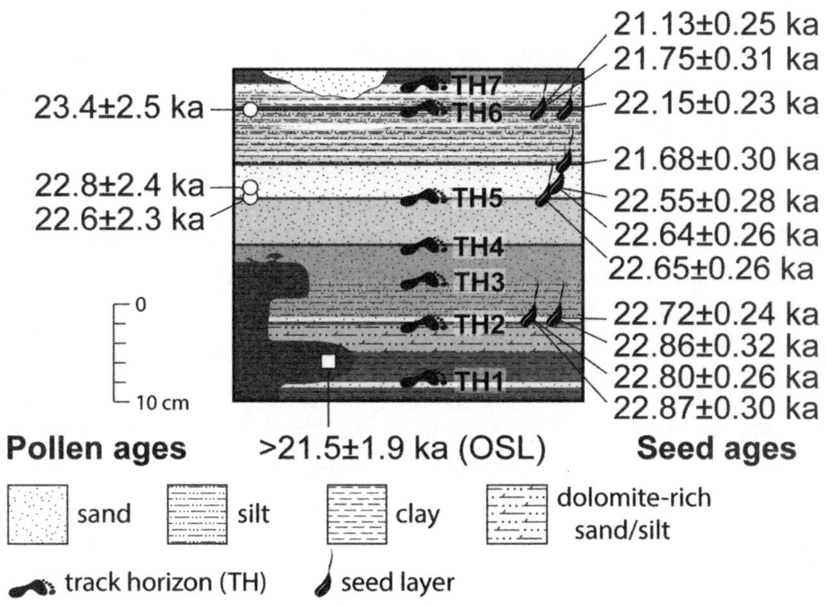

Figure 4.13. New pollen and OSL dates confirm the original stratigraphy and age of the footprint layers.

Therefore, any extraneous seeds would simply add to the error range, rather than skew the mean.

A second line of criticism has focused on our OSL dates. Researchers suggested that we were remiss in our work in 2021 in not using OSL as a corroborating technique. But when we did as they requested, they challenged the methods we used and critically misinterpreted the stratigraphic setting of the site. Finally, some of our critics have taken exception to the use of pollen in dating. They raised several technical issues, suggesting that we may have biased our results by preferentially selecting a particular size and therefore taxa of pollen. We dispute this. They also suggested that reworking of older pollen may have occurred and that our samples were effectively contaminated by pollen that had been on the landscape for a time. There is something in this, since pollen can remain on a landscape for a considerable time, but during this time, it would have become degraded. We do not see any evidence of degraded pollen in our samples consistent with a prolonged landscape residence. We also sampled sediment and pollen from an adjacent modern playa and showed that they contained only modern taxa. No pollen reworking is taking place today, although one could argue that it may have in the past. If you are interested, you can find the technical debate and the back and forth by reading papers by Rhode and colleagues,[11] and the response from our team led by Jeff Pigati.[12]

It is important to recognize that attempts by Rhode and colleagues[13] to dispute our work at WHSA Locality 2 are presented as if the dating techniques and methods operate in a vacuum and are independent of one another.[14] The true strength and power of the work we have completed at WHSA Locality 2 lies in the totality of the evidence. This includes radiocarbon dating of *Ruppia* seeds, radiocarbon dating of pollen from the same stratigraphic levels, and OSL dating of sediments from within the footprint-bearing sediments. The fact that all these lines of evidence agree is the key here; collectively, they have power. The convergence of these various lines of evidence supports the conclusion that humans were present in North America during the last glacial maximum.

Matthew recalls,

> Back in 1991, I was completing my doctoral thesis about glacial geology in the Scottish Highlands—a far cry from footprints! Anyway, several of my peers were putting fancy quotes into their dissertations at the start, and I wanted to do this as well. Being a bit of a rebel, I went for quote from a crime novel, *The Case of Mr. Foggatt* by Arthur Morrison (1894). It is also apposite here: "Often when I have remarked upon the apparently trivial nature of the clues by which [Martin Hewitt] allowed himself to be guided—sometimes, to all seeming, in the very face of all likelihood—he has replied that two trivialities, pointing in the same direction, become at once, by their mere agreement, no trivialities at all but important considerations.

To the outsider, it must all seem rather technical and somewhat esoteric, and it could be summarized cynically as "clever people" arguing among themselves. And to a certain extent, this is true. If you don't like a bit of scientific evidence, it is usually possible to find a problem with it or attempt to dismiss it in another way by developing an alternative explanation. Neither side is necessarily right, since there are no absolutes in science. It is not like a school mathematics problem where the answer can be found in the back of the book. What amounts to certainty in science is achieved through debate. Debate flushes out problems and hopefully focuses minds on getting better, more accurate data. The challenge here is that both sides can become blind to the actual truth as they try to prove the other team wrong. Groupthink[15] is a real thing and can be a major problem in scientific debates like this. To an Indigenous observer, this must all seem unnecessary, since their traditional beliefs and oral traditions place their ancestors on the landscape from the beginnings of time.

There is another way of looking at this, and that is to use the analogy of the four-minute mile. In the 1950s, running a mile in under four minutes was a huge sporting challenge, a record to be set and broken. Roger Bannister achieved this feat in 1954. Today, however, an athlete running a mile in under four minutes is more routine. In fact, by 2022, more than 1,700 athletes had achieved this mark.[16] Records are there to be broken and usually are. One event is noteworthy and open to question, but multiple events become routine. The relevance here? Well, there will be other claims for early people of the Americas over the next decade, based on different types of evidence as well as footprints at other sites. One last glacial maximum date is an anomaly, outside accepted convention and therefore a legitimate target, but when you have five, 10, or more sites, it is no longer an anomaly. Arguing about the dating at White Sands will not achieve much and will no doubt continue for years to come, but finding new sites across the American Southwest to confirm or refute the findings will change the debate in time. That is what our research team is focusing on.

People Really Were in New Mexico 23,000 Years Ago!

To conclude, we draw attention to a comment made about our work by Vance Haynes, one of the fiercest critics of sites that predate Clovis. He wrote to the team in October 2023:

> Having just devoured . . . [your paper] on the dating of pollen from the White Sands track strata, including the supplemental data, I am convinced you and your colleagues are right. If the footprints are indeed human footprints, they exceed Clovis in age by essentially

> 10,000 years. The physical and chemical procedures used in concentrating and purifying fossil pollen are about as exacting as could be, so the radiocarbon dates are as exact as they could be. And the OSL dating is equally exact in spite of the challenges involved and overcome. This in no way validates the proposed ages of [other sites]. . . . Congratulations to you and your team on a job well done.

The debate continues, but for the team, there can be no better endorsement than that of Vance Haynes, who was once a critic of our work and is now a supporter.

CHAPTER FIVE

Stepping from the Past into the Future

Everyone likes a good story, whether it is one your grandma used to tell or one from the latest science documentary on your favorite subject. Narratives convey information. They combine knowledge and present it in patterns that offer a pleasing security in an uncertain world. Indigenous people have origin stories based on oral tradition and deepened by a sense of community, ancestry, and belonging. Scientists have narratives too. We tell evidence-based stories that build incrementally on the work of others to help us understand the world around us. Whether based on observed facts or facts passed down via oral traditions, stories help us understand a confusing world, and all such stories are of equal value.

Scientists call their stories paradigms, models, or hypotheses, but let's face it: They are still stories! A paradigm is influenced by the social and cultural norms of its time and can be colored by such things both consciously and unconsciously. Stories help us understand pieces of a puzzle, which hopefully when complete illustrates a single coherent picture. Over time, one may find puzzle pieces—bits of evidence—that don't fit the picture. At first, they are usually disregarded, explained away, and sometimes treated with hostility. If you believe you are piecing together a picture of a white dog, a black piece may be unwelcome. Maybe it belongs to part of the picture yet to be pieced, such as part of a black collar. But if the number of black pieces becomes sufficiently large, then our world picture must change. We have a paradigm shift: There are now two dogs, one black and one white. Paradigm shifts are like revolutions: They may push on a rotten core, are often a response to the procession of ideas, occur rapidly, and are usually overdue. But getting them started is hard. "Revolution is not an apple that falls when it is ripe. You have to make it fall," Che Guevara famously said. To understand why the age

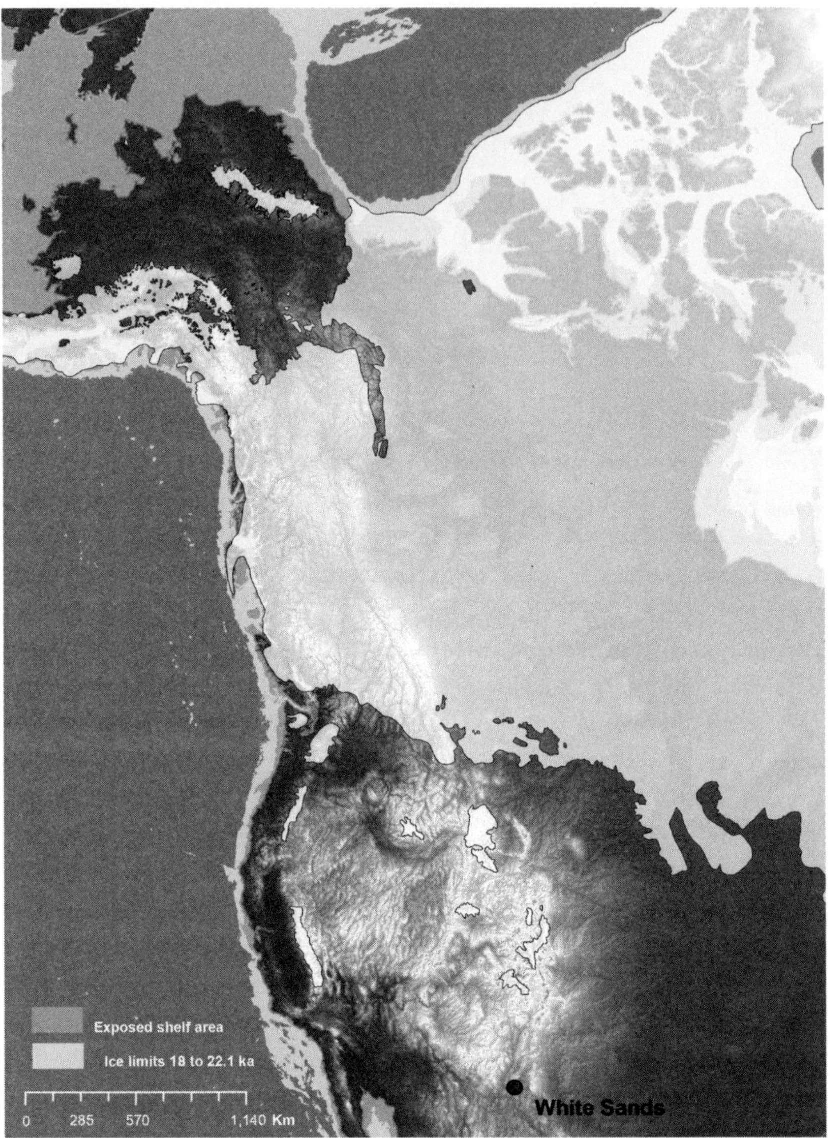

Figure 5.1. North America during the last glacial maximum. Exposure of the continental shelf (reduced sea level) is based on national bathymetry and a range of published sea level curves. Ice margins courtesy of Dalton et al., "Evolution of the Laurentide and Innuitian Ice Sheets."

of the footprints at White Sands is challenging to some archaeologists and has attracted controversy and opposition, it is necessary to understand the prevailing science narrative that it runs counter to.

Barriers to Migration

At the height of the last glacial cycle of the Ice Age, an ice sheet more than 2 miles thick (the Laurentide Ice Sheet) covered much of the northern continent, centered over Hudson Bay (Figure 5.1).[1] Its southern boundary followed the 49th parallel, although ice sheet lobes encroached farther south around the Great Lakes and Long Island. To the east, the ice sheet's margins lay along the edge of the continental shelf, and to the west it merged with a smaller ice sheet, the Cordilleran ice sheet, located over the Pacific ranges and the Rocky Mountains. From coast to coast, there was an ice sheet barrier. The ice within an ice sheet must come from somewhere, and that source is the ocean. Evaporation of ocean waters leads to rain and snow, which accumulate as snow in an ice sheet. The result is that sea levels are lowered as ice sheets grow, revealing land that is submerged today. The Bering Strait to the north of the Pacific Ocean currently separates Russia from Alaska. But at the height of the last glacial cycle, the sea level was lower, and you could walk between the two continents (Figure 5.1). In fact, that may be how the first Americans arrived from Asia. So toward the last glacial maximum, as the ice sheets reached their greatest size (about 21,000 years ago), it was possible for people to walk into Alaska from Asia. The Bering Land Bridge was probably dry land as early as 35,000 years ago, and until around 23,000 years ago,[2] a route south led between the Cordilleran and Laurentide ice sheets. But once this corridor closed, all routes south were barred.

Following this glacial maximum, climates began to warm. The ice sheets began to melt, and consequently their margins retreated, but it was not until somewhere between 14,000 and 12,000 years ago that the corridor between these ice sheets became ice-free, allowing bison to move both north and south (Figure 5.3).[3] The exact age at which this ice-free corridor became open is subject to debate, but traditionally it was

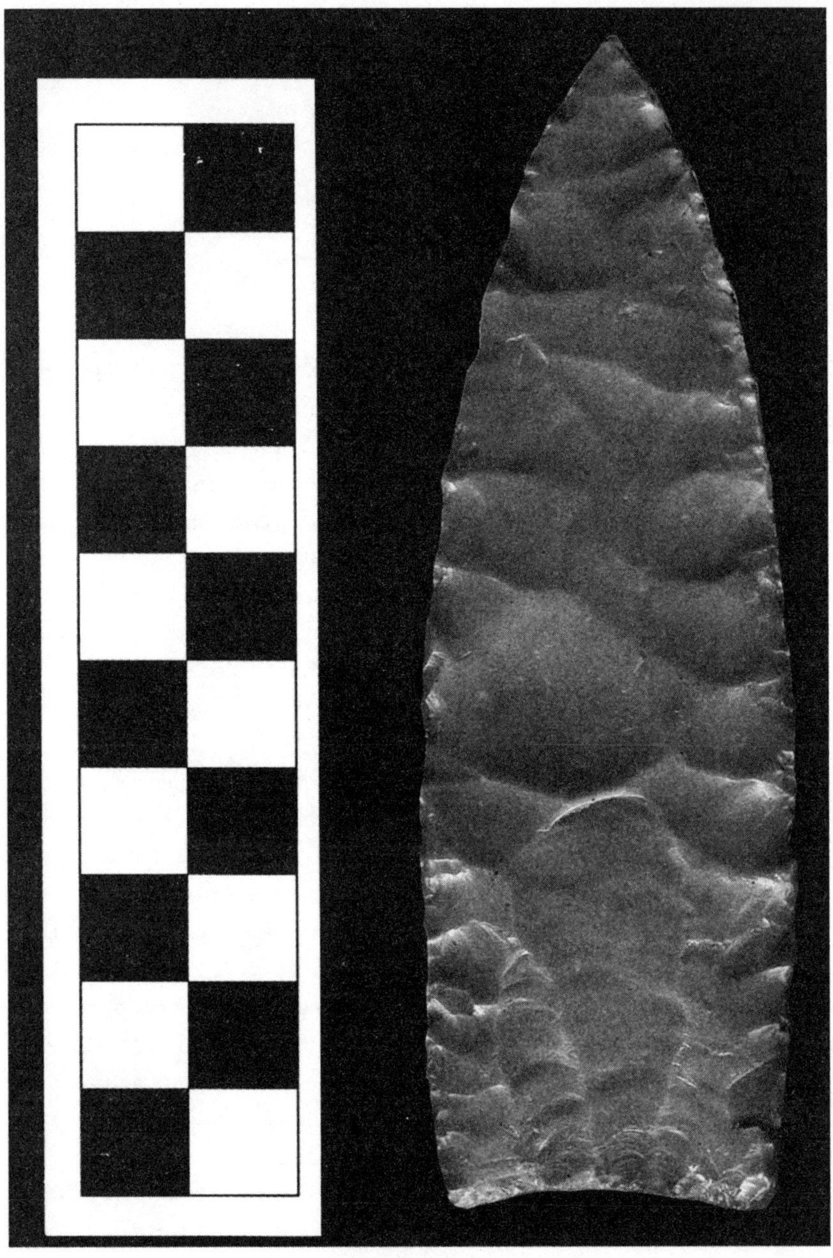

Figure 5.2. A cast of a Clovis point. Photograph by and courtesy of Vance Holliday, from the collection of C. V. Haynes, School of Anthropology, University of Arizona.

thought to be open around 12,000 years ago. In the prevailing narrative, this becomes the route south for the Indigenous people waiting in Alaska as climates warmed and ice sheets shrank. At this time, the evidence for people in the Americas south of the 49th parallel increases rapidly with the widespread occurrence of a distinctive type of spear/dart tip known as a Clovis point. This flaked tool is an elongated (lancelet) point with a central groove, presumably to assist with hafting the flake to a wooden shaft (Figure 5.2). Slightly younger are Folsom points, which show even greater refinement but are variants on this theme. The Clovis point is named after the town of Clovis in New Mexico and is probably the most well-known and well-distributed stone tool in North America. It represents a rapid and widespread cultural diffusion in which everyone was suddenly making, and presumably using, the same type of tool. Archaeologists refer to this as a cultural event horizon, and it helps correlate sites in time: one tool, one culture, one time. The science of radiocarbon dating can place ages on Clovis artifacts, and in 1964 Vance Haynes assigned an age to Clovis sites: between about 11,500 and 10,800 years ago. Emerging from the discovery of all these Clovis points was a conundrum, however, since there was little evidence of earlier occupation and precursor technology. As a crude modern analogy, it was if the iPhone arrived suddenly in our lives and everyone was using it, with no evidence of any earlier type of smartphone. The absence of pre-Clovis technology begged the question of where the precursor populations were located. Were the Clovis people, in fact, the first Americans? This fitted into a nice narrative in which post–Ice Age pioneers swept south through the ice-free corridor to expand and flourish on the prairies of North America hunting Ice Age megafauna. This story has become known as the Clovis First hypothesis. Indigenous people are not keen on this narrative, since it is at odds with their own oral traditions, which place them on the landscape much earlier and, in fact, timelessly. Indigenous paleoarchaeologist Paulette Steeves has gone as far as to call out this narrative as an unconscious repression of the Indigenous voice.

Clovis First became a paradigm that was hard to overturn,[4] and the last few decades are littered with sites proposed and then challenged. Claims and counterclaims around many sites focus on three basic things: (1) the artifacts are not artifacts at all; (2) the artifacts are not in situ; and (3) the dates are corrupted in some way and therefore too old. Part of the challenge here is that everyone is clear what a Clovis point looks like, and there is a good chronology of later technologies, but what should an earlier technology look like? Should it have Asian affinities, or should it be unique? Should the technology be consistent across several old sites? We don't have a clear idea of what went before, so fitting a new find into this narrative is not easy.

There are also lots of natural geological processes, especially in caves, that might give rise to something that looks manufactured, and this is the essence of "geofact versus artifact" debate. This debate has played out recently at the Chiquihuite Cave site in Mexico, which claimed a date of 30,000-plus years back in 2020.[5] The artifacts proposed to be the result of human manufacture are claimed by others to simply be the product of cave collapse and perhaps animal trampling, leaving uncertain the question of whether humans were there at these early periods.[6] The same is true of a claim for 130,000 years in California, where the proponents argued for worked bone[7] while the community shouted that it was trampled bone.[8] Artifacts can also move in natural sediment through bioturbation—the simple action of earthworms, termites, gophers, and other creatures on soil. Several pre-Clovis claims have been dismissed based on artifacts ending up deep in a stratigraphy due to the agency of a burrowing animal. And then we come to sites that have been criticized for their dating. Meadowcroft is one such site. On its face, it has a good claim for being old, and it has fought the pre-Clovis battle bitterly over many years.[9] It is in Pennsylvania, part of the coal belt, and the old radiocarbon dates have been criticized as being contaminated by ancient coal deposits seeping via groundwater. This idea has never been systematically refuted. Our point here is not to debate specific sites, but to point out that to overturn a good narrative with a lot of supporting data, one needs good evidence.

One site that has stood up to this integration is Monte Verde in Chile. It added 1,200 years to the established history and, crucially, 10,000 miles to the migrants' journey.[10] The site's champion was Tom Dillehay, who started to excavate at the site in 1977. It's located along the Chinchihuapi Creek, some 8 miles from the Rio Maullín estuary, which drains into the Pacific. The site was waterlogged and the level of preservation astounding, with wooden artifacts, hut timbers, animal hides, fish and fruits and berries of all types—even human poo, or coprolite, to give it its scientific name. There was an abundance of material to date by radiocarbon methods, which yielded an age of around 14,700 years. In the floor of one hut, close to the hearth, was a footprint of a child—one of three footprints recovered from the site. If anything was totally left of field in the story of the Americas, it was this site, both old and way down in South America. It took time for the archaeological community to accept the site, but after a show and tell with all the protagonists involved, it was accepted,[11] at least by most researchers. About 100 miles to the north lies the archaeological site of Pilauco in the city of Osorno. Here, human footprints have also been recorded and recently dated as 15,600 years old.[12]

In the summer of 2020, while our research team struggled with inactivity due to COVID, the academic journal *Nature* proudly announced to the world the Chiquihuite Cave discovery in Mexico.[13] This was a more conventional archaeological find, with several layers interpreted as occupation and, at depth, some primitive-looking stone tools that were associated with dates of 31,000 to 33,000 years. Matthew recalls,

> It felt a bit like being pipped at the post, to be honest, but that is the way with records. There will always be something along that is older in age, sexier, or somehow more fashionable. Our work was not as old, but was based on different types of evidence. While you can argue that a footprint is not human, it is quite hard when you have such beautiful tracks as those at White Sands to dispute them. The two sites are like comparing apples and pears, but still, it does dent your enthusiasm a little! When our work was published, Ciprian Ardelean, who was first author on the Chiquihuite Cave paper, reached out to congratulate us. By that stage, he was having a heavy time with naysayers about his site and its age and felt that the White Sands footprints offered some support for his case.

David adds,

> We met Ciprian a year or so after our paper in *Science* was published in 2021. The Canadian Broadcasting Corporation was making a documentary for Discovery and filming at White Sands. The program focused on Ciprian's journey in the context of the wider debate about the peopling of the Americas. He is a lovely guy, and I spent more time with him in 2023 in Rome, where I was speaking at a conference session he organized. One of the key issues is "what should an early

stone tool look like?" The answer is that no one really knows, and it is easy to dismiss the tools from Chiquihuite as not fitting any standard model.[14] Until lots of sites are found with early stone tools, it is hard to create a typology.

Prior to the Chiquihuite Cave announcement, the oldest widely accepted site was Cooper's Ferry on the Salmon River in western Idaho.[15] Here, on a river terrace, evidence of human occupation includes unfluted stemmed projectile points like those from Asia that date from around 16,500 years ago, indicating human occupation well before the ice-free corridor became navigable. Cooper's Ferry had broken the pre-Clovis barrier, and with it came evidence of earlier stone tool traditions that represent pre-Clovis technologies. Quite how these earlier technologies relate to Clovis artifacts is still a little uncertain, but a pre-Clovis addendum to the established narrative has slowly emerged in recent years. And with this addendum, alternative migration routes to the ice-free corridor, such as movement along the Pacific coast, began to emerge. But crucially, all these narratives still placed human arrival south of the 49th parallel after the glacial maximum, when the ice sheet barrier was at its peak.

In 1979 Carl Sagan expressed an idea that, for some, has become central to the advancement of knowledge across several scientific disciplines. In what has come to be called the Sagan standard,[16] he said rather simply that extraordinary claims require extraordinary evidence (often abbreviated as ECREE).[17] Essentially, if you want to upset a well-established and evidenced narrative, you must have good evidence and cause. To some extent, Sagan was right. Knowledge accumulates bit by bit through the meticulous work of many researchers, often over decades. Each discovery builds on the last, and ideas are gradually adjusted and refined to account for them. Just as it took the extraordinary site of Monte Verde to convince most archaeologists that Clovis wasn't first after all, it will take extraordinary evidence to convince people that humans were present in the Americas far earlier—during the height of the last ice age, for example. We assess in the next section whether the evidence at White Sands meets these criteria or not.

White Sands: Extraordinary Evidence?

The question that comes to mind here is simple: Is the evidence at White Sands extraordinary? Could it be interpreted differently? If not, what are the implications of that evidence? It is easy to get carried away with your own hubris here. So let us break it down.

Is the White Sands footprint site unique in the world today? The answer is yes, but it may not remain unique for long. Footprint sites around the world are quite limited in their extent—a few hundred yards at most. There are some exceptions, like the footprints of Willandra Lakes,[18] those on the shores of Lake Natron in Tanzania,[19] and those just south of Walvis Bay in Namibia.[20] These sites are bigger than the norm, perhaps a mile or two in extent, but compared to the tens of miles at White Sands and the literally hundreds of thousands of prints present, they are small by comparison. It is the sheer size of the footprint horizons, plus the number of tracks upon them, that makes White Sands unique, especially when you consider that the site continues northward beyond the margins of the national park into the missile range. So in this respect, the site is extraordinary. Nowhere else in the world can you currently literally track an extinct giant ground sloth over such distances. There is a but coming, however. There are many other dried lakebeds and playas in the American Southwest, all of which potentially contain footprints. Once these have been explored, will White Sands be unique? Perhaps not, but it will be the site that pointed the way to this remarkable and currently unexplored archaeological archive of evidence.

The footprints were clearly made by humans, are consistent in quality with tracks recorded at other sites around the world, and are anatomically consistent with modern humans. Moreover, the human tracks are crosscut and overprinted by those of extinct megafauna, such as mammoths and giant ground sloths. The tracks collectively behave in a way that is consistent with a natural ecosystem in which one animal interacts with another.

Are the footprints as old as we think they are? Currently, that is a matter of opinion. The *Ruppia* seed and pollen dating was done by good geoscientists in the United States, and they believe their results. Combined with the OSL dating, you can make a strong case that there are three independent lines of evidence that give dates in the correct stratigraphic order. Furthermore, the paleoenvironmental reconstruction fits the correct time period; the plants and other environmental proxies are consistent with a last glacial maximum age. Therefore dating, stratigraphy, and paleoenvironmental analysis form a coherent whole consistent with a last glacial maximum age.

One site is always going to take the flack, but multiple sites change the dynamic. Our research team already has several footprints sites beyond White Sands that show a consistent age. In 10 years, will White Sands be unique? No! This will no doubt change the dynamic of the current debate, and our guess is that White Sands won't be the last word on the age of the peopling of the Americas. Records are there to be broken. On balance, therefore, as we write in the fall of 2024, we would argue that the evidence at White Sands is extraordinary and supports the claim that humans really were in New Mexico at the height of the Ice Age.

Continuity on a Landscape

A couple of fundamental questions stem from the footprints at White Sands and their age. These questions might mean that both the Clovis and the White Sands narratives coexist as versions of the same story. The first issue is one of continuity of occupation, while the second looks at the discrepancy of scale between the evidence for Clovis people and early footprint pioneers at sites like White Sands. It has been put to us on several occasions that while the footprints evidence early colonization, they don't necessarily provide evidence of successful colonization.

Each footprint layer may have been left by a small band of pioneers who found their way south of the ice sheet barrier by chance in what is called a sweepstakes dispersal. They either perished in an unfamiliar and potentially hostile land or simply were too few in number to make any lasting impact on such a vast landscape. Sweepstakes dispersal is an established concept. For example, Madagascar is famous for its lemurs—King Julien of the *Madagascar* film franchise comes to mind. The island has the only natural surviving lemur population in the world, and they got to Madagascar on rafts formed from fallen trees washed out to sea from the African mainland, where they became extinct in time. There are lots of

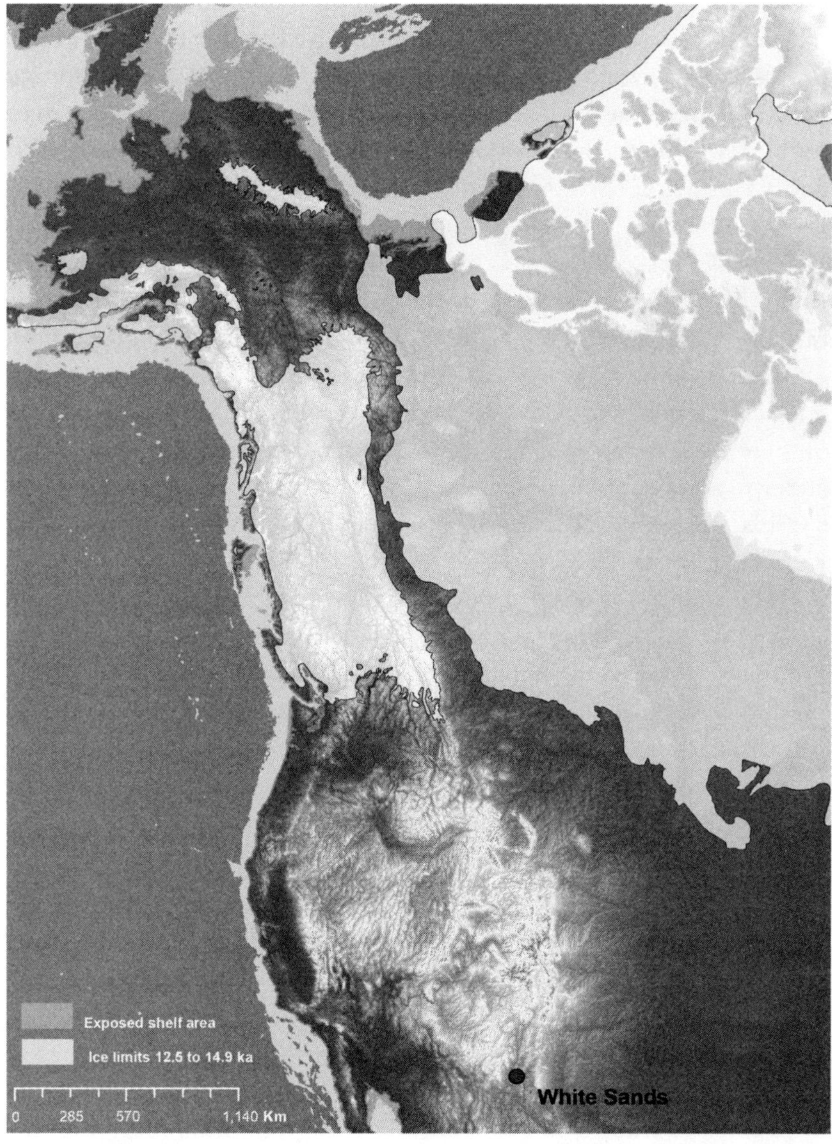

Figure 5.3. North America about 14,000 years ago, showing the ice-free corridor between the Laurentide and Cordilleran ice sheets. Exposure of the continental shelf (reduced sea level) is based on national bathymetry and a range of published sea level curves. Ice margins courtesy of Dalton et al., "Evolution of the Laurentide and Innuitian Ice Sheets."

other examples, such as hippopotami that arrived on small Mediterranean islands in this way and promptly became a dwarf species. Some adventurous human pioneers, or hapless individuals (take your pick), could have been swept down the Pacific coast, moving inland thereafter. Finding food is not the only issue. Breeding and genetics are also critical to survival. You must have enough folks swept south to form a viable genetic population and to avoid inbreeding—otherwise, they go extinct. You can get a lot of lemurs in a few big trees, but we are talking about a lot of boats with human cargo to deliver a viable population. There are other types of sweepstakes dispersal than the sea as well. Some people may have managed to cross the ice sheet barrier or passed south before the ice-free corridor closed. Any of these mechanisms might account for a small population of "pioneers," either with repeated arrivals or simply one or more groups moving over a vast landscape and occasionally returning to the same spot. Is this what we have at White Sands?

The simple answer is that we don't know, but the repetition of footprint layers at White Sands over time speaks to repeated visits. This might imply continuity of occupation but does not prove it, since proof involves joining the dots between occurrences, some of which are separated by thousands of years. Indigenous people believe in this continuity, and they are probably right, but scientifically it is hard to prove. It is also important to recognize that continuity is not just a simple question of genetics but is also about cultural identity and a sense of history with a place or landscape. You may not be related to the folks who lived in your town in the past, but you can share an identity with them defined by that town and its history. Evidence at WHSA Locality 2 points to repeated visitation over two millennia. With more exploration at other sites in the park, the gaps between visits will likely fall, and links with more recent conventional archaeology will be made.

The second issue raised at the start of this section is the discrepancy in scale between the footprint evidence and later Clovis layers throughout North America. This discrepancy may change as more footprint sites are found and dated, but currently we have only one early site with evidence of a few folks and then a huge arrival, as evidenced by multiple stone tools dispersed widely across the continent. Why is this? The answer likely comes down to numbers and, crucially, the exchange of information. Clovis clearly represents the arrival of a sufficient number of people to create a viable network of communities that could share and exchange information. Information is as important as the size of a genetic pool to the survival of a population. You need a stable environment, rich in resources, to allow a population to grow, which both supports and drives information and genetic exchange. It is no surprise, therefore, that the greatest concentration of Clovis points is in eastern North America. In the arid Southwest, the population may have been much more isolated, focused on water, as at White Sands both during Clovis times and earlier. People would have been spread thin across a vast landscape, and this is not conducive to information exchange or to keeping healthy genetic populations. If we were to find cultural artifacts, they might be very different at different locations. The rapid growth of the Clovis culture may also come down to the presence of a small population already living south of the 49th parallel.

In a way, both the Clovis First and the pre-Clovis occupation narratives are part of the same complementary story and are not in conflict. You have early pioneers spread thin across a vast landscape, low in numbers, perhaps focused on reliable water sources that concentrate vital resources. Technological and genetic sharing is limited, and people may have solved the same problem multiple times and potentially in different ways. These populations would have been at constant risk of local extinction, and their lack of numbers reflects the lack of cultural artifacts left on the landscape. We may know only that they walked through the landscape due to their footprints. Accelerate to Clovis times, and suddenly you have a route open for a larger, more viable, and therefore denser population to arrive, especially in the resource-rich East. This allows rapid cultural diffusion of technology and problem solving, which in turn accelerates population growth, information exchange, and the distribution of similar artifacts. The key difference between the success of these peoples and the uniformity of the traces they left is their ability to share information and learn collectively.

Migration Routes

How did these early pioneering folks arrive south of the 49th parallel? To reach the Americas, you must either cross wide oceans by boat or figure out how to survive in the polar North so you can use the Bering Land Bridge.

It is easy to underappreciate just how sophisticated ancient humans were. And while boating and adapting to the subarctic pose certain challenges, neither ability was likely to be beyond the ancestors of the people who walked the shores of Lake Otero. After all, they were anatomically modern humans, with large modern brains capable of learning, innovating, and adapting in remarkable ways. So did they arrive by boat or on foot? Let us look at what we know about each possibility. Before we do, however, we need to discuss Beringia.

Beringia is the name given to the vast region between Canada's Mackenzie River and the Verkhoyansk Range near Russia's Lena River. The name was coined in 1937 by Swedish botanist and Arctic explorer Eric Hultén, who recognized common past plant and animal communities across the region. The region includes the Bering Strait, the body of water that now separates Asia and North America. During the Ice Age, sea levels dropped, at times by as much as 150 m, so the shallow Bering Strait would have been exposed as dry land, enabling the movement of plants, animals, and people across the region. Ice sheets waxed and waned throughout the Ice Age, so the Bering Land Bridge would have emerged and been flooded several times. The term *land bridge* implies a narrow corridor of land, but in truth, Beringia was huge—perhaps as much as 620 miles north to south. The distance was such that the people and animals who called it home might never have seen the ocean.

The first obstacle was moving east, and the lowering of the sea level solved this. But once you arrive from Asia in Alaska, you probably want to head south quite quickly. It's cold, after all, and there lies our second obstacle: the ice sheet barrier. These two obstacles work in subtle opposition to one another. You need the ice sheets to lower the sea level, but those very ice sheets may hinder your route south.

The Bering Strait is generally no deeper than about 50 m. So it would not have taken huge ice sheets to lower global sea level sufficiently for the strait to become passable. Scope out the first door created when the strait first dries, and you can then head south as the climate continues to deteriorate and the ice sheets grow. At some point, the barrier to southward migration becomes total as the Laurentide and Cordilleran ice sheets merge and the Pacific coast becomes icebound. At this point, you are trapped to the south and isolated from Asia by the ice sheets.

The Bering Strait fluctuated between land and water from about 60,000 to 30,000 years ago, after which it was continuously land until

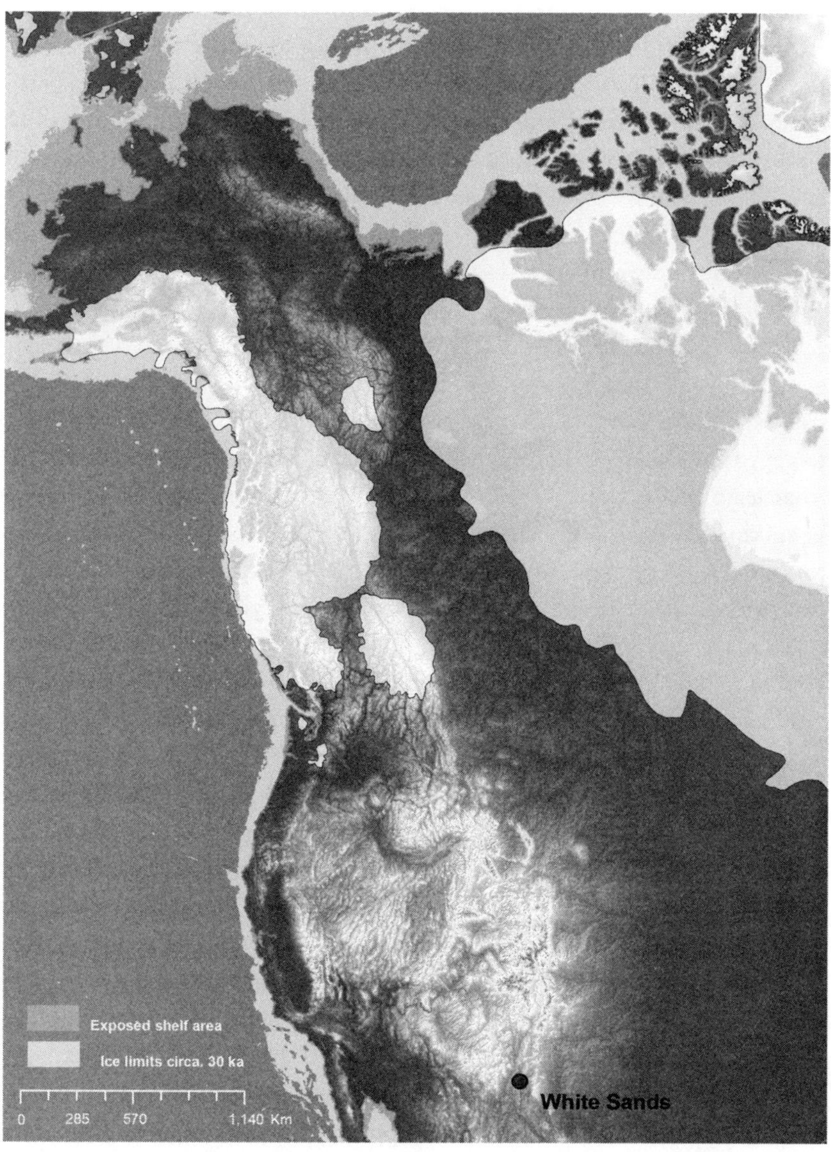

Figure 5.4. North America before the last glacial maximum, about 30,000 years ago, as the ice-free corridor opened. Exposure of the continental shelf (reduced sea level) is based on national bathymetry and a range of published sea level curves. Ice margins courtesy of Dalton et al., "Evolution of the Laurentide and Innuitian Ice Sheets."

around 11,000 years ago. This is good timing for those moving east via Beringia. The Cordilleran and Laurentide ice sheets did not merge to create a complete barrier until around 23,000 years ago, so there was an opportunity for people to head south and perhaps end up on the shores of Lake Otero (Figure 5.4). Of course, they could have set off earlier if they had a boat. The coastline of Beringia would have been an obvious navigational aid, and nearshore boating is far preferable to a major ocean crossing. The oldest direct evidence for boats dates back only a bit over 10,000 years, to a dugout canoe found in the Netherlands.[21] But archaeologists generally agree that boating is much older than that. Humans arrived in Australia more than 50,000 years ago and had to have crossed deep water to get there. On islands in the Mediterranean, Mousterian artifacts dated to at least 35,000 years ago suggest that Neanderthals were also using boats there.[22] And in Southeast Asia, we see the movement of obsidians found only on offshore islands around 35,000 years ago and fishing for pelagic fish even earlier. So it is at least technologically feasible that people reached the Americas by boat. Even if they didn't venture out of sight of land to cross the open ocean, they could still have worked their way north, gradually expanding along the coast from Southeast Asia. If they set out around 35,000 years ago, they might have continued along the coast of the Bering Land Bridge into what is now Alaska and worked their way south to British Columbia and beyond. Archaeological evidence for such voyages is sparse at best, not least because the areas that were coastal back then were drowned by rising seas as the ice sheets melted back into the ocean at the end of the Ice Age.

Such a voyage would have been far more challenging during the last ice age than it would be today. Current reconstructions of glacial history suggest that much of the coastline from the Alaska Peninsula to southern British Columbia was covered in ice by 35,000 years ago and that dry land along that route may not have appeared until around 17,000 years ago, long after people first walked the shores of Lake Otero. We think of that part of the world today as having an amazingly productive ecosystem, with salmon and other fish, sea mammals, shellfish, and the terrestrial resources of the forest all easily accessible from the shore. A lot of work has gone into understanding the evolution of the region's ecology following deglaciation, but there is still much to be done to understand what it was like during the period prior to and during the last glacial maximum. Were there offshore islands where people could have camped? How far would they have had to travel to get past the glaciers? Can we reasonably expect a group of people large enough to form a founding population to have traveled in these conditions? Some say the ocean offered a logical migration route, often referred to as the Kelp Highway.[23]

The Kelp Highway is a popular idea since the Clovis First model collapsed, especially since the corridor between the Cordilleran and Laurentide ice sheets did not become ice-free until around 14,000 years ago.[24] The route would have enabled people to reach southern Chile via the Pacific coast quite quickly. Some archaeologists say that similarities between tools from a handful of sites in the Pacific Northwest and those in Japan indicate an early coastal migration. Others remain unconvinced. Sometimes, such similarities are a product of historical connections: Migrating people carry tools and make similar ones along the way; ideas about how to make a particular type of tool spread through trade and exchange. But stylistic similarities can also arise through convergent evolution, with form following function; independently derived solutions often resemble one another because they perform the same tasks. We haven't found archaeological sites from the key time periods in the region between Japan and the Pacific Northwest, so archaeologists are left to fall back on arguments based on plausibility and similarity. Arguments in favor of a coastal route for early migrations are intriguing, but they are not definitive.

What else can we say about the people who lived at White Sands and left their tracks along the shores of Lake Otero so long ago? This is a difficult question. The best answer at present is that more data are needed. But to the Indigenous peoples who call this region home today, the tracks around Lake Otero are the tracks of their ancestors. It is difficult to dispute their logic. After all, according to their cultural traditions, they have been in the landscape forever, so if there are ancient human tracks, they had to have been made by their ancestors. Others might counter that perhaps someone else lived in the area before the ancestors of today's Indigenous Americans arrived. While this could be true, it doesn't necessarily mean that the Indigenous people are mistaken. All people have a complex mix of ancestry if one traces their history far enough back in time. The folks who walked the shores of Lake Otero more than 23,000 years ago were what scientists call anatomically modern humans (AMH). They arose in Africa, but migrated north in a couple of distinct waves between 100,000 and 60,000 years ago, spreading quickly across the globe, replacing and absorbing earlier Archaic *Homo* species such as the Neanderthals and

Denisovans. Setting aside issues of when and how they arrived at White Sands, we can say a few things about them using evolutionary principles. For example, scientists generally agree that for a viable human population, you need between 250 and 500 individuals. So we are talking more than just a small band of hunters or a couple of boatloads of mariners. This does not mean there were 500-plus folks at White Sands—just that these folks were in contact across the region. In primate evolution, there is a theory of fission and fusion: Groups come together, perhaps during periods of hardship, leading to the fusion of groups; at other times, they split and disperse. This maintains a healthy gene pool over time without everyone living on top of one another. Was the White Sands population isolated from its source? Again, we don't know. It might be that a viable population made its way south and became isolated, perhaps as the ice sheets grew. Alternatively, the pioneers might have maintained a continuous link with their ancestorial population. In this case, a gradual expansion of hunting ranges may have added more folks over vast distances, but occasionally the movement of people within this range continued. We know from historical times that great distances are not an obstacle to maintaining gene flow, as the arrival of the Polynesians in Hawaii or the Norse in Greenland demonstrates. Of course, answers to many questions lie in the genome of Native Americans and in recovered skeletal remains, should DNA analysis of them be allowed.

As of this writing, the oldest human genome from anywhere in the Americas comes from a sample taken from a young boy who was buried around 12,500 years ago at a site called Anzick in southern Montana.[25] The Anzick child postdates the arrival of humans at White Sands by more than 10,000 years. He was a member of the widespread group that archaeologists call Clovis. For geneticists, the Anzick boy is part of a biological population termed Southern Native American (SNA), which includes peoples living in the area from southern Canada to Tierra del Fuego at the southern tip of South America. SNA is distinct from, but related to, a population called Northern North American (NNA), living in Alaska and northern Canada. The two groups are thought to have diverged from a common ancestor population sometime between 17,500 and 14,600 years ago. Because White Sands was occupied long before this split occurred, the relationship between the people who lived there and the population that later gave rise to SNA is unclear. Were they part of the population that is ancestral to both SNA and NNA? If so, that implies that SNA/NNA ancestors were in North America earlier than some archaeologists and geneticists believe. This idea fits with the age of the White Sands footprints. Alternatively, were there other, more distantly related human populations already present in the Americas when the SNA arrived? Some geneticists believe they have found evidence for such a population as faint echoes in the genetic profiles of some ancient and modern individuals from South America. Whether the genetic profiles of ancient or modern individuals in North America also contain such evidence is uncertain. As of now, there are simply too little data available to enable a thorough investigation of this question using genetic analyses. Whether the people of Lake Otero were biologically ancestral to SNA/NNA or were members of another group is interesting to science, but doesn't necessarily answer the question of whether they are ancestral to today's Native Americans. It is entirely possible under either scenario that they could be. What is clear, however, is that regardless of what biological population they might have been part of, almost anything that can be learned about the people of Lake Otero is information that is new to science.

The challenge for archaeology posed by sites like White Sands is the absence of conventional archaeology, such as stone tools. Many North American archaeologists feel more at home with stone tools than other types of evidence. Therefore, the almost constant question raised by researchers when we present the White Sands work is, "Where are the stone tools? It would be so much better if we had tools!" There is an element of discipline difference here. Historically, footprints (mainly of dinosaurs, to be honest) are the preserve of earth science, of which ichnology is a branch. Archaeologists are taught to excavate and value cultural artifacts. To them, human presence is about hearths, tools, fibers, and animal remains. But if you walk on a lonely beach today, the only presence you will leave is a set of footprints. The evidence is equal in value to a dropped smartphone or litter—but not to some. In demonstrating human presence, we would put our money on footprints every time!

The real challenge currently is that White Sands is one point on a huge map, and until we have lots of points with subtle variations in age, discussion of migration routes is just discussion. The legacy, at least in our view, is that White Sands points the way to finding those map points by finding more sites with footprints and literally tracing the footfall of the first Americans. In a decade's time, there will be many points on the map, and with them a greater understanding of the Indigenous colonization of the Americas. As we step into the future, we can use the footfall of the past to guide us and constrain our ideas.

The Human Hunter

Today's human impact on the environment is current news: The threat of climate change to people's security and the extinction of endangered animals are widely discussed. Human impact on the environment is such that some scientists wish to define a new geological period, the Anthropocene,[26] to draw attention to the fact. They just can't agree on how to define its start.[27] In truth, the environment is always changing. The climate has never been stable, and over the last few million years, the earth's climate has been naturally variable in the extreme. The cause of change, natural or human, is less relevant than managing the impact on those changes on vulnerable communities and ecosystems. Ever since the early 1970s, the idea that human hunters were responsible for mass extinction at the end of the last glacial cycle has been encapsulated in something known as the overkill hypothesis,[28] which in some ecological quarters is believed as an article of faith rather than fact.[29] When people first arrived in the Americas as hunters is now a key part of this debate.

The evolution of new species and the extinction of old are part of the natural rhythm of our planet, and extinction has occurred on a grand scale at least six times in its 4.6 billion-year history. The asteroid strike some 65 million years ago that wiped out the dinosaurs comes to mind, and further back, at the end of the Permian (about 250 million years ago), a toxic ocean wiped out 81 percent of the earth's marine species. Although vulgar, this phrase sums it up—shit happens!

At the end of the last glacial cycle, 10,000 years ago, the earth experienced a smaller mass extinction when a range of large animals went extinct (except in Africa). Today, people travel to Africa's savanna to view the big five—lions, leopards, buffalos, elephants, and rhinos—to which we could add the giraffe and hippo. All are defined as megafauna based on their size. In America, by contrast, the equivalent megafauna—mammoths, mastodons, giant armadillos, camels, horses, saber-toothed cats, and giant ground sloths—went extinct. Australia and Eurasia also lost megafauna in the same way. The big question is why.

The Pleistocene Ice Age has lasted more than 2 million years and continues today. Climate has oscillated during this time between glacial periods, when large ice sheets covered North America and Europe, to interglacial (now), when ice sheets are restricted to the poles. The last glacial maximum, 23,000 years ago, was at the height of the last glacial period. The switch from glacial to interglacial is one of extreme environmental change, with a major reorganization of ecological biomes during each transition. Such periods of transition are going to cause the extinction of vulnerable species. If the Arctic grasslands shrink as they did 10,000 years ago, where can the cold-adapted mammoth graze? The problem lies in the fact that some 125,000 years ago, at the start of the last interglacial—before the current one we are living through—a mass extinction did not occur. Climate changed rapidly before—many times, in fact—and did not have as profound an impact as it did 10,000 years ago, when the current interglacial started. So what is different?

The answer is modern humans, of course. The argument goes that humans arrived post-glacial and hunted aggressively, such that they caused the extinction of large animals at a time when they were facing maximum environmental stress. Paul Martin coined the term *overkill* and argued that human hunters were like a blitzkrieg that swept across North and South America, causing a mass extinction. These ideas have caused a lot of scientific debate over the years, and the story is much more complex than the overkill hypothesis suggests. The gradual pushing back of first arrival dates for humans in North America, of which the White Sands dates are just the latest part, challenges the overkill hypothesis. If people arrived earlier, they would have coexisted with the megafauna for much longer periods of time than previously thought.

The extinction dates for different megafauna have also become more nuanced over time, especially with the advent of environmental DNA. In building a mass extinction story, you want the different species of animal to die out at about the same time. Ideally, you want the last living animal of a given species to die in such a way that it gets fossilized and can be dated accurately. You also need extinction to occur rapidly across a region. Neither is likely. Fossilization is a random process, and the fewer animals of a given species there are, the less chance there is of it occurring neatly. Moreover, as we know from the study of endangered species today, animals disappear from different regions gradually. Also, environmental DNA recovered from frozen Arctic lakes paints a subtle picture of species lingering on in different areas. Think of hair, skin, and bodily fluids finding their way into a lake or being blown on the wind into that lake. The material slowly accumulates in sediment on the lake floor. Once frozen, it is preserved, and that is the source of fragments of DNA that tell us about the animals within the basin's catchment.[30] Therefore, you are never going to have a precise stratigraphic juxtaposition between animal extinction and human arrival.

Elephants are eco-engineers today. They modify plant ecology through their grazing to suit their needs. Mammoths would have done the same.[31] The so-called Arctic mammoth steppe, which allowed the various species of mammoths to roam widely across northern latitudes during glacial cycles, is a result of grazing. Mammoths maintain and basically cultivate the ecosystem they favor. By nibbling fresh tree buds, they prevent trees from getting hold even when climate is warming and thereby prevent a forest invasion. The interaction here is subtle and dependent on population. Think of all the lawns in your hometown. If there is only one shared lawn mower, it won't be able to keep things tidy, but if every house has its own mower, the chances are greater. The larger the population of mammoths, the more mouths there are to keep those pesky trees at bay. But should the population become stressed by climate, the trees might get the upper hand, reducing food supply and thereby causing mammoth populations to decline further. These ecological balances are subtle and complex, and when we view the issue of extinction through this broader lens, mass extinction of megafauna at the end of the Ice Age ceases to be so simple.

Bison survived this mass extinction, yet were hunted in their thousands in the early Holocene by human hunters. Abundant archaeological and paleontological sites show huge collections of bison skulls. Early hunters drove herds over cliffs and killed thousands, yet the animal did not go extinct. Why? In this case you must look at gestation times. Bison have a gestation time of about 280 days, and one calf is born in the spring of each year. Those calves can stand and run within a few minutes of birth.

In contrast, a mammoth gestates for typically 660 days, and the calf is small and needs nursing for longer. So predation of young and female mammoths has a much greater impact on the viability of a herd than it does for other animals.

Earlier arrival of human hunters also plays into this story. As arrival times have slowly become older, and much older as evidenced at White Sands, the juxtaposition of extinction and human arrival no longer holds. If people arrived before the height of the last glacial maximum, then they coexisted with the megafauna for at least 10,000 years before the megafauna went extinct. We have evidence of hunting during this time. The sloth hunt discussed in an earlier chapter is an example,[32] and there are examples from elsewhere in the Americas of mammoth skeletons with spear/dart points embedded in them.[33] But were such practices common? Risk versus reward comes into play here. Would you like to face up to a raging mammoth dressed in nothing but animal skin with a stone-tipped spear in your hand? The chances of getting hurt are high, but the reward is considerable—a mammoth will feed a lot of people. But in truth, a large mammoth carcass takes a lot of processing to exploit its full potential. Contrast this with low-risk, low-reward prey like rabbits. They are easier to catch, and you don't get hurt. They are a dependable food supply, but they don't feed many people. Population numbers are key here. A few hunter-gatherers have little impact. They don't have the human resources to process large animals regularly, and the risk equation in a small band is stacked against doing anything too foolish because the number of adults is small. As human numbers grow, however, this equation changes. There are more mouths to feed, more bodies to help transport and process large animals; the risk equation changes as the group is less dependent on just a few adults. Consequently, the impact on megafauna is more about population size than presence. To put it crudely, it took 10,000 years or so for the number of human hunters to become sufficient to have an ecological impact.

Extinction is complex and likely to have been different for each large animal at the end of the Ice Age; one explanation will not fit all.[34] Did humans play a part? Probably, but only as the human population increased and perhaps only by stressing animals that were already at their ecological limits due to climate change. There is perhaps a lesson here for the future as we face a period of uncertain climate.

Two Ways of Knowing?

The fossil footprints found at White Sands have pushed back the date for the peopling of the Americas by perhaps 8,000 to 10,000 years. No doubt the validity of these ages will continue to be debated by scientists for a few years to come. But it is worth remembering that most Indigenous people believe that their ancestors have lived on the American landscape since the beginning of time. In our work at White Sands, we have tried to develop good relationships with the tribes and pueblos that are indigenous to the region. For the research team, it has been a great honor and privilege to work with the folks whose homeland this is. In some cases, tribal representatives have shared their opinions on the importance of this work in confirming to the rest of the world what they have always known from their oral traditions and histories. Others are more ambivalent and would prefer it if the past was undisturbed.

As is the case in many fields of study, there is a tension between different ways of knowing. Science is pitted against oral tradition, yet both have value. The challenge for many is that media outlets favor science stories over more traditional belief systems. Added to this, we can't state enough how sociopolitical factors have played an often-negative role in promoting the narratives and beliefs of Indigenous peoples. The tribal nations have known White Sands for thousands of years. They have words for the great megafauna that once roamed the area and words for the snow-white gypsum dunes that formed thousands of years after the megafauna had gone. Within the Chihuahuan Desert, the White Sands gypsum dune field and highwater table have been an oasis, providing freshwater and resources to support a rich cultural history from before the park was established, through the arrival of the first Europeans, and for more than 20,000 years of continued human history.

The challenge for everyone now is that this fragile footprint record, not just at White Sands but throughout the American Southwest, is being lost to erosion. Climate change and groundwater use are changing the preservation potential of the dried lakes and playa in this landscape. As water tables fall, the ground dries, and the wind takes fragile sediments and the footprints within them, the record is lost. The legacy of White Sands is not to change the date at which people first arrived in the Americas—in time there will be another oldest claim—but to show the importance of the footprint archive that exists. But we are late for the party, since this resource is in danger of being lost before we unlock its secrets. David summarizes,

> The footprints tell stories of past lifeways, maybe some of the oldest stories in American history, but they are being rapidly lost. I think of it as a wing of the Library of Congress, and it's on fire! We're racing to try and capture these stories, and the pages are burning one by one in front of our eyes, lifting on an updraft of wind. These stories tell of the interaction of ancient people with extinct animals and landscapes different from today. Children are not often well-recorded in the archaeological record—maybe there was little time for toys—but at White Sands we can see them playing in puddles left by extinct animals and moving as part of a group as it goes about the business of survival. Children are everywhere—working, jumping, and playing. We often think of the past as hard, a fight for survival, but White Sands tells a different story, a story of children at play, at home in a landscape that our own children today could not navigate or entertain themselves in, especially without internet! This action of play connects us to the past in a way that cultural artifacts don't. We love to play with our children and value family time today, and so did the people who walked the edges of Lake Otero at the height of the Ice Age. Footprints transcend time, connect people past and present."

CHAPTER SIX

A Journey of Footprints

Nothing quite compares to that first flush of discovery in April 2017 when David and Matthew found the first human footprint together. David had long believed in the presence of human track-makers, a belief that Matthew was able to confirm that fateful day. Our team has been on a journey of discovery and learning ever since. It took time to work out how to find, excavate, and record the footprints at White Sands—a body of learning that this book barely touches upon and is now being deployed at other dried lakebeds throughout the American Southwest.

Not only have we become closer friends, but we have met many interesting people along the way. The journey has changed us too, and we are wiser, stronger, and better for it. It has been a journey into ourselves as much as a journey into the past. It is therefore hard to find a fitting conclusion, especially when our journey of discovery is just starting, with many more footprints to find and stories to tell in the coming years (Figure 6.1). Our story breaks into three logical parts, each with its own flavor. First, there were the initial visits before we had dates; second, the trips to get those dates; and finally, the postdating trips.

Before the Dates

For some of our team, this was the best time of all. There was less scrutiny, fewer bureaucratic hurdles to jump through, and the simple joy of discovery. We spent a lot of time lying flat on the playa floor, with the wind driving sand in our faces, brushing out tracks and reading their stories written

Figure 6.1. An interpretation of life in the vicinity of WHSA Locality 2 at the height of the last glacial maximum. The number of young adolescents seems to be borne out by the size of the footprints at this site. It is a happy, gentle scene, and that is how we like to think of White Sands in the past—as a place of abundance where people met from time to time.

in the dried mud before us. Life was simpler and there was less at stake. Our focus was on discovery: exploring the record and following clues that told us about lifeways on the playa and the interaction of one animal with another. The sloth hunt was a start, followed by our work on the double trackway, which will always have resonance for Matthew in particular because of the birth of his daughter during that work. The joy of finding the sloth tracks used as puddles by playing children was another highlight. We have many stories from this time. Matthew recalls,

> We were working on tracks of the double trackway, brushing out prints in amenable silence when the radio crackled into life. At first, it was hard to hear what was being said . . . something about a parrot. My wife keeps parrots, so this caught my attention. A few static-rich messages later and it became clear that someone had lost a parrot in the dunes. We looked at each other: Why would you bring a parrot to a dune field? The story grew over the next few days. David confirmed that someone had lost a parrot and that a search party had been formed without success. The radio crackled to life throughout the

> following days as we followed the story, which you will be glad to hear had a happy ending, but not before the community of parrot owners far and wide had been called to action. I recall driving back through the dunes and passing huge RVs parked on the side of the road, with a parrot perched behind every window. You would never have guessed that one lost bird would become a rallying cry for parrot owners nationwide! You can't make these stories up, and they form the background to many of my trips, along with the sheer joy of discovery.

Dan continues,

> We were finding sloth tracks and human tracks together, but there were real questions about how old they were and, more importantly, about whether they might be contemporaneous with each other. We knew sloths had been extinct for at least 10,000 years, so we knew their tracks were old, but we didn't know whether the human track-makers had come along sometime later. I remember feeling goosebumps when I realized that I was seeing tracks made by a sloth and humans reacting to each other. The sloth changed direction as it presumably scented the human tracks. For me, this really made the trackways come alive. It was as if we had somehow unearthed an ancient video clip.

We learned a lot during those early trips: just how fickle the footprint record could be, how hostile the weather often was, and over time, the best way to uncover a set of tracks and record them accurately for posterity. We didn't have all the answers, despite having worked at other sites with tracks, but we found them. Our field equipment evolved, and we became skilled in converting innocent items from home improvement stores into perfect excavation tools. We tried to cast tracks in plaster and in latex, with varying degrees of success. We perfected using a long-handled brush trimmer with a GoPro taped to the top for making the best photographic maps (orthomosaics). There was always something to try as we experimented with different geophysical tools. On one occasion, we made a "loom." It consisted of two plastic pipes with holes drilled along their length and 20-foot-long strings attached between—just like a very long loom. It was an awful thing to move, since each strand would tangle with the next, and after a night out on the playa, each string would be crusted in sharp gypsum crystals. You might well ask the purpose of our loom. It was to guide the passage of a magnetometer moving along survey lines just a few inches apart. We replaced it with foam mats when we switched to ground-penetrating radar. These were fun times—times of innovation and learning. Matthew adds,

> David kindly let me borrow some of the latex molds he had made from some of our early plaster casts. I had them on the kitchen table set out in boxes so that I could cast them in plaster. My wife, Sally, and newborn daughter were asleep upstairs, and my son Samuel was helping. All was going well until the handle on the bucket full of plaster broke. We watched in shocked silence as it fell to the floor and a column of plaster shot upward in all directions. It caked us head to toe, but worse was that it sprayed up over the kitchen walls, refrigerator, and stove. A frantic hour later, we had the kitchen clean. Samuel was sent upstairs to tell Sally that all was okay and she could come down. I use those casts to teach with, but can never quite banish that moment of horror!

Dan recalls,

> Those early days of working on the tracks at White Sands were incredible. I remember being impressed with David's unrivaled knowledge of park resources. It is rare these days to come across someone with such a deep, observation-based understanding of a place who is as passionate about sharing his knowledge of that place as he is about protecting it. The chance to work alongside him and Matthew and to learn a whole new way of seeing things really helped me on a new professional journey. Initially, I was focused on how to help David understand and preserve what was being uncovered. It quickly became clear that the tracks were potentially important and unusual. I quickly realized that a career spent excavating archaeological sites in the Arctic hadn't really prepared me for working on ghost tracks preserved in gypsum in the American Southwest.

Getting the Dates

In September 2019, things changed when David and Matthew found the first tracks that we could securely trace into the stratigraphy. The possibility of dating the tracks via the intercalated seed layers became a reality. Matthew recalls,

> For me, this will always be associated with COVID and the painful lockdowns that came with it. I had never had my movements restricted by a government before, and that nagging fear for one's loved ones is hard to shake. January 2020 saw us undertake our first big excavation, and boy, was it a circus. Lots of folks in play, a TV crew, and both welcome and sometimes unwelcome scrutiny from the Park Service. We had a job to do: to find the tracks in the best possible position for dating. For me at least, the joy of discovery, of storytelling, was gone. The dates changed the team dynamic; egos came to the fore and something was lost, at least for me.

COVID put a hold on our fieldwork for almost two years, and they were hard and frustrating years. As we examined the dates and footprints, we had to try and work out the best way to present our evidence at a time when we couldn't rush out and get more. Science can suffer from a wish to be the first, the oldest, the biggest, or the best, and "fast science" like this is often driven by a wish for glory, or at least what passes for it in a science career: public affirmation associated with publishing in a top journal and having one's work broadcast via the media. Wally Herbert's aptly entitled biography of Robert E. Peary comes to mind here: *The Noose of the Laurels*. Big claims need extraordinary data, as we have seen, and if you set out to challenge an established narrative, you are going to get some criticism. And we did—not just from fellow scientists but, more painfully for us, from Indigenous people who felt we were playing fast and loose with their heritage. We went from no one really caring what work we did and how we did it to having our every action scrutinized and, in some cases, criticized. We became victims of our own success. Matthew recalls,

> I had never really cared much about how old the footprints were and recall having a heated debate with Kath Springer in the field about this. My argument was that the richer narrative was to learn about the lifeways on the playa. Her counterpoint was that people always wanted to know how old something was. Perhaps both viewpoints are correct, but for me, the work lost something as we became constrained and limited by the age of the tracks and all that that implied. The footprints were the same and the stories they told were the same; just suddenly people seemed to care more.

Our science agenda was captured by others. Scientists criticize each other, a process that in fact drives progress, by posing questions. Why didn't you date the tracks this way? Why didn't you do this or that? On the face, the process is constructive; we need you to do this so that we can believe your results. But in fact, the criticism is rarely meant to be genuinely constructive. It changes your agenda; you can't carry on as you having been doing because you must address the criticism of your work. And that is exactly what this period was like. Our field program became dominated by more excavation and sampling to address other people's concerns. We no longer had free initiative, and that is hard. The response took two years of method development and work, and much of this work remains unpublished. The pollen dating method developed by our colleagues in the USGS took time, and while it validated our original stratigraphy when published in October 2023, we are still only at the start of a scientific journey, the end point of which is validation (or not) of the age of the White Sands footprints—with all the implications for the peopling of the Americas that holds.

Postdating Future

Our team has much still to publish about its work at White Sands, and the story is not yet complete. But in truth, White Sands is already in our rearview mirror. Our team has moved on to explore new sites, find new footprints, and discover new stories about the peopling of the American Southwest. It is an exciting time to be a footprint expert, since every dried lakebed may contain footprints that tell a story. They may not be as old as those at White Sands, but these discoveries tell us about the way people lived in this landscape in the past. We are often asked what the legacy of the footprint work will be, and we each have different answers.

Matthew says, "The legacy of White Sand is not the age; records are always broken in time. There will be another site that is older or better in some way. The true legacy is that White Sands points to the fact that people leave footprints that are preserved in the landscapes of the American Southwest. In time, this footprint archive will rewrite early American history for sure. We just need to trace the footfall of these pioneers and embrace their spirit of exploration."

Through the process of discovery at White Sands, we have learned that the preservation of trackways is common in playa systems throughout the American Southwest. White Sands stands as a remarkable example and pioneer in this area of research. David explains,

> The discovery of these living repositories of early human migrations is not only exciting, but also reinforces tribal beliefs that people have inhabited the region since time immemorial. What is truly exhilarating is the realization that countless stories remain untold—stories hidden in the mud that await someone to reveal and read them. But there is a real risk here. These stories are being lost as these ancient lakebeds are eroded by the wind as climates change. Let us not forget that we are in a race to preserve the stories in this footprint archive before it is lost. It as a race that everyone can get involved with. You can start now by putting this book down, reaching for your boots, and learning to become a footprint detective.

POSTSCRIPT

Definitions, Methods, and Additional Details

At one stage, we thought to add the following sections as cutaways into the main text, but they just kept getting in the way. Another idea was to place them at the end of each chapter, and at one point, we entitled these as "Random Bits of Geology!" This final title is perhaps most apt. Many readers won't want to dwell on these sections for long; others will already know this stuff. But those who want more information or clarity on a term or method can read on; the material is cross-referenced to the main text. Browse, read, or ignore as you wish; this postscript is not intended to be read from start to finish.

Understanding Geological and Archaeological Time

All superheroes have an origin story, and many of our favorite characters have more than one. Just think of how many times Superman has been rebooted over the years. Planet earth is a superhero, supporting a rich diversity of life, and has more than one origin story. For example, Indigenous peoples have a rich folklore of such stores, which include such ideas as people descending from the stars. All origin stories are valid, but scientists tend to favor stories based on the interpretation of the rocks and fossils that make up our planet.

According to the science of geology, planet earth is around 4.6 billion years old, a middle-aged planet in an average solar system in the Milky Way. How do geologists know? Well, we can date the rocks that make up our planet, and those rocks tell a story of the evolution of life, of moving continents, mountain building, and both sea level and climate change. Geologists break up time into eons, eras, and periods. For example, the Jurassic period is that which occurred between 201 to 145 million years ago (made famous, of course, by the *Jurassic Park* franchise). The current period is known as the Quaternary, and it is made up of the epochs of the Pleistocene and Holocene. The Pleistocene started some 2.6 million years ago and ended just 10,000 years ago, when the last glacial cycle came to an end (Figure 7.1). Our story here is focused on a parcel of time that starts at the end of the Pleistocene and extends into the early Holocene, perhaps 30,000 to 8,000 years ago. This is the story that the rocks and landforms of White Sands tell.

Throughout geological time, the earth's continents have moved, trading places, colliding to create mountains, subducting under one another to create chains of volcanoes. This process is referred to as plate tectonics, since the earth's crust is split up into thin plates that move across the surface of the planet at about the rate that your fingernails grow. We live on a restless earth. The climate has also changed from periods when it was warmer than it is today—greenhouse times—to icehouse times. Yes, we live in an icehouse, despite the rate at which our planet is currently warming due to human use of fossil fuels. The oscillation of climate between these states is controlled by carbon dioxide, which is the main product of volcanoes and is removed from the atmosphere by the weathering of new mountain ranges. Carbon dioxide is the climate king, and ignoring human pollutants, the atmospheric budget is controlled by the relative abundance of volcanoes and mountain building, both of which are controlled by plate tectonics. Shortwave radiation from the sun cuts through the atmosphere to warm the earth's surface. In turn, the earth radiates long-wave radiation back to space, but this is intercepted in the atmosphere by an amount proportional to the level of carbon dioxide in the atmosphere. The more carbon dioxide, the more heat is retained. Consequently, our planet gets warmer.

About 65 million years ago, the age of the dinosaurs came to a fiery end when an asteroid hit the Yucatán Peninsula of Mexico. Ever since, the earth's climate has cooled progressively. The collision of India and Eurasia created the Himalayas, the weathering of which drew down carbon dioxide levels in the atmosphere, cooling our planet, as has the isolation of Antarctica over the South Pole. At the start of the Pleistocene, the earth entered the current ice age, during which vast ice sheets waxed and waned over much of the northern hemisphere. Intervals of time when the ice

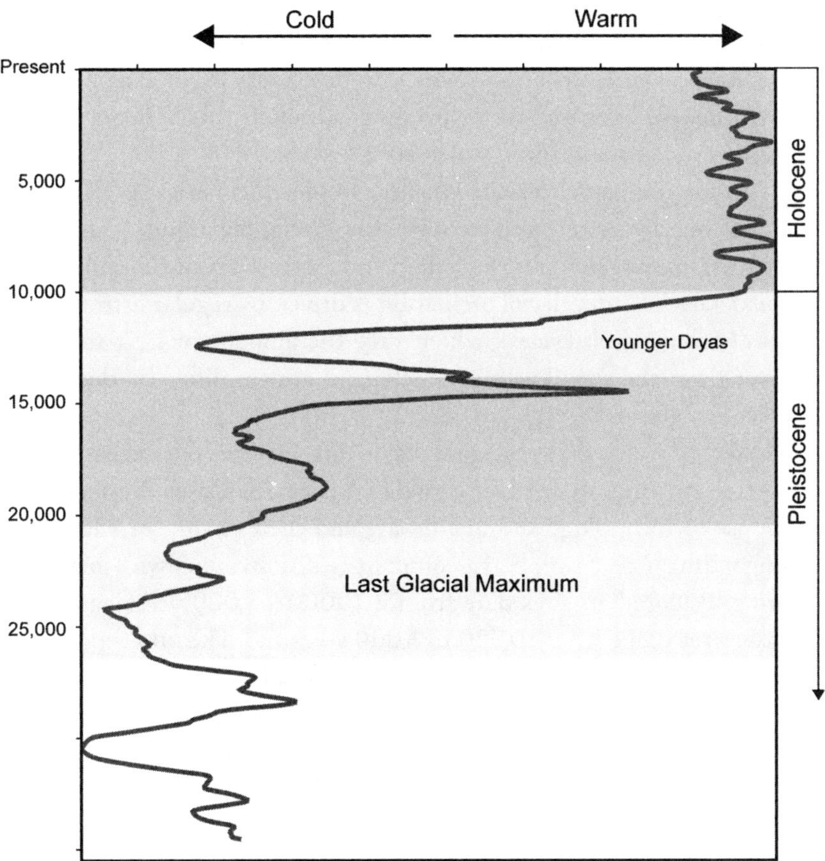

Figure 7.1. Key features in the terminal Ice Age or Pleistocene. The graph shows the variation in oxygen isotopes (temperature) extracted from ice cores in Greenland. The Holocene is the current interglacial. The last glacial maximum is shown, as is the Younger Dryas. The latter was a short, sharp return to glacial conditions right at the end of the Pleistocene.

sheets were at their maximum are known as glacials and are separated by interglacials. The Holocene, in which we live today, is an example of an interglacial. And yes, the ice will return, although this is being delayed by human use of fossil fuels, which are a key source of carbon dioxide.

The last glacial cycle reached its peak in North America about 21,000 years ago in what is referred to as the last glacial maximum (Figure 7.1). Since then, the ice sheets have melted and retreated, and the climate has warmed. Glacial–interglacial oscillation is driven by regular astronomical cycles (Milankovitch cycles), which vary the amount of heat the earth receives from the sun. These small changes are amplified by the oceans to drive the glacial–interglacial seesaw.

In the same way that geologists divide time into periods, archaeologists also partition time to create a shorthand that links sites. Implicit here is the use of technology and/or lifeways and their change or adaptation through time. For example, Paleoindian is synonymous with big game hunting. Paleoindian sites date from 20,000 to 8,000 years ago, while Archaic sites range from 10,000 to 3,000 years ago. The other important complication here is that geologists and archaeologists use a wide range of different age-related nomenclatures. Most people are aware of the abbreviations BC and AD, relating to before and after the birth of Jesus, and also the secular alternatives BCE and CE ("before common era" and "common era"). Scientists also use the term BP, which stands for "before present," based on the year 1950. The difference between BP and AD, therefore, is 1,950 years. Finally, calendar years are sometimes used, and these usually refer to something's age relative to the current year. We try, where we can, to use calendar years. If no caveat is added, that is what we are referring to.

Figure 7.2 (*opposite page, above*). Key families and species in the order Proboscidea. The ticks indicate whether fossil footprints have been recovered. Tracks from the United Arab Emirates (UAE) are some of the oldest known proboscidean tracks, while those of *Palaeoloxodon* have been recently documented from Portugal.

Figure 7.3 (*opposite page, below*). The proboscidean track from White Sands on the left consists of a series of concentric ridges. The actual track is the inner ring, and those around it are pushed up by the weight of the foot, as shown on the right.

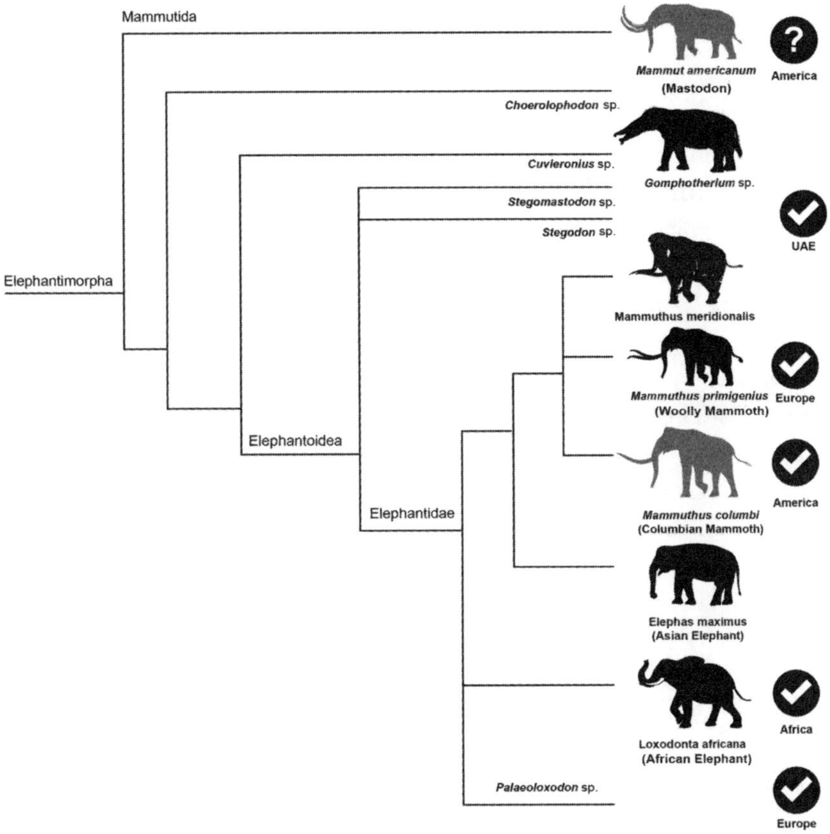

Mammutida
Mammut americanum
(Mastodon)
America
Choerolophodon sp.
Cuvieronius sp.
Gomphotherium sp.
Stegomastodon sp.
Stegodon sp.
UAE
Elephantimorpha
Mammuthus meridionalis
Mammuthus primigenius
(Woolly Mammoth)
Europe
Elephantoidea
Mammuthus columbi
(Columbian Mammoth)
America
Elephantidae
Elephas maximus
(Asian Elephant)
Loxodonta africana
(African Elephant)
Africa
Palaeoloxodon sp.
Europe

Apparent size
Actual size

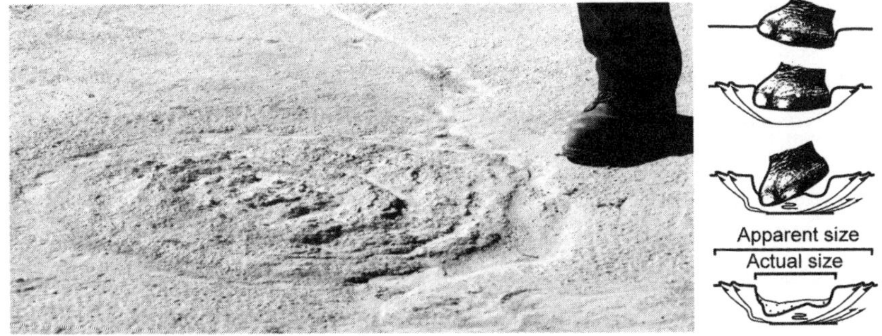

Mammoths and Their Tracks

So far in our story, we have referred to the large circular tracks as those of mammoths, but in practice, there are several possible animals that could have made them, since the remains of mastodons have been found in the Tularosa Basin. To understand this family of animals, it is worth unpacking their family tree a little.[1]

Proboscidea is a taxonomic name for the order of elephant-like animals, and modern elephants are the only living members of this large order of mammals. The name derives from ancient Greek words meaning "elephant trunk." The family Elephantidae, which lives today, contains the African bush, forest, and Asian elephants. The family tree is sketched out in Figure 7.2. The elephant family contains the extinct mammoths and the genus *Palaeoloxodon*. Members of this genus were typically straight-tusked. They were the largest ever members of the elephant family; some claim that some species were the largest ever land-based mammals.

For many, mammoths are probably the most iconic Ice Age animals. There were the woolly mammoth of Eurasia (*Mammuthus primigenius*) and the Columbian mammoth of the Americas (*Mammuthus columbi*). The latter are likely the main source of elephant-like tracks at White Sands. However, Columbian mammoths were not the only proboscideans to roam the Americas during the Ice Age. Gomphotheres are known from Ice Age deposits in the Americas, as are mastodons. Mastodons split from the main evolutionary line of the proboscideans before the gomphotheres, were restricted to North America, and became extinct at the end of the Ice Age, as did Columbian mammoths. It is entirely possible that some of the tracks at White Sands were made by mastodons, and fossil fragments have been recovered from the Tularosa Basin. The problem is that a proboscidean foot is similar across different species. Yes, they vary subtly in size and gait, but a small proboscidean track could be a young Columbian mammoth or a mastodon.

Maybe in time, we will have enough proboscidean tracks from around the world to begin to separate out different track-making species, but currently, we don't. The sheer number of proboscidean tracks at White Sands tends to suggest that they were made by Columbian mammoths, and we lapse into referring to these tracks rather loosely as mammoth tracks in the text for ease of reference, but one must always keep an open mind. One of the problems with proboscidean tracks is that the foot area in contact with the ground (plantar area) is often hard to define because a mammoth frequently deforms soft sediment way beyond the literal extent of the track,[2] as illustrated in Figure 7.3.

Salt Flats and Playas

There are many names for the same thing in science, and in this case, a playa is also known as a pan or salt flat. The Spanish word *playa* simply means beach. The name varies with geography: *pan* is common in Africa and Australia; *salt flat* tends to be used in the Americas. In geology, the designation refers, although not exclusively, to a closed (endorheic) basin, which is one that has internal drainage and limited or no outflow to a river or ocean. Here, the mountains or uplands that surround a low-lying area (a basin) prevent water flowing anywhere else, and all rivers feed into this one low point. In semiarid areas, where water evaporation is equal to or greater than annual rainfall, any lake that forms is going to be very salty because there is no outflow to flush the dissolved sediment away. This type of lake doesn't form in wet areas because rainfall exceeds evaporation in them, and the water will simply rise unchecked until it reaches the lowest pass in the surrounding uplands and drains over it. Erosion of this overflow will reduce its elevation over time, and the basin will no longer be closed. So playas are features of semiarid regions that form in closed basins that may or may not be seasonally by a lake. In the past, ancient lakes (paleolakes) may have persisted in these basins during wetter climates, and in some cases these former lakebeds eroded to create modern playas; Alkali Flat is one such playa. It is important to note that not all playas contain salt pans or flats. Any ephemeral lake counts as a playa, and on the high plains of Texas and New Mexico, there are tens of thousands of ephemeral lakes and therefore playas.

During the Ice Age, weather systems were different from those today. Precipitation fell as snow in certain areas to build ice sheets, while rain may have fallen in areas that are arid today. In old school geology, a glacial cycle was equated to a pluvial or wet period in a desert, but we now know that such simple equivalency does not apply. However, at times during the Ice Age, it was much wetter in arid areas, such as the American Southwest, and large paleolakes and wetlands developed. Lake Otero at White Sands is an example of such an ancient lake. During this pluvial event, sediment built up on the lake floor, and once the lake drained it was eroded by the wind. Thus, playa basins can be filled by a complex stratigraphy of lake, wetland, and windblown sediments that have been eroded and deposited several times.

Playas can be predominantly depositional, erosional, or some combination of the two, which may vary over time. There are lots of variables at play here, such as the length of time the basin is water-filled and therefore sediment can be laid down on the playa floor and how this may have varied in the past with changes in climate. Also, a high water table may allow salt-tolerant vegetation to grow on the playa floor, and damp sediment is harder to erode than sediment that is dry. The rate of sediment accumulation in playas is also controlled by the nature of the surrounding hill slopes and the degree to which those slopes are vegetated. Vegetation is good at slowing erosion. These factors vary geographically from one location to another and over time at each location. Consequently, the depositional history in any one playa may be different from that of its neighbor, and that history will determine the likely presence or absence of footprints and, crucially, at what depth they are to be found.

Let's take a basin that often has a lake within it and receives a lot of sediment from surrounding areas. It lies at the wet end of a playa spectrum. Footprints that formed around the margin of the lake (or on the playa floor) in the past will be deeply buried, while recent tracks will be closer to the current surface. If it remains wet, then only a little erosion of this layer cake of sediment and footprints may have occurred. At the other end of our spectrum is an arid playa that has been deeply eroded by the wind. Here, there may have been lots of footprints formed on sediment layers in the past, but they may now be long gone due to erosion; or if we are lucky, only the old ones survive. White Sands lies somewhere between these two extremes. There was once a large lake and wetland into which lots of sediment was deposited. Footprints were imprinted during low stands of the lake—dry periods when water levels were low. At other times, during wetter periods, these footprints were buried by more sediment.

This ancient lakebed has now been eroded to reveal these footprints on the current playa surface. Moreover, that surface appears to have been stable during the last 10,000 years or so. The water table may have played a role in preventing further incision. As salts evaporate to create crystals (blooms), they form a protective surface layer. The wind deflates this layer and not the subsurface. The bloom of salt crystals gives the wind something to erode and is replenished after every episode of rainfall. It is the Goldilocks of playas—not too much erosion, but just enough to reveal its footprint treasure.

Sediments and the Graphic Log

Describing and recording the vertical succession of sediment layers is a key job for the geologists on our research team. We need to describe the layers so that we can say something about the depositional environment in which those layers were deposited (Figure 7.4). The key to linking sediment to the environment in which it was deposited is the principal of uniformitarianism, or the "present is the key to the past." The idea originated with James Hutton (1726–1797), who was part of the Scottish Enlightenment in the eighteenth century.[3] He was a landowner south of Edinburgh for much of his life, and he used to look out over his fields as they were slowly eroded by winter rains. If nature had always worked this way, then erosion was a slow process, he inferred. He believed the laws of nature (physics, really) must have always operated in the same way, and therefore present-day process rates applied to the past. Thanks to the work of Charles Lyell (1797–1875), a contemporary of Charles Darwin (1809–1882), this idea developed into the principle of uniformitarianism. By studying the way present-day processes produce characteristic deposits, you can infer those processes wherever you find the same deposits. This remains a basic tenant of modern geology. If a river leaves a specific type of deposit, then when you find similar deposits in the geological record, you know that a river once flowed there.

When a geologist is faced with a natural cliff or a soil pit cut into the ground, they set to work to describe each layer of rock or sediment. The

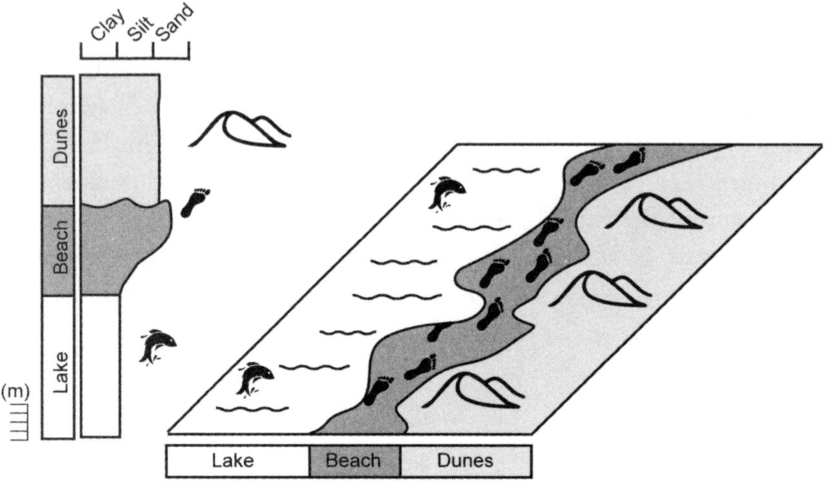

Figure 7.4. A schematic illustration of a graphic log and an associated environmental picture using Walther's Law. The vertical succession of environments in the log represents the spatial pattern on the ground. It involves substitution for time and space.

thickness of the layer or unit comes first, then an estimate of its grain size and whether it is made of clay, sand, or pebbles, for example. Its color may come next, along with any internal structure (bedding) that it may contain. This information is presented in the form of a vertical log, known as a graphic log, in which each layer is represented by a scale thickness and symbols to summarize the characteristics of that layer. The process is descriptive and as objective as possible. Interpretation takes no part in this process, at least to start with. Later, based on the descriptive evidence, inferences are made as to whether the layer was deposited in a lake, in a river, or by windblown sand, for example. Collectively, a sequence of layers tells a story about a depositional environment, a picture of the landscape in which each layer was laid down.

There is one other useful geological principle used here: Walther's law. This states that what occurs in vertical succession will also occur laterally. Crudely, if you lay a graphic log on its side, you have a picture of the environments that were once next to one another in the landscape. It is a classic case of substituting time for space. Imagine a lake, a shoreline, and a gentle slope across a landscape. The lake is associated with clays that settle out in still water. The shoreline has evidence of coarse sediments, crushed shells, and perhaps small ripples. The slope has a mix of windblown sand and material washed downslope in the rain (Figure 7.5). If rain falls and persists, the water level in the lake will rise. Clays will now be deposited on the shoreline sediments, which in turn will move to overlie the slope deposits. In this way, the vertical succession of sediments now represents what was once laid out laterally. It is a powerful tool that allows you to create a cinematic vision of the past, to which you can add footprints!

Excavation Strategies

In chapter 2, we discussed some of the principal elements to be considered in excavating tracks at a site like White Sands. Because we believe that track sites of this type occur throughout the American Southwest, it is perhaps worth spending a few more moments on this subject. Figure 7.5 shows the different excavation settings relevant to White Sands and to similar playas or ancient lakebeds. There are four common scenarios. Perhaps the simplest is natural exposure (Figure 7.5A), where an existing erosional bluff is simply cleaned of fallen debris to reveal natural indurated benches, which often contain tracks. This is the lightest approach with respect to ground disturbance, since only loose and eroded material is removed. With a slightly more aggressive approach, shallow steps are cut into the face to reveal the stratigraphy (Figure 7.6). This has been practiced by our team at other sites, but not at White Sands. Trenching is the next strategy and involves block removal to reveal the stratigraphy in the side walls of the trench (Figure 7.5B). A particularly useful approach at White Sands has been to hinge indurated blocks and thereby reveal tracks on bedding surfaces. A pry bar may cause the bedding surface to part cleanly in the same way that a chisel splits slate. Removal of the intact or split block, either entirely or by hinging it upward, often reveals tracks. Elsewhere at White Sands, and at other similar sites, tracks are often found very close to the surface, below a thin crust composed of salt and silt (Figure 7.5C). Using a trowel to expose the in situ surface below the tracks frequently reveals them in two dimensions, picked out by different sediment colors, textures, and faint outlines. A variant of this scenario is common around

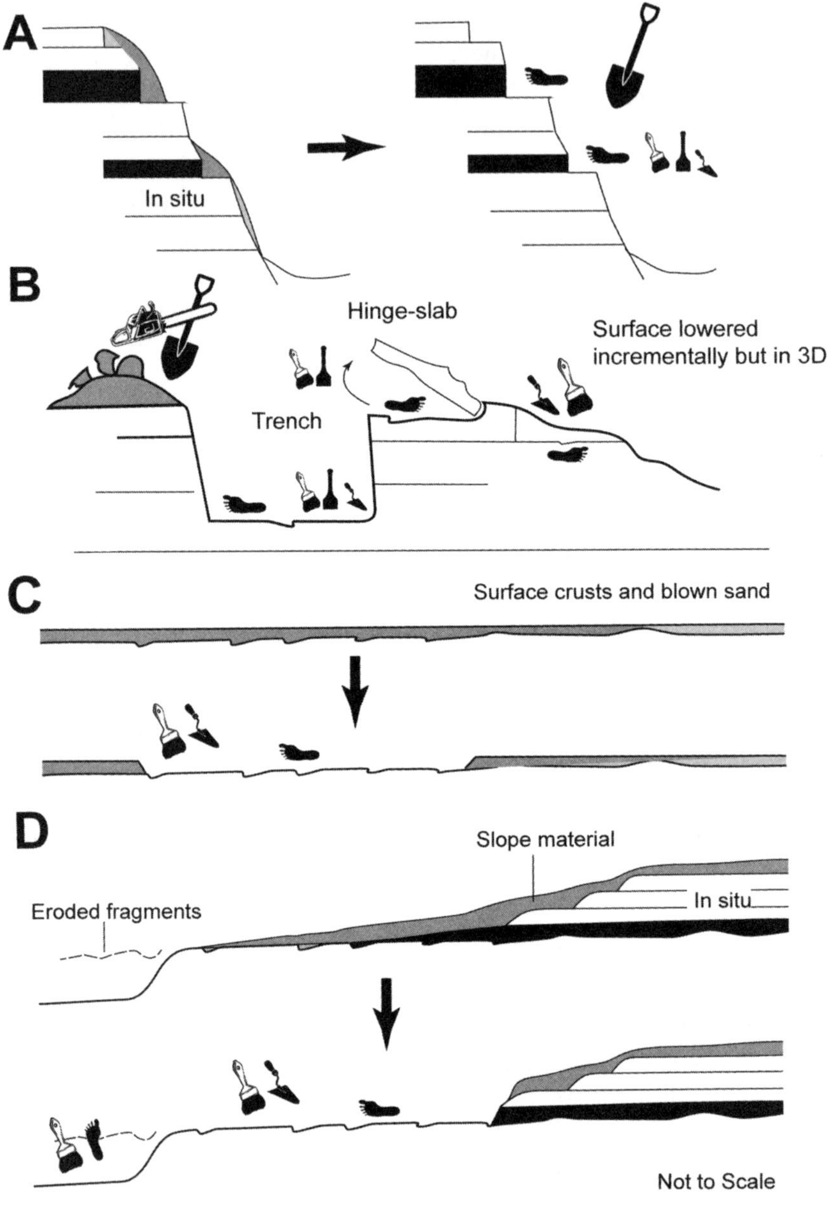

Figure 7.5. A schematic illustration of the different types of excavation undertaken at White Sands and similar sites in the American Southwest. A: A natural bluff or cliff with benches. B: A trench. C and D: How natural surfaces can be exposed.

Figure 7.6. At an ancient lakebed with tracks (not White Sands), Sally Reynolds cleans a vertical face to reveal the stratigraphy. A series of benches is cut into the face so that true bed thickness can be measured. Benches often contain footprints.

1

Arrival at Field Site

2

Pause

- Do you have the necessary permits and permissions?
- What are the objectives of the study?
- Where are the main areas of interest?
- Are the tracks exposed or do they need to be excavated?
- What is known? What is the working hypothesis or hypotheses?
- Why and how were the tracks preserved? Keep an open mind.
- Who, what made the tracks? Keep an open mind.
- Actions should be proportional to the objectives and permissions.

3

Assess and Preserve

- How large is the surface? Is there more than one surface/site?
- What are the stratigraphic context and dating potential?
- What were the environmental conditions at the time the tracks were made?
- What are the current weather conditions?
- What can be excavated and uncovered easily? Do you have permission?
- What are the temporal relationship between the prints?
- How are you assessing/storing removed material?

4

Evidence Recovery Plan

- Risk assessment, health and safety considerations.
- Prioritize vulnerable tracks and consider sequence of documentation.
- Constantly change the line of sight and use different lighting options.
- Leave as much in situ as possible.
- Ensure excavation approach does not damage the tracks as they are uncoverd.

Record Throughout (1-4)

- Known information prior to attending.
- Site assessment and recovery plan.
- Surfaces searched.
- Types of surfaces.
- Location of all tracks recovered/documented.
- Sample list and list of all 3D files.

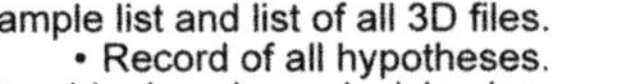

- Record of all hypotheses.
- Consider keeping a decision log.

5

Review

- New evidence may come to light, so always be prepared to evolve your plan.
- Review and learn from experience and mistakes if made.

Figure 7.7. This is a typical excavation strategy for footprints. Note that it may need tailoring if there are archaeological considerations on the site. Modified from Bennett and Budka, *Digital Technology*.

gentle bluffs, such as those found at WHSA Locality 2. Here, slope wash and windblown material form a veneer over the bedding surfaces, and these surfaces can be revealed by gently removing the overlying debris. In some cases, the bedding surfaces can be traced, via shallow excavation, into the bluff to reveal tracks below in situ sediment layers (Figure 7.5D).

We emphasize the importance of having a field-based excavation strategy that can evolve with the program of work. It is often necessary to outline such a strategy as part of the permit application process, but as military strategists say, the best plans frequently have to change "in contact with the enemy"—or, in our case, with the practical reality of discovery. Figure 7.7 is a generic strategy for track excavation that emphasizes the importance of flexibility. Tracks like those at White Sands and similar sites degrade rapidly once exposed and/or excavated. Moreover, in our experience, tracks are so frequent on surfaces that decisions need to constantly be made to prioritize recovery as one proceeds to excavate and uncover the surfaces. It is perhaps of little comfort to those interested in excavating tracks themselves, but experience is essential, and conventional archaeological experience does not prepare you for an ichnological excavation.

How Fast Was Someone Running?

Do you have children of different ages? Find a beach and let them run together, keeping pace with one another. As they stretch their legs and gain speed, the footprints they leave on the sand will become farther apart, and this spacing will increase in proportion to their running speeds. The child with the smallest legs will have to take more steps, and they will be closer together than those of the child with longer legs. To work out the speed at which they were running from their footprints alone, you need to know two things: the spacing between the tracks and the length of their legs (Figure 7.8). Specifically, you need to know the length of the leg from the hip to the sole of the foot. For a fossil track, you can work this out from empirical relationships that give you total stature; just like the relationship between foot length and stature, hip height is also correlated neatly with stature. If you collect the data set out below, you can plug it into an empirical relationship that predicts the speed at which the folks

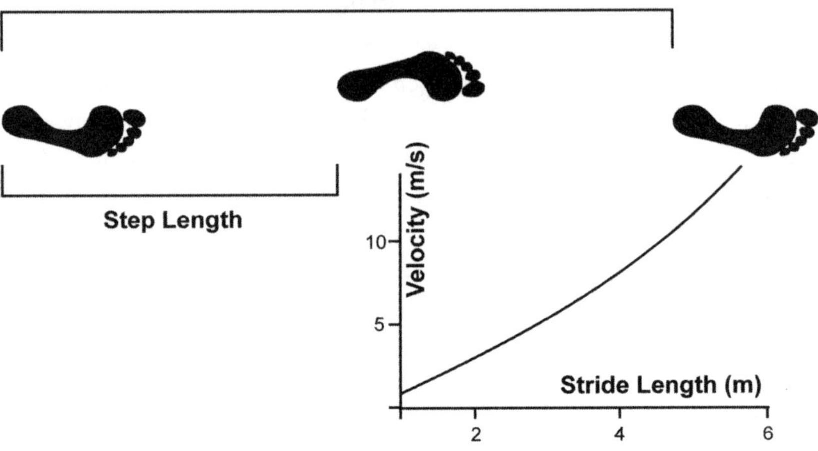

Figure 7.8. An illustration defining step and stride length in a trackway. The inset graph shows the empirical relationship between velocity and stride length.

who left the tracks were running or walking. The empirical relationship works just as well for a dinosaur as for a human.

The relationship looks like this[4]:

$$v \cong 0.25\, g^{0.5}\, \lambda^{1.67}\, h^{-1.17},$$

where g is the gravitational constant (~10 m/s), λ is the stride length (m), and h is hip height (m).

A couple of Spanish researchers have simplified this to the following power law,[5] which does not require hip height:

$$v = 0.794\, \lambda^{1.67}$$

A word we have used a lot is *empirical*, which means there is a statistical link between two variables rather than a physical law. Think about all the members of your family. There are bound to be some folks who have little feet but are tall—exceptions to the rule. But given enough data, these exceptions become less relevant, and the general rule "Tall people have big feet" holds. That is what we mean by empirical, and any predictions made by empirical relationships are just those: predictions.

A set of fossil tracks left on an ancient lakebed in Australia, the Willandra Lakes tracks, are similar in some respect to those at White Sands. One of the claims made about these long trackways is that the folks who made them were running very fast—in fact, as fast as an Olympic athlete (~10.3 m/s).[6] The Spanish researchers referred to above used their new equation on this data and downgraded these estimates to around 7 m/s, which is still fast.

Proboscidea, and Inferring Age and Size from Tracks

As one of the big five animals, elephants hold a special place in the public's imagination. Threatened by poaching, all three of the living elephant species—African bush elephants (*Loxodonta africana*), African forest elephants (*Loxodonta cyclotis*), and Asian elephants (*Elephas maximus*)—are protected and well-studied. One of the consequences of this attention is that their growth history has been documented, and growth curves, just like those used to monitor the development of children, exist. Modern elephants belong to the family Elephantidae, as do mammoths (*Mammuthus* sp.) and the order Proboscidea. It is worth noting that during the Ice Age in the Americas, there were three different species of Proboscidea roaming the landscape: mammoths, mastodons, and gomphotheres. You probably haven't heard of the latter, but they were relatively small, with elongated and low-vaulted skulls and straight tusks. They evolved from species with tusks extending from both the upper and the lower jaws.

The fancy names hide a simple fact: the animals are all related and, in theory, should have similar body plans and growth patterns. So if you have data on the height of an elephant at different stages of maturity, this should theoretically at least provide a first approximation for data on a mammoth. This idea has been tested by using frozen mammoths from the Arctic. Here the ground is permanently frozen into permafrost, but the top layer becomes unfrozen in summer and deep melt ponds may form and refreeze over time. In some cases, mammoths stumbled into such ponds and were preserved, frozen in the ground, and their carcasses have been recovered. The maturity of a mammoth can be determined from its bone structure, and you can measure the height, so in theory you have data to add to an elephant growth curve to check if the two are equivalent. The data points are limited, but the growth data are applicable from one animal to the other.

This has allowed folks to make inferences from mammoth tracks in the same way inferences are made about human tracks. The shoulder height, sex, and age of mammoth track-makers have all been inferred for several sites. It is not a precise business, but a first-order approximation is possible. Some caution is required because, as we have said before, the proboscidean tracks at White Sands may not all be from mammoths. Some may be from mastodons, and these are a bit more distant from modern elephants in terms of genetics. Figure 7.9 shows some elephant growth curves that have been used.

Stature from Foot Length: A Gruesome Perspective

The forensic and anthropological literature is full of studies looking at the size of feet and relating it to stature.[7] Different ethnic groups have subtly different empirical relationships between size and stature and therefore justify their own studies. These simple scientific studies are popular in part because they appeal to students. You can simply get folks to draw around their feet and measure their height or use skin-safe vegetable dyes or paints to make footprints on paper. In either case, you then measure the length of the track that is made. If there is a school sandpit or long jump pit, you could make actual footprints there and measure them. Simply graph the results, foot size against stature, and you have your own predictive tool that will be valid to the folks in your sample. The empirical relationships can be quite sophisticated, separating out males from females, each with their own regression equations. Within the literature, there are a huge number of such equations.

Aside from the ease with which such studies can be conducted, what is the underlying rationale for doing this? Well, here comes the gruesome bit. In a plane crash or terrorist explosion, your feet have a better chance of

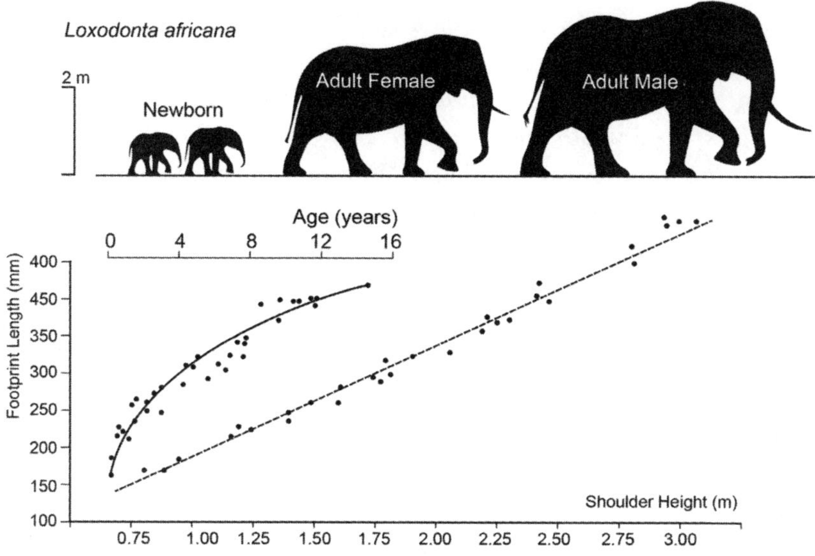

Figure 7.9. The modern growth curve for African elephants. By analogy, we can use this information to make a first approximation of the height and age of a mammoth.

surviving than some other body parts. They are usually protected by shoes or boots and are therefore more likely to survive than, say, your hands. When forensic scientists have the grim task of identifying survivors' stature, estimates can provide a first-order characterization. *CSI*-type TV programs use DNA to identify victims with a zip and zap, but in truth it is not all that easy, and DNA degrades quickly in certain conditions and climates.

Setting aside the grim part of this, one might think these data are of real value in footprints studies, and to a certain extent that is true. But you can't assume the ethnicity or sex of a fossil footprint, and therefore must fall back on more generic empirical relationships.

Some folks believe you can tell the sex of a track-maker simply by looking at the track. To test this, we gave a couple of expert forensic podiatrists exactly that challenge, and the best they could do was about 56 percent, which is not much better than even odds. But with artificial intelligence, an algorithm trained to do exactly this can get it right around 90 percent of the time. The first step is to set aside data for testing and then to train a machine learning algorithm on the rest, providing both images and metadata such as a sex and age. The algorithm breaks each image down into components and looks to see what components correspond with what information. Budka and colleagues used this approach with around 5,000 black-and-white track prints from a UK National Health Service hospital that specializes in podiatry.[8] With each image, there was a lot of anonymous identifying information such as sex and age. The software worked like a dream and was soon returning accurate assessments based on the test data. When the algorithm was asked to both assign decadal age and determine sex, the success rate was around 90 percent. The problem with such an approach is that you have no idea what the computer is effectively seeing and the expert is not. One solution is to overlay a heat map on each image, identifying those areas that are crucial for the decision the algorithm makes. This at least gives you an idea of which parts of the foot are important.

In Budka's study, differences around the toes stood out, as did an area just forward of the heel. The biggest bone in the human heel is the calcaneus, and it is known to be sexually dimorphic—that is, it shows a difference between males and females, and there is a modest literature using heel X-rays to confirm this. The age of the track-makers completely baffled the researchers, though. In theory, your foot stops growing in your late teens and stays the same size throughout your adult lifetime, but the algorithm was detecting something apart from size. Currently, we are not sure what this is.

Can algorithms like this work on fossil tracks? The answer is yes in theory, but not yet. A machine learning algorithm is only as good as the training data it is given, which in this case was neat black-and-white footprint images. Fossil tracks are messy, and while some progress has been made using depth maps of nice footprints, applying the approach to a fossil dataset is not yet possible. Our guess is that it will happen at some point soon. This does beg the question that is often asked about artificial intelligence: Will it, in time, replace the expert? The answer in this case and others like it is probably not, but the expert who uses artificial intelligence as part of their tool kit is likely to have more time to study the complex cases.

The Future

We believe the archaeological and geological communities are on the cusp of a breakthrough in understanding the peopling of the Americas. In our view, footprints have been neglected as a source of evidence, yet they are more common than one thinks. The work at White Sands points to the potential for footprint evidence on ancient lakebeds throughout the Americas and especially in the American Southwest. Careful prospection using satellite images should reveal locations that have tracks of Ice Age megafauna, such as mammoths and giant ground sloths. That is the first step. The second step is to go out, provided you have the landowner's permission, and look at those tracks on the ground. In our experience, chances are there will be human tracks there too. It is not always easy to see tracks on these surfaces, and conditions often must be just right, but perseverance will pay off in time. We hope to train a new generation of ichno-archaeologists to tackle this challenge. In the meantime, thank you for reading to the end.

Notes

Chapter One

1. B. Gross, "White Sands Mystery Solved," *DARCOM News*, November 1981, 11; B. Gross, "Range's Giant Footprints May Become Historical," *Missile Ranger*, February 19, 1982, 16.
2. White Sands became a national park in December 2019. Before that, it was a national monument. For simplicity, we refer it to as White Sands National Park throughout this book.
3. For simplicity, we are going to stick with the term *mammoth* here, but strictly speaking these tracks were made by a proboscidean, a member of the same order elephants belong to. Mastodons belong to this order as well and were potentially present at White Sands, but the size of the tracks leads us to believe that most of them belong to *Mammuthus columbi*, the main proboscidean species in the Americas during the Pleistocene.
4. S. G. Lucas, B. D. Allen, G. S. Morgan, R. G. Myers, D. W. Love, and D. Bustos, "Mammoth Footprints from the Upper Pleistocene of the Tularosa Basin, Doña Ana County, New Mexico," *Cenozoic Vertebrate Tracks and Traces* 42 (2007): 149–54.
5. The postscript to this book includes a short section defining *Ice Age* and other key geological terms.
6. Bruce D. Allen, Dave W. Love, and R. G. Myers, "Evidence for Late Pleistocene Hydrologic and Climatic Change from Lake Otero, Tularosa Basin, South-Central New Mexico," *New Mexico Geology* 31, no. 1 (2009): 9–25.
7. Vance T. Holliday, Allison Harvey, Matthew T. Cuba, and Aimee M. Weber, "Paleoindians, Paleolakes and Paleoplayas: Landscape Geoarchaeology of the Tularosa Basin, New Mexico," *Geomorphology* 331 (2019): 92–106.
8. Anna Szynkiewicz, Craig H. Moore, Mihaela Glamoclija, David Bustos, and Lisa M. Pratt, "Origin of Coarsely Crystalline Gypsum Domes in a Saline Playa Environment at the White Sands National Monument,

New Mexico," *Journal of Geophysical Research* 115 (2010): 1–14, https//doi:10.1029/2009JF001592.

9. Allen et al., "Evidence for Late Pleistocene Hydrologic and Climatic Change," 9–25.
10. Gary Kocurek, Mary Carr, Ryan Ewing, Karen G. Havholm, Y. C. Nagar, and A. K. Singhvi, "White Sands Dune Field, New Mexico: Age, Dune Dynamics and Recent Accumulations," *Sedimentary Geology* 197, no. 3–4 (2007): 313–31, https://doi.org/10.1016/j.sedgeo.2006.10.006; Holliday et al., "Paleoindians, Paleolakes and Paleoplayas," 92–106.
11. "White Sands National Park History," National Park Service, September 3, 2022, https://www.nps.gov/whsa/learn/historyculture/white-sands-national-park-history.htm.
12. HABS is the Historic American Building Survey. HAER is the Historic American Engineering Record.
13. M. R. Bennett, J. W. Harris, B. G. Richmond, D. R. Braun, E. Mbua, P. Kiura, D. Olago et al., "Early Hominin Foot Morphology Based on 1.5-Million-Year-Old Footprints from Ileret, Kenya," *Science* 323 (2009): 1197–1201.
14. M. R. Bennett and S. A. Morse, 2014. *Human Footprints: Fossilised Locomotion?* (Springer, 2014), 1–12.
15. F. S. Worman, A. Kurota, and P. Hogan, "Dunefield Geoarchaeology at White Sands National Monument, New Mexico, USA: Site Formation, Resource Use, and Dunefield Dynamics," *Geoarchaeology* 34, no. 1 (2019): 42–61; you can find definitions of these time periods at the end of the chapter.
16. See, e.g., Mary D. Leakey and R. L. Hay, "Pliocene Footprints in the Laetolil Beds, at Laetoli, N. Tanzania," *Nature* 278 (1979): 317–23; Mary D. Leakey, "Tracks and Tools," *Philosophical Transactions of the Royal Society of London* B292 (1981): 95–102.
17. Anna K. Behrensmeyer and L. F. Laporte, "Footprints of a Pleistocene Hominid in Northern Kenya," *Nature* 289, no. 5794 (1981): 167–69.
18. See, e.g., Andreas Pastoors, Tilman Lenssen-Erz, Tsamkxao Ciqae, Ui Kxunta, Thui Thao, Robert Bégouën, Megan Biesele et al., "Tracking in Caves: Experience Based Reading of Pleistocene Human Footprints in French Caves," *Cambridge Archaeological Journal* 25, no. 3 (2015): 551–64.
19. P. Willey, P. J. Watson, G. Crothers, and J. Stolen, "Holocene Human Footprints in North America," *Ichnos* 16, no. 1–2 (2009): 70–75.

20. M. R. Bennett and S. C. Reynolds, "Inferences from Footprints: Archaeological Best Practice," in *Reading Prehistoric Human Tracks*, ed. Andreas Pastoors and Tilman Lenssen-Erz (Springer, 2021), 15.
21. Leakey and Hay, "Pliocene Footprints."
22. Fidelis T. Masao, Elgidius B. Ichumbaki, Marco Cherin, Angelo Barili, Giovanni Boschian, Dawid A. Iurino, Sofia Menconero et al., "New Footprints from Laetoli (Tanzania) Provide Evidence for Marked Body Size Variation in Early Hominins," *eLife* 5 (2015): e19568.
23. Bennett et al., "Early Hominin Foot Morphology."
24. Kevin G. Hatala, William E. H. Harcourt-Smith, Adam D. Gordon, Brian W. Zimmer, Brian G. Richmond, Briana L. Pobiner, David J. Green et al., "Snapshots of Human Anatomy, Locomotion, and Behavior from Late Pleistocene Footprints at Engare Sero, Tanzania," *Scientific Reports* 10 (2020), https://doi.org/10.1038/s41598-020-64095-0.
25. David Webb, Marius Robu, Oana Moldovan, Silviu Constantin, Bogdan Tomus, and Ionel Neag, "Ancient Human Footprints in Ciur-Izbuc Cave, Romania," *American Journal of Physical Anthropology* 155, no. 1 (2014): 128–35.
26. P. Willey, "Preservation of Prehistoric Footprints in Jaguar Cave, Tennessee," *Journal of Cave and Karst Studies* 67, no. (2005): 61–68.
27. H. Gregory McDonald and Oscar Carranza-Castañeda, "Increased Xenarthran Diversity of the Great American Biotic Interchange: A New Genus and Species of Ground Sloth (*Mammalia, Xenarthra, Megalonychidae*) from the Hemphillian (Late Miocene) of Jalisco, Mexico," *Journal of Paleontology* 91, no. 5 (2017): 1069–82.
28. H. Gregory McDonald and Gary S. Morgan, "Ground Sloths of New Mexico," *New Mexico Museum of Natural History and Science Bulletin* 53 (2011): 652–63.
29. Meaghan M. Emery-Wetherell, Brianna K. McHorse, and Edward Byrd Davis, "Spatially Explicit Analysis Sheds New Light on the Pleistocene Megafaunal Extinction in North America," *Paleobiology* 43, no. 4 (2017): 642–55.
30. Donald K. Grayson and David J. Meltzer, "A Requiem for North American Overkill," *Journal of Archaeological Science* 30, no. 5 (2003): 585–93.
31. Paul S. Martin, "The Discovery of America: The First Americans May Have Swept the Western Hemisphere and Decimated Its Fauna Within 1,000 Years," *Science* 179, no. 4077 (1973): 969–74.

32. P. L. Falkingham, K. T. Bates, L. Margetts, and P. L. Manning, "The 'Goldilocks' Effect: Preservation Bias in Vertebrate Track Assemblages," *Journal of the Royal Society Interface* 8, no. 61 (2011): 1142–54.
33. Daniel Marty, André Strasser, and Christian A. Meyer, "Formation and Taphonomy of Human Footprints in Microbial Mats of Present-Day Tidal-Flat Environments: Implications for the Study of Fossil Footprints," *Ichnos* 16, no. 1–2 (2009): 127–42.

Chapter Two

1. D. Marty, A. Strasser, C. A. Meyer, "Formation and Taphonomy of Human Footprints in Microbial Mats of Present-Day Tidal-Flat Environments: Implications for the Study of Fossil Footprints," *Ichnos* 16, no. 1–2 (2009): 127–42.
2. M. R. Bennett and S. A. Morse, *Human Footprints: Fossilised Locomotion?* (Springer, 2014).
3. T. M. Urban, M. R. Bennett, D. Bustos, S. W. Manning, S. C. Reynolds, M. Belvedere, D. Odess et al., "3-D Radar Imaging Unlocks the Untapped Behavioral and Biomechanical Archive of Pleistocene Ghost Tracks," *Scientific Reports* 9, no. 1 (2019): 16470.
4. M. Belvedere, M. Budka, A. L. A. Wiseman, and M. R. Bennett, "When Is Enough, Enough? Questions of Sampling in Vertebrate Ichnology," *Palaeontology* 64, no. 5 (2021): 661–72.
5. M. R. Bennett and M. Budka, *Digital Technology for Forensic Footwear Analysis and Vertebrate Ichnology* (Springer, 2018).
6. M. R. Bennett and S. C. Reynolds, "Inferences from Footprints: Archaeological Best Practice," in *Reading Prehistoric Human Tracks*, ed. Andreas Pastoors and Tilman Lenssen-Erz (Springer, 2021), 15.
7. Bennett and Budka, *Digital Technology*.
8. D. C. Adams, F. J. Rohlf, and D. E. Slice, "Geometric Morphometrics: Ten Years of Progress Following the 'Revolution,'" *Italian Journal of Zoology* 71, no. 1 (2004): 5–16; M. Zelditch, D. Swiderski, H. D. Sheets, and W. Fink, *Geometric Morphometrics for Biologists: A Primer* (Academic Press, 2012).
9. M. Belvedere, M. R. Bennett, D. Marty, M. Budka, S. C. Reynolds, and R. Bakirov, "Stat-Tracks and Mediotypes: Powerful Tools for Modern Ichnology Based on 3D Models," *PeerJ* 6 (2018): e4247.

10. M. R. Bennett, J. W. Harris, B. G. Richmond, D. R. Braun, E. Mbua, P. Kiura, D. Olago et al., "Early Hominin Foot Morphology Based on 1.5-Million-Year-Old Footprints from Ileret, Kenya," *Science* 323 (2009):1197–1201.
11. "Past 5—the Past of the Future," University of Oslo Natural History Museum, www.nhm.uio.no/english/research/resources/past.
12. M. R. Bennett, S. C. Reynolds, S. A. Morse, and M. Budka, "Laetoli's Lost Tracks: 3D Generated Mean Shape and Missing Footprints," *Scientific Reports* 6, no. 1 (2016): 21916.
13. J. Y. Kim, K. S. Kim, M. G. Lockley, and N. Matthews, "Hominid Ichnotaxonomy: An Exploration of a Neglected Discipline," *Ichnos* 15, no. 3–4 (2008): 126–39.
14. D. J. Meldrum, M. G. Lockley, S. G. Lucas, and C. Musiba, C., "Ichnotaxonomy of the Laetoli Trackways: The Earliest Hominin Footprints," *Journal of African Earth Sciences* 60, no. 1–2 (2011): 1–12.
15. B. D. Allen, D. W. Love, and R. G. Myers, "Evidence for Late Pleistocene Hydrologic and Climatic Change from Lake Otero, Tularosa Basin, South-Central New Mexico," *New Mexico Geology* 31, no. 1 (2009): 9–25.
16. S. A. Morse, M. R. Bennett, S. Gonzalez, and D. Huddart, "Techniques for Verifying Human Footprints: Reappraisal of Pre-Clovis Footprints in Central Mexico," *Quaternary Science Reviews* 29, no. 19–20 (2010): 2571–78.
17. T. J. Cole, "The Development of Growth References and Growth Charts," *Annals of Human Biology* 39, no. 5 (2012): 382–94; F. Lifshitz, "Nutrition and Growth," *Journal of Clinical Research in Pediatric Endocrinology* 1, no. 4 (2009): 157.
18. A. L. A. Wiseman and I. De Groote, "One Size Fits All? Stature Estimation from Footprints and the Effect of Substrate and Speed on Footprint Creation," *Anatomical Record* 305, no. 7 (2022): 1692–1700; J. Duveau, "From Footprint Morphometrics to the Stature of Fossil Hominins: A Common but Uncertain Estimate," *L'Anthropologie* 126, no. 4 (2022): 103067.
19. A. Hrdlička, *Physiological and Medical Observations Among the Indians of Southwestern United States and Northern Mexico*, Bureau of American Ethnology Bulletin 34 (US Government Printing Office, 1908).
20. A. Hrdlička, "Anthropology of the Old Americans. II: Stature," *American Journal of Physical Anthropology* 5, no. 3 (1922): 209–35.

21. K. T. Bates, R. Savage, T. C. Pataky, S. A. Morse, E. Webster, P. L. Falkingham, L. Ren et al., "Does Footprint Depth Correlate with Foot Motion and Pressure?" *Journal of the Royal Society Interface* 10, no. 83 (2013): 20130009.
22. A. Pastoors, T. Lenssen-Erz, T. Ciqae, U. Kxunta, T. Thao, R. Bégouën, M. Biesele et al., "Tracking in Caves: Experience Based Reading of Pleistocene Human Footprints in French Caves," *Cambridge Archaeological Journal* 25, no. 3 (2015): 551–64; A Pastoors, T. Lenssen-Erz, B. Breuckmann, T. Ciqae, U. Kxunta, D. Rieke-Zapp, and T. Thao, "Experience Based Reading of Pleistocene Human Footprints in Pech-Merle," *Quaternary International* 430 (2017): 155–62.
23. L. Liebenberg, *The Art of Tracking: The Origin of Science* (New Africa Books, 1990).
24. C. Feller, G. G. Brown, E. Blanchart, P. Deleporte, and S. S. Chernyanskii, "Charles Darwin, Earthworms and the Natural Sciences: Various Lessons from Past to Future," *Agriculture, Ecosystems & Environment* 99, no. 1–3 (2003): 29–49.
25. R. W. Yarnell, M. Pacheco, B. Williams, J. L. Neumann, D. J. Rymer, and P. J. Baker, "Using Occupancy Analysis to Validate the Use of Footprint Tunnels as a Method for Monitoring the Hedgehog Erinaceus europaeus," *Mammal Review* 44, no. 3–4 (2014): 234–38.
26. S. Jarvie and J. M. Monks, "Step on It: Can Footprints from Tracking Tunnels Be Used to Identify Lizard Species?" *New Zealand Journal of Zoology* 41, no. 3 (2014): 210–17; T. D. Harker, N. F. Harker, F. R. Harker, J. Peace, M. Barry, M. R. Ludbrook, and W. Ji, "Analysis of Footprints Provides Additional Insights During Monitoring of Duvaucel's Geckos (Hoplodactylus duvaucelii)," *New Zealand Journal of Zoology* 44, no. 4 (2017): 305–18.
27. Z. C. Jewell, S. Alibhai, P. R. Law, K. Uiseb, and S. Lee, "Monitoring Rhinoceroses in Namibia's Private Custodianship Properties," *PeerJ* 8 (2020): e9670.
28. S. Alibhai, Z. Jewell, and J. Evans, "The Challenge of Monitoring Elusive Large Carnivores: An Accurate and Cost-Effective Tool to Identify and Sex Pumas (Puma concolor) From Footprints," *PLOS One* 12, no. 3 (2017): e0172065.

Chapter Three

1. T. C. Chamberlin, "The Method of Multiple Working Hypotheses," *Science* 366 (1890): 92–96.
2. H. N. Poinar, M. Hofreiter, W. G. Spaulding, P. S. Martin, B. A. Stankiewicz, H. Bland, R. P. Evershed et al., "Molecular Coproscopy: Dung and Diet of the Extinct Ground Sloth Nothrotheriops shastensis," *Science* 281 (1998): 402–6; J. I. Mead, B. A. Schroeder, and C. L. Yost, "Late Pleistocene Shasta Ground Sloth (Xenarthra) Dung, Diet, and Environment from the Sierra Vieja, Presidio County, Texas," *Texas Journal of Science* 73, no. 1 (2021).
3. H. G. McDonald and G. S. Morgan, "Ground Sloths of New Mexico," *New Mexico Museum of Natural History and Science Bulletin* 53 (2011): 652–63.
4. G. G. Politis, P. G. Messineo, T. W. Stafford Jr., and E. L. Lindsey, "Campo Laborde: A Late Pleistocene Giant Ground Sloth Kill and Butchering Site in the Pampas," *Science Advances* 5, no. 3 (2019): eaau4546.
5. J. Ruprecht, C. E. Eriksson, T. D. Forrester, D. B. Spitz, D. A. Clark, M. J. Wisdom, M. Bianco et al., "Variable Strategies to Solve Risk–Reward Tradeoffs in Carnivore Communities," *Proceedings of the National Academy of Sciences* 118, no. 35 (2021): e2101614118.
6. T. C. Pataky, T. Mu, K. Bosch, D. Rosenbaum, and J. Y. Goulermas, "Gait Recognition: Highly Unique Dynamic Plantar Pressure Patterns Among 104 Individuals," *Journal of the Royal Society Interface* 9, no. 69 (2012): 790–800.
7. O. Panagiotopoulou, T. C. Pataky, M. Day, M. C. Hensman, S. Hensman, J. R. Hutchinson, and C. J. Clemente, "Foot Pressure Distributions During Walking in African Elephants (Loxodonta africana)," *Royal Society Open Science* 3, no. 10 (2016), 160203; O. Panagiotopoulou, T. C. Pataky, Z. Hill, and J. R. Hutchinson, "Statistical Parametric Mapping of the Regional Distribution and Ontogenetic Scaling of Foot Pressures During Walking in Asian Elephants (Elephas maximus)," *Journal of Experimental Biology* 215, no. 9 (2012): 1584–93.
8. K. T. Bates, R. Savage, T. C. Pataky, S. A. Morse, E. Webster, P. L. Falkingham, L. Ren et al., "Does Footprint Depth Correlate with Foot Motion and Pressure?" *Journal of the Royal Society Interface* 10, no. 83 (2013): 20130009.
9. T. M. Urban, M. R. Bennett, D. Bustos, S. W. Manning, S. C. Reynolds, M. Belvedere, D. Odess et al., "3-D Radar Imaging Unlocks the Untapped

Behavioral and Biomechanical Archive of Pleistocene Ghost Tracks," *Scientific Reports* 9, no. 1 (2019): 16470.

10. M. R. Bennett, D. Bustos, M. Belvedere, P. Martinez, S. C. Reynolds, and T. Urban, "Soft-Sediment Deformation Below Mammoth Tracks at White Sands National Monument (New Mexico) with Implications for Biomechanical Inferences from Tracks," *Palaeogeography, Palaeoclimatology, Palaeoecology* 527 (2019): 25–38.
11. B. F. Platt and S. T. Hasiotis, "Novel Neoichnology of Elephants: Nonlocomotive Interactions with Sediment, Locomotion Traces in Partially Snow-Covered Sediment, and Implications for Proboscidean Paleoichnology," in *Experimental Approaches to Understanding Fossil Organisms: Lessons from the Living* (Springer, 2014): 371–93; C. W. Helm, M. G. Lockley, L. Moolman, H. C. Cawthra, J. C. De Vynck, M. G. Dixon, W. Stear et al., "Morphology of Pleistocene Elephant Tracks on South Africa's Cape South Coast and Probable Elephant Trunk-Drag Impressions," *Quaternary Research* 105 (2022): 100–14.
12. M. R. Bennett, S. A. Morse, C. Liutkus-Pierce, J. McClymont, M. Evans, R. H. Crompton, and J. F. Thackeray, "Exceptional Preservation of Children's Footprints from a Holocene Footprint Site in Namibia," *Journal of African Earth Sciences* 97 (2014): 331–41.
13. M. R. Bennett, J. W. Harris, B. G. Richmond, D. R. Braun, E. Mbua, P. Kiura, D. Olago et al., "Early Hominin Foot Morphology Based on 1.5-Million-Year-Old Footprints from Ileret, Kenya," *Science* 323 (2009): 1197–1201.
14. F. Altamura, M. R. Bennett, K. D'Août, S. Gaudzinski-Windheuser, R. T. Melis, S. C. Reynolds, and M. Mussi, "Archaeology and Ichnology at Gombore II-2, Melka Kunture, Ethiopia: Everyday Life of a Mixed-Age Hominin Group 700,000 Years Ago," *Scientific Reports* 8, no. 1 (2018): 2815; F. Altamura, M. R. Bennett, L. Marchetti, R. T. Melis, S. C. Reynolds, and M. Mussi, "Ichnological and Archaeological Evidence from Gombore II OAM, Melka Kunture, Ethiopia: An Integrated Approach to Reconstruct Local Environments and Biological Presences Between 1.2 and 0.85 Ma," *Quaternary Science Reviews* 244 (2020): 106506.
15. M. R. Bennett, D. Bustos, D. Odess, T. M. Urban, J. N. Lallensack, M. Budka, V. L. Santucci et al., "Walking in Mud: Remarkable Pleistocene Human Trackways from White Sands National Park (New Mexico)," *Quaternary Science Reviews* 249 (2020):106610.

Chapter Four

1. Kirsten M. Menking, Victor J. Polyak, Roger Y. Anderson, and Yemane Asmerom, "Climate History of the Southwestern United States Based on Estancia Basin Hydrologic Variability from 69 to 10 ka," *Quaternary Science Reviews* 200 (2018): 237–52.
2. Matthew R. Bennett, Davis Bustos, and Daniel Odess, "Evidence of Humans in North America During the Last Glacial Maximum," *Science* 373, no. 6562 (2021): 1528–31.
3. A range of papers responded to the 2021 claim. They include C. Vance Haynes, "Evidence for Humans at White Sands National Park during the Last Glacial Maximum Could Actually be for Clovis people ~13,000 Years Ago," *PaleoAmerica* 8, no. 2 (2022): 95–98; David B. Madsen, Loren G. Davis, David Rhode, and Charles G. Oviatt, "Comment on 'Evidence of Humans in North America During the Last Glacial Maximum,'" *Science* 375 (2022); Charles G. Oviatt, David B. Madsen, David Rhode, and Loren G. Davis, "A Critical Assessment of Claims That Human Footprints in the Lake Otero Basin, New Mexico Date to the Last Glacial Maximum," *Quaternary Research* 111 (2023): 138–47; David M. Rachal, Robert Dello-Russo, and Matthew Cuba, "The Pleistocene Footprints Are Younger Than We Thought: Correcting the Radiocarbon Dates of Ruppia Seeds, Tularosa Basin, New Mexico," *Quaternary Research* 117 (2024): 67–78.
4. Michael Strevens, *The Knowledge Machine: How an Unreasonable Idea Created Modern Science* (Penguin, 2020).
5. J. Iversen, "Viscum, Hedera and Ilex as Climate Indicators: A Contribution to the Study of the Post-Glacial Temperature Climate," *Geologiska Föreningen i Stockholm Förhandlingar* 66, no. 3 (1944): 463–83.
6. Jeffery S. Pigati, Kathleen B. Springer, Jeffrey S. Honke, David Wahl, Marie R. Champagne, Susan R. H. Zimmerman, Harrison J. Gray et al., "Independent Age Estimates Resolve the Controversy of Ancient Human Footprints at White Sands," *Science* 382, no. 6666 (2023): 73–75.
7. David Rhode, Christina M. Neudorf, David Rachal, and Loren G. Davis, "Unresolved: Persistent Problems with the White Sands Locality 2 Geochronology," *PaleoAmerica* 10 (2024): 10–27. See also J. S. Pigati et al., "The Geochronology of White Sands Locality 2 Is Resolved," *PaleoAmerica* 10 (2024): 28–44.

8. Oviatt et al., "A Critical Assessment"; Rachal et al., "The Pleistocene Footprints Are Younger Than We Thought."
9. Pigati et al., "The Geochronology of White Sands Locality 2 Is Resolved."
10. D. M. Rachal, J. I. Mead, R. Dello-Russo, and M. T. Cuba, "Deep-Water Delivery Model of *Ruppia* Seeds to a Nearshore/Terrestrial Setting and Its Chronological Implications for Late Pleistocene Footprints, Tularosa Basin, New Mexico," *Geoarchaeology* 37, no. 6 (2022): 923–33.
11. Rhode et al., "Unresolved." See also Pigati et al., "The Geochronology of White Sands Locality 2 Is Resolved."
12. Pigati et al., "The Geochronology of White Sands Locality 2 Is Resolved."
13. Rhode et al., "Unresolved." See also Pigati et al., "The Geochronology of White Sands Locality 2 Is Resolved."
14. Pigati et al., "The Geochronology of White Sands Locality 2 Is Resolved.".
15. W. H. Whyte, "Groupthink," *Fortune*, March 1, 1952, 114–17, 142, 146. For a modern take on the concept, see M. Akhmad, S. Chang, and H. Deguchi, "Closed-Mindedness and Insulation in Groupthink: Their Effects and the Devil's Advocacy as a Preventive Measure," *Journal of Computational Social Science* 4 (2021): 455–78.
16. "The Sub-4 Alphabetic Register," National Union of Track Statisticians, June 30, 2022, https://nuts.org.uk/sub-4/Sub-4%20register%20 6%20June%202022.pdf.

Chapter Five

1. Daniel R. Muhs, John F. Wehmiller, Kathleen R. Simmons, and Linda L. York, "Quaternary Sea-Level History of the United States," *Developments in Quaternary Sciences* 1 (2008): 147–83; Jorie Clark, Jerry X. Mitrovica, and Jay Adler, "Coastal Paleogeography of the California-Oregon-Washington and Bering Sea Continental Shelves During the Latest Pleistocene and Holocene: Implications for the Archaeological Record," *Journal of Archaeological Science* 52 (2014): 12–23; Dan H. Shugar, Ian J. Walker, Olav B. Lian, Jordan B. R. Eamer, Christina Neudorf, Duncan McLaren, and Daryl Fedje, "Post-Glacial Sea-Level Change Along the Pacific Coast of North America," *Quaternary Science Reviews* 97 (2014): 170–92.

2. April S. Dalton, Chris R. Stokes, and Christine L. Batchelor, "Evolution of the Laurentide and Innuitian Ice Sheets Prior to the Last Glacial Maximum (115 ka to 25 ka)," *Earth-Science Reviews* 224 (2022): 103875; April S. Dalton, Martin Margold, Chris R. Stokes, Lev Tarasov, Arthur S. Dyke, Roberta S. Adams, Serge Allard et al., "An Updated Radiocarbon-Based Ice Margin Chronology for the Last Deglaciation of the North American Ice Sheet Complex," *Quaternary Science Reviews* 234 (2020): 106223.

3. Peter D. Heintzman, D. Froese, J. W. Ives, A. E. R. Soares, G. D. Zazula, B. Letts, T. D. Andrews et al., "Bison Phylogeography Constrains Dispersal and Viability of the Ice Free Corridor in Western Canada," *Proceedings of the National Academy of Sciences* 113, no. 29 (2016): 8057–63.

4. Paulette F. Steeves, *The Indigenous Paleolithic of the Western Hemisphere* (University of Nebraska Press, 2021).

5. Ciprian F. Ardelean, Lorena Becerra-Valdivia, Mikkel Winther Pedersen, Jean-Luc Schwenninger, Charles G. Oviatt, Juan I. Macías-Quintero, Joaquin Arroyo-Cabrales et al., "Evidence of Human Occupation in Mexico Around the Last Glacial Maximum," *Nature* 584, no. 7819 (2020): 87–92.

6. James C. Chatters, Ben A. Potter, Anna Marie Prentiss, Stuart J. Fiedel, Gary Haynes, Robert L. Kelly, J. David Kilby et al., "Evaluating Claims of Early Human Occupation at Chiquihuite Cave, Mexico," *PaleoAmerica* 8 (2022): 1–16.

7. Steven R. Holen, Thomas A. Deméré, Daniel C. Fisher, Richard Fullagar, James B. Paces, George T. Jefferson, Jared M. Beeton et al., "A 130,000-Year Old Archaeological Site in Southern California, USA," *Nature* 544 (2017): 479–83.

8. Mark Q. Sutton, Jennifer A. Parkinson, and Martin D. Rosen, "Observations Regarding the Cerutti Mastodon," *PaleoAmerica* 5, no. 1 (2019): 8–15.

9. J. M. Adovasio, D. R. Pedler, J. Donahue, and R. Stuckenrath, "Two Decades of Debate on Meadowcroft Rockshelter," *North American Archaeologist* 19, no. 4 (1999): 317–41.

10. David J. Meltzer, *First Peoples in a New World: Populating Ice Age America* (Cambridge University Press, 2021).

11. David J. Meltzer, Donald K. Grayson, Gerardo Ardila, Alex W. Barker, Dena F. Dincauze, C. Vance Haynes, Francisco Mena et al., "On the Pleistocene Antiquity of Monte Verde, Southern Chile," *American Antiquity* 62, no. 4 (1997): 659–63.

12. Karen Moreno, Juan Enrique Bostelmann, Cintia Macías, Ximena Navarro-Harris, Ricardo De Pol-Holz, and Mario Pino, “A Late Pleistocene Human Footprint from the Pilauco Archaeological Site, Northern Patagonia, Chile,” *PLOS One* 14, no. 4 (2019): e0213572.
13. Ardelean et al., “Evidence of Human Occupation in Mexico.”
14. Chatters et al., Evaluating Claims of Early Human Occupation.”
15. L. G. Davis, D. B. Madsen, L. Becerra-Valdivia, T. Higham, D. A. Sisson, S. M. Skinner, D. Stueber et al., “Late Upper Paleolithic Occupation at Cooper’s Ferry, Idaho, USA, 16,000 Years Ago,” *Science* 365, no. 6456 (2019): 891–97.
16. *Cosmos: A Personal Voyage*, episode 12, “Encyclopaedia Galactica,” featuring Carl Sagan, Public Broadcasting Service, December 20, 1980. For an investigation into the history of ECREE and ECREE-like claims, see “Quote Origin: Extraordinary Claims Require Extraordinary Evidence,” Quote Investigator, December 5, 2021, https://quoteinvestigator.com/2021/12/05/extraordinary.
17. David Deming, “Do Extraordinary Claims Require Extraordinary Evidence?” *Philosophia* 44 (2016): 1319–31.
18. S. Webb, M. L. Cupper, and R. Robins, “Pleistocene Human Footprints from the Willandra Lakes, Southeastern Australia,” *Journal of Human Evolution* 50 (2006): 405–13.
19. Kevin G. Hatala, William E. H. Harcourt-Smith, Adam D. Gordon, Brian W. Zimmer, Brian G. Richmond, Briana L. Pobiner, David J. Green et al., “Snapshots of Human Anatomy, Locomotion, and Behavior from Late Pleistocene Footprints at Engare Sero, Tanzania,” *Scientific Reports* 10, no. 1 (2020): 7740.
20. S. A. Morse, M. R. Bennett, C. Liutkus-Pierce, F. Thackeray, J. McClymont, R. Savage, and R. H. Crompton, “Holocene Footprints in Namibia: The Influence of Substrate on Footprint Variability,” *American Journal of Physical Anthropology* 151, no. 2 (2013): 265–79.
21. W. van Zeist, “De steentijd van Nederland,” *Nieuwe Drentse Volksalmanak* 75 (1957): 4–11.
22. George Ferentinos, Maria Gkioni, Maria Geraga, and George Papatheodorou, “Early Seafaring Activity in the Southern Ionian Islands, Mediterranean Sea,” *Journal of Archaeological Science* 39, no. 7 (2012): 2167–76.
23. J. M. Erlandson, M. H. Graham, B. J. Bourque, D. Corbett, J. A. Estes, and R. S. Steneck, “The Kelp Highway Hypothesis: Marine Ecology,

the Coastal Migration Theory, and the Peopling of the Americas," *Journal of Island and Coastal Archaeology* 2, no. 2 (2007): 161–74.

24. Ben A. Potter, James F. Baichtal, Alwynne B. Beaudoin, Lars Fehren-Schmitz, C. Vance Haynes, Vance T. Holliday, Charles E. Homes et al., "Current Evidence Allows Multiple Models for the Peopling of the Americas," *Science Advances* 4, no. 8 (2018): eaat5473.
25. Morten Rasmussen, Sarah L. Anzick, Michael R. Waters, Pontus Skoglund, Michael DeGiorgio, Thomas W. Stafford Jr., Simon Rasmussen et al., "The Genome of a Late Pleistocene Human from a Clovis Burial Site in Western Montana," *Nature* 506, no. 7487 (2014): 225–29.
26. Simon L. Lewis and Mark A. Maslin, "Defining the Anthropocene," *Nature* 519, no. 7542 (2015): 171–80.
27. Will Steffen, Reinhold Leinfelder, Jan Zalasiewicz, Colin N. Waters, Mark Williams, Colin Summerhayes, Anthony D. Barnosky et al., "Stratigraphic and Earth System Approaches to Defining the Anthropocene," *Earth's Future* 4, no. 8 (2016): 324–45. See also P. Gibbard, M. Walker, A. Bauer, M. Edgeworth, L. Edwards, E. Ellis, S. Finney et al., "The Anthropocene as an Event, Not an Epoch," *Journal of Quaternary Science* 37, no. 3 (2022): 395–99.
28. Paul S. Martin, "The Discovery of America: The First Americans May Have Swept the Western Hemisphere and Decimated Its Fauna Within 1,000 Years," *Science* 179, no. 4077 (1973): 969–74.
29. Lisa Nagaoka, Torben Rick, and Steve Wolverton, "The Overkill Model and Its Impact on Environmental Research," *Ecology and Evolution* 8, no. 19 (2018): 9683–96.
30. Tyler J. Murchie, Alistair J. Monteath, Matthew E. Mahony, George S. Long, Scott Cocker, Tara Sadoway, Emil Karpinski et al., "Collapse of the Mammoth-Steppe in Central Yukon as Revealed by Ancient Environmental DNA," *Nature Communications* 12 (2021): 1–18.
31. Norman Owen-Smith, "Pleistocene Extinctions: The Pivotal Role of Megaherbivores," *Paleobiology* 13 (1987): 351–62.
32. David Bustos, Jackson Jakeway, Tommy M. Urban, Vance T. Holliday, Brendan Fenerty, David A. Raichlen, Marcin Budka et al., "Footprints Preserve Terminal Pleistocene Hunt? Human–Sloth Interactions in North America," *Science Advances* 4, no. 4 (2018): eaar7621.
33. D. Mothé, L. S. Avilla, H. I. Araújo-Júnior, A. Rotti, A. Prous, and S. A. K. Azevedo, "An Artifact Embedded in an Extinct Proboscidean Sheds

New Light on Human–Megafaunal Interactions in the Quaternary of South America," *Quaternary Science Reviews* 229 (2020): 106125.

34. J. M. Broughton and E. M. Weitzel, "Population Reconstructions for Humans and Megafauna Suggest Mixed Causes for North American Pleistocene Extinctions," *Nature Communications* 9, no. 1 (2018): 1–12.

Postscript

1. Faysal Bibi, Brian Kraatz, Nathan Craig, Mark Beech, Mathieu Schuster, and Andrew Hill, "Early Evidence for Complex Social Structure in Proboscidea from a Late Miocene Trackway Site in the United Arab Emirates," *Biology Letters* 8, no. 4 (2012): 670–73; Carlos Neto de Carvalho, Zain Belaústegui, Antonio Toscano, Fernando Muñiz, João Belo, Jose María Galán, Paula Gómez et al., "First Tracks of Newborn Straight-Tusked Elephants (*Palaeoloxodon antiquus*)," *Scientific Reports* 11, no. 1 (2021): 7311.
2. Matthew R. Bennett, David Bustos, Matteo Belvedere, Patrick Martinez, Sally C. Reynolds, and Tommy Urban, "Soft-Sediment Deformation Below Mammoth Tracks at White Sands National Monument (New Mexico) with Implications for Biomechanical Inferences from Tracks," *Palaeogeography, Palaeoclimatology, Palaeoecology* 527 (2019): 25–38.
3. James Hutton, "X. Theory of the Earth; or an Investigation of the Laws Observable in the Composition, Dissolution, and Restoration of Land upon the Globe," *Earth and Environmental Science Transactions of the Royal Society of Edinburgh* 1, no. 2 (January 2013): 209–304.
4. R. M. Alexander, "Estimates of Speeds of Dinosaurs," *Nature* 262 (1976): 129–30.
5. J. Ruiz and A. Torices, "Humans Running at Stadiums and Beaches and the Accuracy of Speed Estimations from Fossil Trackways," *Ichnos* 20, no. 1 (2013): 31–35.
6. S. Webb, M. L. Cupper, and R. Robins, "Pleistocene Human Footprints from the Willandra Lakes, Southeastern Australia," *Journal of Human Evolution* 50 (2006): 405–13; S. Webb, "Further Research of the Willandra Lakes Fossil Footprint Site, Southeastern Australia," *Journal of Human Evolution* 52: (2007): 711–15.

7. K. Krishan, T. Kanchan, and J. A. DiMaggio, "Emergence of Forensic Podiatry—A Novel Sub-discipline of Forensic Sciences," *Forensic Science International* 255 (2015): 16–27; T. Kanchan, R. G. Menezes, R. Moudgil, R. Kaur, M. S. Kotian, and R. K. Garg, "Stature Estimation from Foot Dimensions," *Forensic Science International* 179, no. 2–3 (2008): 241; J. Duveau, "From Footprint Morphometrics to the Stature of Fossil Hominins: A Common but Uncertain Estimate," *L'Anthropologie* 126, no. 4 (2022): 103067; E. A. Okubike, N. M. Ibeabuchi, O. A. Olabiyi, and M. E. Nandi, "Stature Estimation from Footprint Dimensions in an Adult Nigerian Student Population," *Journal of Forensic Science and Medicine* 4, no. 1 (2018): 7–17.
8. M. Budka, M. R. Bennett, S. C. Reynolds, S. Barefoot, S. Reel, S. Reidy, and J. Walker, "Sexing White 2D Footprints Using Convolutional Neural Networks," *PLOS One* 16, no. 8 (2021): e0255630.

Index

Acahualinca footprint site, Nicaragua, 46
Alamorgordo, NM, 6, 7, 55
Alaska, 55, 127, 129, 138, 140, 142
Alkali Flat, 2, 4, 5, 6, 7, 8, 10, 12, 24, 26, 30, 58, 63, 73, 79, 83, 163
Apache Peoples, 69
archaic sites, 160
anatomically modern humans (AMH), 141
Anzick, MT, 142
Ardelean, C., 131–32
Australopithecus afarensis (Lucy), 14, 44, 45, 46

Back to the Future, 102
BC/AD or BCE and CE, 160
Bering Straits (land bridge), 127, 138
Before present (BP), 109
behavioral ecology, 96
biomechanics, definition, 50, 63. *See also* gait
biostratigraphy, 94
British Columbia, 140

calibration curve, dating, 106–8
calendar versus radiocarbon age, 108
California, 16, 54, 130
Captain Kirk, 48
Chamberlain, T. C., 60
Chester Zoo, 70
children at play, 69–75
Chihuahua, Mexico, 4, 148
Chiquihuite Cave, Mexico, 131–32
Clovis, 49; first hypothesis, 127–29; points, 49, 53, 109, 123–24, 128–37, 141, 142
Columbian mammoths (*Mammuthus columbi*), 16, 17, 46, 66, 67, 161, 162
Copper's Ferry (Salmon River), ID, 132
Cordilleran Ice Sheet, 127, 138
Covid, 103, 109, 110, 115, 131, 154
crosscutting relationships or patterns, 34, 36, 94, 96
Cuevera, C, 125

Darwin, C., 165
dating footprints, 91–124
Davis, J., 87
Denisovans, 142
Dillehay, T. 130
dire wolf (*Canis dirus*), 17
ditch grass, 11, 89, 97, 98, 103. *See also Ruppia sp.*
dolomite, definition, 18, 103
double trackway, 75–80

elephants, species, 173. *See also* Elephantidae
Elephantidae, 161, 162, 173
Ellis Wright, 1, 3, 59
environmental DNA, 145
Estancia Basin, NM, 113
Ethiopia, 72

flow cytometry, 118
Folsom point, 51, 53, 129

footprints: in caves, 15; erosion of, 148; ethics 30; excavation, 36–41, 167–71; formation, 32; ghost tracks, 8; morphology, defined, 38, 42; paleo-tracking, 50; preservation 91–92; puddles, 74; recognition of, 48; sandbox, 57; sexing of, 176; stature from, 174–76; tunnels, 56; types of relief, 17–18

gait, 172. *See also* biomechanics
Generalized Procrustes Analysis (GPA), 38, 43
geoartifact versus artifact, 130
geological time, 157–61. *See also* Holocene; Pleistocene; Quaternary
geometric morphometrics, 42
geophysics, 26; ground penetrating radar, 27, 28, 29, 63, 83
giant beavers (*Castoroides*), 88
giant ground sloth, 12, 13, 18, 19, 26, 47, 49, 50, 58–63, 65, 69, 72, 73, 80, 88, 94, 133, 147, 151, 152; hunting of, 58–63; *Northrotheriops shastensis*, 16, 61, 62, 63, 64, 69; *Paramylodon harlani*, 16, 61. *See also* megafauna
glacial-interglacial cycles, 160
Gloshay, S., 89
graphic log, 165
Great Lakes, 127
Greenland, 159
groupthink, 123

Hallux, 42
hardwater effect, 111–15
handprints, 73, 77
Haynes, V., 124, 129
hearth mounds, 13
Hebert, W. 154
Holocene, 146, 158, 159, 160
Homo erectus, 14, 4, 72
Homo heidelbergensis, 72
Hrdlička, A., 49
Hudson Bay, 127
Hueco Mountains, 4
Hulten, E, 138
Hutton, J. 165

Ice Age Trail, White Sands National Park, 24
ichnology, 15; computational ichnology, 44; ichnotaxa, 46; neo-ichnology, 57, 86
Idaho, 132
Ileret, Kenya, 9, 15, 44
Indigenous Peoples, 30, 89, 114, 123, 125, 129, 136, 141, 144, 148, 154, 157; colleagues, 88, 89; site monitors, 87; trackers 52
iron rules of explanation, 114
Ivensen, J, 118

Kelp Highway, 141
King Julien, *Madagascar* Film Franchise, 134
Knowledge Machine, The, 114

La Brea Tar Pits, CA, 16, 17
Laurentide Ice Sheet, 127, 138
Linnaeus, C., 45
Lake Lucero, NM, 2, 23
Lake Natron, Tanzania, 15, 133. *See also* Tanzania
Lake Otero, NM, 2, 7, 138, 21, 23, 140, 141, 143, 149, 164
landmark, 43

laser scanner, 41
Laetoli, Tanzania, 14, 15, 41, 44, 46. *See also* Tanzania
Libby W. F., 105
Library of Congress, 149
lithification, 92
Long Island, NY, 127
Lylell, C., 165

Mackenzie River, Canada, 138
Madagascar, 134
manus (front) foot, 68
Martin, P., 145
mass extinction, 16, 144–46
mammoths: head impression, 71; mammoth steppe, 146; tracks, 2, 6, 9, 11, 16, 17, 34, 36, 46, 48, 58, 62–68, 69, 70, 80, 89, 94, 110, 133, 146, 147, 162–65, 173–74, 177
Meadowcroft, PA, 130
megafauna: definition, 15, 133; *Glytopdont*, 16; *Gomphotheres*, 16; mastodons, 16, 162. *See also* giant ground sloth; mammoths
magnetometer, 153
Melka Kuntura, Ethiopia, 72, 73
Mesopotamia, 87
migration routes, 137–44
Milankovitch cycles, 160
Monte Verde, Chile, 130
Mousterian artifacts, 140
multiple working hypotheses, 60

Namibia, 52, 72, 92, 133
Neanderthals, 140, 141
Noose of the Laurels, 154
Northern Native American (NNA), 142

optical stimulated luminescence (OSL), 111, 119, 120, 121, 122, 124, 133
Oscura Mountains, NM, 4, 7
Osorno, NM, 131
Otero Mesa, NM, 4
overkill hypothesis 144–47

Pacific Ocean, 127
Paleoindian, 160
Palaeoloxodon, 162
paradigm, 125
parrots, 151–52
peer review, 111
Pennsylvania, 130
Paleolake Otero, 2, 7, 21, 23, 138, 140, 141, 143, 149, 164. *See also* Lake Otero
Peary, R. E., 154
Peppa Pig, 69
pes (back) foot, 68
photogrammetry, 41
plantar pressure, 63
Pleistocene, 80, 94, 96, 120, 145, 158, 159
pressure depth relationship, 63
Proboscideans, 161, 162–63
playas, 2, 163–65
pollen, 116; dating from, 115–17, 121
Poole Harbour, United Kingdom, 86
von Post, L, 115

Quaternary, 158

radiocarbon dating, 103–9
radiocarbon age versus calendar age, 108
Reacher, J., 87
relative dating (ages), 94

Rio Grande, 4
Rio Maulin Estuary, Chile, 130
risk versus reward in hunting, 147
Rocky Mountains, 127
Ruppia sp., 11, 97, 98, 101, 103, 109, 115, 119, 120, 122, 133. *See also* ditch grass

saber-tooth cat (*Smilodon Californicus*), 17
Sacremento Mountains, NM, 4, 7
Sagan standard, 132
San Luis Valley, NM, 4
Sand Andres, NM, 4, 7
selenite crystals, 4, 5
Sierra Blanca, NM, 4, 7
Southern Native American (SNA), 142
Spock, 48
Steeves, P. 129
step length, 172
stride length, 172
Stokes' law, 93
superposition, principle of, 92
sweepstake dispersal, 134

Tanzania, 14, 15, 41, 44, 46, 133
taphonomy, definition, 32
topology, definition, 42
tortuosity, definition, 46, 47, 52
tracks. *See* footprints
trackways: inter-trackway, 44; intra-trackway, 44
travois, 80–89
tree rings, 105–8
Trinty Nuclear Test, 6
Tularosa Basin, 2, 4, 6, 7, 14, 90, 113, 120, 162

uranium/thorium dating, 113
uniformitarianism, 165

Verkhoyansk Range, Russia, 138

walking/running speed, 171–73. *See also* gait
Walther's law, 166
White Sands National Park (WHSA), 1, 7, 18, 20, 30
WHSA Locality 2, 85, 88, 95, 96–123, 136, 151, 171
Willandra Lakes, Australia, 173

Younger Dryas, 159
Yucatan Peninsula, Mexico, 158